Y0-EDW-664

THE IBM
PERSONAL COMPUTER

THE **IBM** PERSONAL COMPUTER

BY ROBERT J. TRAISTER

TAB BOOKS Inc.

BLUE RIDGE SUMMIT, PA. 17214

NOTICE: IBM Personal Computer is a trademark of IBM Corporation. VisiCalc is a registered trademark of Personal Software, Inc. DIF is a trademark of Software Arts, Inc. Time Manager is a trademark of the Image Producers, Inc.

FIRST EDITION
FIRST PRINTING

Copyright © 1983 by TAB BOOKS Inc.
Printed in the United States of America

Reproduction or publication of the content in any manner, without express permission of the publisher, is prohibited. No liability is assumed with respect to the use of the information herein.

Library of Congress Cataloging in Publication Data

Traister, Robert J.
The IBM Personal Computer.

Includes index.
1. IBM Personal Computer. I. Title.
QA76.8.12594T73   001.64   82-5719
ISBN 0-8306-2696-4   AACR2
ISBN 0-8306-1496-6 (pbk.)

Cover illustration by Keith Snow.

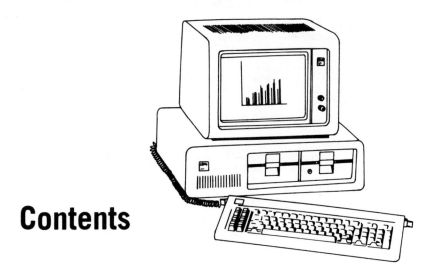

Contents

Introduction

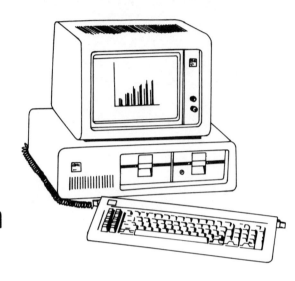

Home computers have fully arrived now that IBM, the giant among large, mainframe computer manufacturers has, at last, introduced their own personal computer for home and business use. This book is designed to guide IBM Personal Computer users through many of the unique features and expanded capabilities offered by this fine unit. Whether your interests range from simple home use to small business applications, you will find needed information in the following pages.

From the story of how IBM developed its machine to valuable information on applications, peripheral equipment, and hands-on programming guidance, you will be able to decide if the IBM Personal Computer is the right machine for your needs. There is an authorita-

tive look at software that is available, as well as information on a wealth of programs that will appear as this computer continues to make headway in the marketplace.

Background on the design characteristics of the IBM Personal Computer and a thorough explanation of the 16-bit chip, which is used to allow expanded computer operations, is provided together with information on how IBM has transferred large, mainframe reliability to the small, personal microcomputer unit.

I hope that everyone with an interest in the ongoing development of personal computers and especially those considering purchase of the IBM Personal Computer will find this book a highly fascinating and informative source book.

Other TAB books by the author:

No. 909 *How To Build Metal/Treasure Locators*
No. 996 *Treasure Hunter's Handbook*
No. 1198 *All About AIRGUNS*
No. 1254 *How to Build Hidden, Limited-Space Antennas That Work*
No. 1316 *The Master Handbook of Telephones*
No. 1409 *Build a Personal Earth Station for Worldwide Satellite TV Reception*
No. 1433 *Make Your Own Professional Home Video Recordings*
No. 1486 *32 Electronic Power Supply Projects*
No. 1487 *The Shortwave Listener's Antenna Handbook*
No. 1506 *Making Money with Your Microcomputer*
No. 2097 *All About Electric & Hybrid Cars*
No. 2321 *The Joy of Flying*

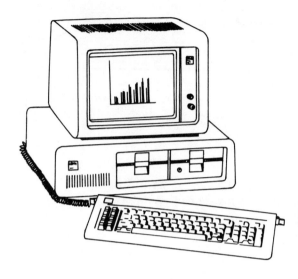

Acknowledgments

I thankfully acknowledge the assistance of the IBM Corporation, which generously supplied me with the complete IBM Personal Computer system, along with a wealth of support information and documentation on their hardware and available software.

I also wish to thank Intel Corporation for providing information on their 8088 microprocessor, which is used in the IBM Personal Computer.

To my dear friend, Mimi M., who assisted me throughout the writing of this book. Without her help, this work would never have been completed.

Chapter 1

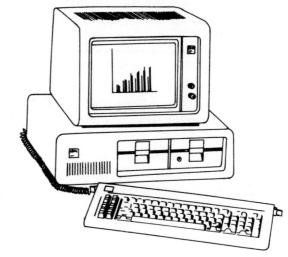

The IBM Company

The primary reason for the tremendous interest in the IBM Personal Computer long before anyone had even an inkling of the machine's capabilities is because it was being offered by IBM, the best-known computer manufacturer in the world today. Because of their long-known reputation for mainframe computers, IBM use was bound to attract worldwide attention for and avid interest in their personal computer for home and business. While most persons are familiar with the name IBM, many are not fully aware of this company's progress since its inception in 1911.

HISTORY

The value of tabulating machines was established in the late nineteenth century when machine compilation of the 1890 United States census cut the tabulation time from seven to three years. Dr. Herman Hollerith, who worked as a statistician in the United States census office, had devised a series of electrical machines to perform adding and counting operations on data stored on punched cards. In 1896, Hollerith formed the Tabulating Machine Company, with a plant in Washington, D.C.

The first computing scale was patented in 1885 by Julius E. Pitrat of Gallipolis, Ohio. His patents were bought by Edward Canby and Orange O. Ozias, businessmen in Dayton, Ohio, who incorporated the Computing Scale Company in 1891.

A mechanical time recorder was devised in 1888 by Willard Bundy, a jeweler in Auburn, New York. The next year, his brother Harlow organized the Bundy Manufacturing Company to produce time recorders. The company later relocated in Endicott, New York, as the International Time Recording Company.

In 1911, at the suggestion of merchant-banker Charles R. Flint, the International

Time Recording Company, the Computing Scale Company, and the Tabulating Company merged and incorporated in New York State as the Computing-Tabulating-Recording Company (C-T-R). It manufactured commercial scales, and tabulating and time-recording equipment. This was the beginning of what was to become IBM. The new company came under single management for the first time in 1914 when the company had 1,300 employees. In that year, the late Thomas J. Watson, Sr. left National Cash Register Company to join C-T-R as general manager. He soon became president.

In 1924, the name International Business Machines Corporation (IBM) was adopted. As president and later as chairman of the board, Mr. Watson served as chief officer of the company until May, 1956. Thomas J. Watson, Jr., who had been elected president in 1952, became chief executive officer in 1956 and was elected chairman of the board in 1961. He relinquished his responsibilities as chairman of the board and chief executive officer in 1971, when he became chairman of the executive committee of the board of directors. Mr. Watson, Jr., retired on January 31, 1974 but continued to serve as chairman of the executive committee of the board of directors until his appointment as U.S. Ambassador to the Soviet Union in 1979.

T. Vincent Learson was elected IBM president in 1966 and chairman of the board and chief executive officer in 1971. Mr. Learson retired on December 31, 1972, but he continues to serve as a member of the executive committee of the board of directors. Frank T. Cary, who was president of IBM from 1971 to 1974, became chairman of the board and chief executive officer on January 1, 1973. John R. Opel was elected president on February 26, 1974, and became chief executive officer on January 1, 1981.

In the company's early days, little emphasis was placed on its tabulating machine products, which included a keypunch, a hand-operated gang punch, a vertical sorter and a nonprinting tabulator. In 1928, the increase data capacity of a punched card from 45 to 80 columns of information paved the way for a new series of machines introduced in the early 1930s, machines that could not only add and subtract, but could also perform full-scale accounting operations.

The company's first educational building and an engineering laboratory were constructed in Endicott, New York, in 1933. During the depression of the 1930s, IBM added salesmen, increased efforts to develop new machines, and continued to produce parts without cutback. These efforts proved to be fruitful, for in 1936, the company was in a position to provide the machines and services for what has been called the "biggest accounting operation of all time," the Social Security Program.

IBM entered the electric typewriter business in 1933, when it purchased Electromatic Typewriters, Inc., a company of 36 employees. The first IBM electric typewriter appeared two years later.

When World War II started, all company facilities were put at the disposal of the government. More than five thousand IBM accounting machines were used in Washington to keep track of men and materials. Other machines were installed in mobile units. These units followed U.S. troops overseas.

The first general-purpose digital computer, the Automatic Sequence Controlled Calculator, was completed in 1944 after six years of development work in cooperation with Harvard University's Professor Howard Aiken. It was an electromechanical computer that used relays and tape-controlled programming devices. The machine was presented to Harvard by IBM. In 1948 the Selective Sequence Electronic Calculator followed. In 1952, the company introduced its first production computer, the IBM 701, which did 21,000 calculations a second. Today, IBM's most powerful computers can perform millions of instructions per second.

The advent of electronics brought substantial changes in data processing machines and methods. Equally important has been the development of data processing as a technique for advanced management and operational control.

With continuing improvements in computer programming techniques, data processing machines can now help to evaluate overall company plans that affect product scheduling, inventory management, capital investment, and other fundamentals of business management. By using computers to simulate a plant's performance, today's manager can turn hindsight into foresight. The computer thus becomes an important aid to decision making at the highest levels.

IBM HIGHLIGHTS

1914. Thomas J. Watson, Sr., age 40, joined Computing-Tabulating-Recording Company as general manager. He codified three basic policies: profit for customers, profit for employees, and profit for stockholders. One hundred shares of C-T-R were worth less than $3,000, and the company had only 770 stockholders.

The Endicott plant was devoted primarily to producing time-recording equipment. The Dayton plant made scales, and Washington produced cards. The use of accounting machines began to spread.

The accounting product line included a mechanical key punch, hand-operated gang punch, vertical sorter, and tabulator. Customers included railroads, chemical companies, utilities, and life insurance companies. By the end of the year, company personnel had grown to 1,346 and gross income from sales, service, and rentals in the United States were $4 million.

1915. Thomas J. Watson, Sr. was elected president and general manager of C-T-R. The first sales convention was held, forerunner of the Hundred Percent Club conventions. The sales force was reorganized and strengthened.

1916. The first steps were taken in setting up the educational program. An education department was established with its own manager and a study session for employees was held in New York. The program later expanded to include employee courses in sales, customer engineering, and manufacturing, as well as general education courses for customers.

1917. C-T-R entered the Canadian market under the name of International Business Machines Co., Ltd. , and an office in Brazil opened.

1919. C-T-R was introduced in Europe. The electric synchronized time clock system was introduced.

1920. The printing tabulator was introduced. At the start of the year, the company had more than 3,000 employees. Gross income had tripled since 1914.

1923. Sales posts opened in other Latin American countries and in the Far East. The electric keypunch was introduced.

1924. C-T-R adopted the name of International Business Machines Corporations. The Quarter Century Club was organized. The rotary card press was developed to produce cards at high speed. IBM introduced a self-regulating time system. The first issue of "Business Machines" appeared. Plant locations included Endicott, New York; Washington, D.C.; Dayton, Ohio; France; and Germany.

1925. IBM opened an office in the Philippines. The horizontal sorting machine was introduced. The first stock dividend was paid at a rate of 20 percent.

1926. IBM stock split three for one. All three company divisions won grand prizes for products at the Sesquicentennial Exposition in Philadelphia. The company had 3,953 employees.

1928. The punched card was made to hold 80 columns, almost double its previous capacity. The subtracting-accounting machine was introduced. The Customer Engineering training course was organized. IBM established a Suggestion Program for employees, and a 5 percent stock dividend was declared.

1929. The stock market crashed, but IBM declared a 5 percent stock dividend. Gross income passed the $18 million mark.

1930. Despite the depression, IBM increased its employment, trained more salesmen, and increased their engineering efforts. A 5 percent stock dividend was declared.

1931. Accounting machines were introduced in Japan. New products included the 400-series alphabetical accounting machines and the first of the 600-series calculating machines, which handled multiplication and division. The first permanent installation of the Filene-Finlay Translator was set up at the League of Nations in Geneva. A 5 percent stock dividend was declared.

1933. A new education building and engineering laboratory was built at Endicott. The development of the Carroll Carriage improved alphabetical accounting machines by automatic handling of special forms and variable line spacing, IBM acquired Electromatic Typewriters, Inc., of Rochester, New York.

1934. The Company sold Dayton Scale Division to Hobart Manufacturing Company. The 405 Alphabetical Accounting Machine was introduced. The Group Life Insurance Plan was initiated for employees. IBM dropped piecework and declared a 5 percent stock dividend.

1935. The first commercially successful electrical typewriter appeared on the market from IBM's Electric Typewriter Division. The first issue of Think appeared. The international proof machine, to clear bank checks, was introduced. The survivor benefit payment was introduced in addition to group life insurance, and a 5 percent stock dividend was declared.

1937. Although paid holidays were not generally granted by major companies, IBM announced a policy of paying employees for six holidays. A paid vacation plan was also introduced. The company now had more than 10,000 employees. The 77 collator appeared and a test-scoring machine was introduced. Gross income passed $30 million, and a 5 percent stock dividend was declared.

1940. IBM had 12,656 employees and announced a service benefit plan for employees entering the armed forces. The company declared a 5 percent stock dividend.

1941-1945. IBM offered its entire facilities to the government for the World War II effort and accepted nominal 1 percent profit on war materials. Among wartime products were naval and aircraft fire control instruments, Browning automatic rifles, .30 caliber carbines, director and prediction units for 90-mm anti-aircraft guns, bombsights, and aircraft supercharger impellers.

The Washington card plant turned out war bond assemblies. In addition, thousands of IBM accounting machines handled wartime paperwork in Washington, D.C., and on the war fronts, IBM accounting machines in mobile units followed U.S. troops in battle.

The company built a plant in Poughkeepsie, New York, in 1942 and added an extension to the plant in Endicott. Both plants won Army-Navy "E" awards. In 1944, IBM's first large-scale computer, the Automatic Sequence Controlled Calculator, was presented to Harvard University. The same year, Watson Scientific Computing Laboratory was founded at Columbia University.

The company announced a Sickness and Accident Plan for employees and a Retirement Plan a year later. A 5 percent dividend was declared in each year.

1946. IBM announced the first small commercial electronic calculator, the 603 Multiplier. The IBM Hospitalization Plan for employees was announced and Family Dinners were launched. Thomas J. Watson, Jr. was elected to the board of directors. Employees now totaled 22,492 and stocks split five for four.

1947. IBM Total and Permanent Disability Income Plan was announced. A vested rights provision was added to the IBM Retirement Plan.

1948. IBM's first large-scale digital calculating machine, the Selective Sequence Electronic Calculator, was announced. The 604 Calculating Punch was introduced. The IBM Model A typewriter was introduced. IBM began active support of the United Negro College Fund. Group life insurance was provided for retired employees. Gross income was $156.4 million, and stockholders voted for a 75 percent stock split.

1949. Thomas J. Watson, Sr. was elected Chairman of the Board. The World Trade Corporation was formed as an independently operated but wholly owned subsidiary to handle overseas operations. The IBM Model A "Executive" Electric Typewriter with proportional spacing was introduced. Employment was now 27,236, and a 5 percent stock dividend was declared.

1950. During the Korean war, IBM again placed facilities at the government's disposal.

The company was assigned military projects, including bombing-navigational systems for Air Force bombers and giant and high-speed electronic calculators for the country's air defense.

1951. The IBM Model A Decimal Tabulation Typewriter was introduced, and a 5 percent stock dividend was declared.

1952. Thomas E. Watson, Jr. became IBM president. IBM announced the 701, its first production computer designed primarily for scientific calculations. The company now had more than 40,000 employees, and a 5 percent stock dividend was declared.

1953. The Suggestion Plan's top award was increased from $2,500 to $5,000. The company announced the 702 computer for commercial use and the 650, an intermediate size electronic computer, to handle widely diversified accounting and scientific computations. The IBM Model A Toll Biller was introduced, and a 5 percent stock dividend was declared.

1954. A new plant was completed at Greencastle, Indiana, and a heat-treat-plating plant was built at Endicott. A new research laboratory was completed at Poughkeepsie. The faster, more powerful 704 computer succeeded the 701, and the 705 replaced the 702. The New Model B Standard and "Executive" Typewriters were introduced. The stock split five for four, a 2½ percent stock dividend was declared, and IBM now had over 50,000 employees. The fastest, most powerful electronic computer of its time was developed and built by IBM for the U.S. Navy's Bureau of Ordnance.

1955. Electric Typewriter and Military Products became autonomous divisions. IBM's engineers developed magnetic core storage units. New products included the 608 transistor calculator, 858 Carda-type accounting machines, a series of high speed printers, the 83 sorter, and the central control system (introduced by Time Equipment Division to control mechanical devices electronically). Gross income was $563 million.

1956. The company entered a consent decree with the government, which began an antitrust-suit against IBM in 1952. Thomas J. Watson, Jr. became chief executive of IBM. The IBM Family Major Medical Plan was announced.

New products included the 305 RAMAC, the 27 Card Proof Punch, and 28 Printing Card Proof Punch. The Electric Typewriter Division announced an electronic "reading" device for electric typewriters and an electronic input-output device to automatically type work done by computers. The Time Equipment Division introduced an automatic production recording system.

Thomas J. Watson, Sr. died at age 82. Construction was completed on the Kingston plant. The Military Products Division continued production of its large-scale computer for a vast air warning system known as SAGE and advanced bombing and navigational systems for the U.S. Air Force. IBM reorganized into six autonomous divisions and the subsidiary World Trade Corporation. A Corporate Staff was formed to advise and assist the divisions in specialized areas. The Travel Accident Insurance Plan was announced. Stock split five for four, a 2½ percent stock dividend was declared, and employment reached 72,504.

1957. IBM's gross annual income topped the billion dollar level. The company made a public offering of 1,050,233 shares of additional stock to help finance continued growth. The Service Bureau Corporation was formed as wholly owned but independently operated subsidiary. The Thomas J. Watson Memorial Scholarship program was established. The 709

computer was announced. The plant facility at Burlington, Vermont was completed. Plant and laboratory facilities were completed at Oswego, New York, and San Jose, California. A card plant in Sherman, Texas was completed and the Data Processing Division moved its headquarters to White Plains, New York. The stock split two for one, and the company had 83,588 employees.

1958. All workers previously paid on an hourly basis were placed on salary. The Electric Typewriter Division, during its twenty-fifth anniversary year, produced its one-millionth typewriter. The Stock Purchase Plan allowed employees to buy IBM stock at 85 percent of the market price. The company announced a Tuition Refund Plan for employees' after-hours education. IBM sold the Time Equipment Division to Simplex Time Recorder Company. New products included the 7090 high-capacity computer, 7070 intermediate data processing system, Series 50 basic accounting machines, and 632 Electronic Typing Calculator for card output. Plants were completed at Rochester, Minnesota; Dayton, New Jersey; and Lexington, Kentucky. The first issue of *Management Briefing* appeared. RAMAC 305 answered questions on world history in ten languages at the Brussels World Fair. The 704 computer aided in design and tracking of space missiles and in monitoring missile trajectories during firing. A 2½ percent stock dividend was declared.

1959. The company announced the Matching Grants program to match employees' gifts to institutions of higher learning up to $1,000. The Speak Up program was introduced, and the Maximum Suggestion Plan award was raised from $5,000 to $25,000. New products included the 1401 data processing system, 1620 scientific computer, and the 357 data collection system. The IBM 9090 reservation system permitted automatic airlines reservations through central control. IBM introduced the new Model C Standard and "Executive" Typewriters and the IBM Model C Hektowriter. The company reorganized the Data Processing Division into Data Systems, General Products and a new marketing division that retained the Data Processing title. The Military Products Division was renamed Federal Systems Division. Advanced Systems Development, a new division, was set up to explore new markets.

Stockholders, meeting at New York City's Coliseum, voted a three-for-two stock split, and a 2½ percent stock dividend was declared. The Federal Systems Division moved its headquarters to Rockville, Maryland. Construction started on Yorktown Heights, New York, Research Center. The Concord, Massachusetts, card plant was completed. The World Trade Corporation opened new Belgium headquarters and dedicated the European Education Center at Blaricum, the Netherlands. The company had 108,915 stockholders and 94,912 employees.

1960. New developments included the solid-state 7000-series computers to replace the 700-series of vacuum tube machines; the 410 computer; STRETCH computing system, the world's most powerful to date; "Execucary", the first dictation equipment marketed by the Electric Typewriter Division; and the 632 Electronic Typing Calculator with paper tape output.

The 305 RAMAC scored the Winter Olympic Games in California and tallied votes at both political conventions and processed presidential election returns on TV. IBM computers provided data for launching and tracking Project Echo, the nation's pioneering experiment in space communications. Mark I, a language translator developed for the Air Force, translated Russian into English.

Construction started on a materials distribution center at Poughkeepsie and on an addition to the Endicott product development laboratory. The Supplies Division completed the Campbell, California, card plant and opened a card design center in Houston. The company started the Systems Research Institute as the first graduate level school in the computer industry to educate people for advanced work in data processing systems engineering. The World Trade Corporation completed a manufacturing plant in Argentina, expanded its plants in Scotland, France, and Japan, and started construction on new laboratory buildings in France, Holland, West Germany, and a new office in West Berlin.

1961. The maximum on suggestion awards was increased to $75,000. The largest suggestion award in company history to date, $56,000, was paid to two employees. The company launched an Invention Award Plan for significant inventions by employees. Executive vice-president Louis H. LaMotte retired. Thomas J. Watson, Jr., was elected chairman of the board, and Albert L. Williams became president.

New products included the "Selectric" Typewriter, an electric typewriter without type bars or movable carriage; the "Execucary" PBX dictation system and portable dictating unit; the 1710 control system; Hypertape system; 1301 disk storage; and the high-speed 1403 printer.

The Thomas J. Watson Research Center at Yorktown Heights, New York, was officially opened, with an annual meeting held there at which stockholders voted for a three-for-two split and an improved Employee Stock Purchase Plan. A Components Division was formed to handle development, manufacture and purchase of solid-state components used in the production of IBM data processing equipment.

After a trial period at Yorktown, New York, IBM decided to move its corporate headquarters to Armonk, New York. The General Products Division and Data Systems Division moved to headquarters near White Plains, New York. IBM had 116,276 employees and 197,509 stockholders.

1962. The company joined President Kennedy's Plan for Progress program, pledging to continue and take action to strengthen IBM's policy of equal job opportunity for all individuals. The first Invention Award Dinner was held to honor 34 outstanding IBM inventors.

New products included the 1440 data processing system; the 7094, one of the most powerful computing systems offered by IBM to date; the 7010 data processing system; the 7710 data communications unit, which permitted computers at different locations to exchange information via high-speed facilities; the 7750, which allowed a single computer to communicate with large numbers of widely separated terminals; the 1420 bank transmit system; the 1062 teller terminal; the 6400 Accounting Machine, and the "Selectric" Input-Output Typewriter.

Work began on an IBM guidance computer that helped steer the two-man Gemini capsule. IBM delivered the first guidance computer for the Saturn series of launch vehicles. IBM scientists succeeded in operating a semiconductor diode laser powered directly by an electric current rather than an external light source. An experimental thin-film memory that operated at a speed of 100 billionths of a second was demonstrated. Using the Telstar satellite, IBM engineers sent computer information back and forth between Endicott and La Gaude, France.

The Supplies Division moved into new headquarters at Dayton, New Jersey. Development laboratories were completed at Poughkeepsie and San Jose. The World Trade Corporation completed a development engineering laboratory at La Gaude, France; dedicated an administration building in West Berlin; built an education center at Cuernavaca, Mexico; and opened Datacenters in Dusseldorf, Tokyo and Toronto.

1963. The company appointed its first eight IBM Fellows in a new Fellowship Program for honoring company scientists, engineers and other professions who had sustained records of innovation and technical achievement. The company formed three new divisions: the Industrial Products Division, the Real Estate and Construction Division, and the Research Division.

New products and applications included the IBM 7094 II, the most powerful computer in the company's product line to date; an electronic filing system composed of new IBM 1302 disk storage files, the 1460, which processed information nearly twice as fast as the 1401; and the 1240 banking system and IBM microprocessing equipment.

IBM introduced several different kinds of teleprocessing systems, including the 1030 data collection system, the 1050 data communications systems and the 7740 communication control unit. IBM people and computing systems were used in NASA's ground-based control network to help track Mercury astronaut L. Gordon Cooper on his 546,000-mile orbital flight around the earth.

The Components Division completed a manufacturing plant in East Fishkill, New York; the Electric Typewriter Division completed an extension to the Lexington, Kentucky plant; the General Products Division completed an addition to the Rochester, Minnesota plant; and the Research Division dedicated a new facility for its laboratory in Zurich, Switzerland.

In World Trade, a new plant near Bombay, India, started production of punched card accounting equipment. A plant in Sindelfinger,

West Germany, began deliveries of IBM 1440 systems. A new development engineering laboratory was dedicated at La Gaude, France; and another was established in Vienna, Austria. IBM had 137,612 employees and 232,761 stockholders.

1964. The company celebrated "50 Years of Progress" with 80,000 IBMers and guests at 231 Family Dinner and Quarter Century Club gatherings. IBM Day at the New York World's Fair had General Dwight D. Eisenhower, Major Robert F. Wagner and Robert Moses, president of the World's Fair Corporation, as featured speakers. Chairman Robert J. Watson Jr. received the Medal of Freedom, the highest civil honor the U.S. President can bestow.

T. Vincent Learson and Arthur K. Watson were named senior vice presidents. The company moved corporate headquarters from New York City to Armonk, New York, and acquired a new subsidiary, Science Research Associates (SRA), a Chicago publisher of education, test, and guidance materials. IBM formed the Field Engineering Division and changed the name of the Electric Typewriter Division to Office Products Division.

System/360, a new concept in IBM computers, spanning almost the entire performance range of IBM's existing lines of computers and incorporating microelectronics, was introduced on April 7 in the most important product announcement in company history to date. Subsequently, IBM introduced the 1800 data acquisition and control system, as well as a graphic data processing system which permitted information to be displayed on a television like screen and changed with a light pen. American Airlines' SABRE system, using IBM computers and linking 1,000 ticket sales desks in 65 U.S. cities, went into full operation.

IBM introduced several teleprocessing units and systems and the Magnetic Tape "Selectric" Typewriter. They developed an experimental device that can electronically position in millionths of a second a laser light beam carrying written and pictorial information, a solid-state optical scanning device that converts images into electrical signals, and a laser transmitter that sends signals great distances over laser light beams.

The Federal Systems Division was awarded a contract for part of the Saturn launch vehicles, the largest space contract in the company's history. IBM computers helped speed the results of both the Winter and Summer Olympics. The company completed new plants at Huntsville, Alabama, and East Fishkill, New York. The stock split five for four. IBM had 149,834 employees and 266,086 stockholders.

1965. IBM Pavillion completed two years at the New York World's Fair with more than ten million visitors. World Trade Corporations' gross income passed the billion dollar mark. The first System/360 was shipped one year after introduction; the Model 44 medium-size computer designed for scientific applications was announced; Models 65 and 75 became part of the System/360 line; Model 67 for time sharing was introduced; and the Model 30 processor was introduced.

Other products introduced included the 1130 low-cost, desk-size computer; 2740 and 2741 typewriter communications terminals; 2321 data cell drive; Document Processing System to prepare computer-printed documents for distribution in one operation; and a 28-ounce Model 224 "Executary" portable dictating unit. The 2361, the largest computer memory even built, was shipped to the NASA Manned Spacecraft Center. IBM scientists completed the most precise computation of the moon's orbit and developed a fabrication technique to connect hundreds of circuits on a tiny silicon wafer.

A 59-pound on-board IBM guidance computer was used on all Gemini flights, including the first spaceship rendezvous. A computer-based communications network linked IBM's major domestic and foreign engineering, manufacturing, and administrative facilities to coordinate work on System/360. The first donated computer centers in European universities opened in London, Copenhagen, and Pisa, Italy.

SRA operated the Rodman Job Corps Center as part of the nation's "War on Poverty" and opened its Canadian subsidiary. Construction started on manufacturing and development facilities near Raleigh, North Carolina and Boulder, Colorado. The company completed plant and laboratory additions at Kingston, Oswego, Poughkeepsie and Yorktown Heights. IBM had 172,000 employees and 275,650 stockholders.

1966. Albert L. Williams retired as IBM president and was named chairman of the executive committee of the board of directors, T. Vincent Learson was elected IBM president and Arthur K. Watson was elected vice chairman of the board of directors. The Corporate Office was established to conduct overall affairs of the corporation and consisted of the chairman of the board, chairman of the executive committee, vice chairman of the board and the president. Mrs. Jeannette K. Watson, widow of Thomas J. Watson, Sr., died at 82.

IBM announced a new employee benefit, the Family Surgical Plan, and a new special care program to assist employees with handicapped children. A new stock offering to shareholders and a three-for-two stock split were approved at the annual meeting. The Supplies Division was renamed the Information Records Division and the Data Processing Group was organized, with Frank T. Cary as general manager.

New products included the "Selectric" Composer and Magnetic Tape "Selectric" Composer for high-quality cold-type composition; 1287 optical reader, which read hand-printed numbers and five characters; 9370 document reproducer; IBM 1500, the first system specifically designed for computer-assisted instruction; IMPACT, a set of computer programs for inventory control of retail operations; 1080 data acquisition system for hospital and laboratory tests; and System/4 Pi, a special family of aircraft and space computers.

IBM computers processed some 19 million Medicare identification cards for the Social Security Administration. The Service Bureau Corporation began implementation of a nationwide computer network that linked 125 System/360s in more than 80 offices.

SRA opened subsidiaries in the United Kingdom and Australia. Federal Systems Division personnel moved into new facilities near Gaithersburg, Maryland. The Office Products Division announced a plant and engineering complex at Austin, Texas. The company acquired a 550-acre site at Boca Raton, Florida. IBM scientists operated an organic dye laser which for the first time provided laser light that "tuned" on a wide range of colors. IBM World Trade dedicated a plant in Vimercate, Italy and a laboratory at Lidingo, Sweden; completed construction of a manufacturing facility in Mainz, West Germany; and announced plans to build a second manufacturing plant at Havant near Portsmouth, England. IBM had 198,816 employees worldwide and 326,427 stockholders.

1967. A Management Committee of senior executives was formed to assist the Corporate Office in management of the overall affairs of the corporation. Thomas J. Watson, Jr. was named "Businessman of the Year" in a Saturday Review magazine poll. Arthur K. Watson was elected president of the International Chamber of Commerce. IBM exhibited computer systems at Canada's Expo '67.

New products and services included the System/360 Model 25; Paper Tape "Selectric" Composer; Model D Typewriter and Model D "Executive" Typewriter; 2680 CRT printer for publishing; QUIKTRAN 2, an improved version of the remote QUIKTRAN terminal system; 1259 magnetic character reader/sorter; Series/500 magnetic tape; and binary synchronous communication, an IBM technique that regulated and sped the flow of data characters into transmission lines.

The cartographic scanner converted maps to binary data for computer processing. IBM scientists produced the first monolithic integrated germanium circuits; made gains in laser technology; and discovered and proved a series of formulas that gave minimum number of steps required for addition, multiplication and comparison of numbers.

An IBM ground team played a key role in successful Saturn V test flight. A trillion-bit photo-digital storage system was built for the Atomic Energy Commission. Customer support included 40 installation centers, 17 field systems centers, four data acquisition and control centers, and six scientific centers. An IBM computer was used to process data for the FBI at the National Crime Information Center in Washington. A data communications experiment was completed between IBM computing centers in the United States and Paris via satellite.

The World Trade Corporation established the European Systems Research Institute. The Real Estate and Construction Division acquired sites in Norman, Oklahoma, and Manassas, Virginia. Construction began on new Data Processing Division headquarters in White Plains, New York. Expansion was completed on the manufacturing plant at Fujusawa, Japan and the technical center at Diegem, Belgium.

Expansion was completed on manufacturing facilities at Mainz, West Germany; Amsterdam; The Netherlands; and Greenock, Scotland. IBM closed the year with 221,866 employees worldwide and 359,495 stockholders. A 2½ percent stock dividend was declared.

1968. Changes in the way IBM charged for and supported its data processing equipment were under study, with results scheduled for a mid-1969 announcement. Control Data Corporation filed a civil antitrust suit against IBM; CDC's allegations were denied. Huyler VanBuren, a Kingston technician, received a $75,000 suggestion award, possibly the largest in American history; 33 other employees shared invention and technical contribution awards totalling $375,000.

Lyle M. Spencer, co-founder and president of SRA, died; he was replaced by Richard A. Giesen. A Voluntary Health Screening Program for employees was announced. IBM's Bedford-Stuyvesant manufacturing plant was established in Brooklyn, and a Harlem Street Academy was sponsored by IBM to aid school dropouts. These were two of more than 100 programs undertaken by IBM in the Equal Opportunity area. The Apollo mission support at the Federal Systems Division played a vital role in the first circumlunar flight; NASA delved deeper into theoretical space exploration using two System/360 Model 95s.

Addition to the System/360 were announced: the Model 85; two versions of the Model 20; the 50 data inscriber and 2495 carriage reader, offered a new data entry technique for System/360; two display units, the 2265 and 2760; a display copier, the 2285; and the 1288 optical reader. Customer engineers completed 100,000 hours of instruction through a System/360 that "taught" at more than 200 branch offices. New models of IBM's "Executary" dictation and transcription units were introduced, as well as the IBM Braille Typewriter.

SRA added new educational programs in mathematics, reading, social studies, language arts and science. Consolidated gross income reached $6.9 billion, increasing $1.5 billion over 1967 on a high level of computer sales; World Trade gross income passed $2 billion; and stockholders voted for a stock split.

Plans were announced for a 52-story office building in Chicago; more than two million square feet of new World Trade facilities and expansions were completed or were under construction in ten countries; and almost six million square feet were added or were under construction in the U.S.

In R&D, a basic patent was received on Gunn-effect devices. IBM scientists developed an experimental laser optical memory system. Widely used SLT modules achieved a reliability rate 1,000 times that of earlier vacuum tubes. IBM employment reached 241,000, and stockholders numbered 501,390.

1969. Thomas J. Watson, Jr. termed the decade of the sixties "the most exciting and productive in the more than 50-year history of the company." A new IBM marketing policy provided that most systems engineering activities, many future computer programs, and most customer education courses would be offered for separate charges. IBM offered a new service, Custom Contract Services, under which the company designed and installed customers' data processing systems. The General Systems Division was formed to develop and manufacture low-cost data processing equipment and provide related programming systems support.

The Federal government filed an antitrust suit against IBM; four civil antitrust actions (three filed this year) were consolidated. IBM denied the allegations and said it would defend all cases vigorously.

Two new computers were announced: System/3 for small businesses, with a new, small punched card; and System/360 Model 195, IBM's most powerful computer to date. Both used IBM monolithic integrated circuits. Major new teleprocessing products were introduced: the 2770 data communication system and the 2790 data communication system. The IBM Mag Card "Selectric" Typewriter was introduced.

IBM research scientists developed experimental devices using laser beams to store huge amounts of information, as well as techniques for word recognition, speaker identification and advanced audio response. IBM computers helped NASA put the first men on the moon. An on-board computer in the Orbiting Astronomical Observatory II operated for a full year. SRA introduced the Distar System in reading, language, and arithmetic.

More than 250,000 suggestions were made by employees; IBM paid more than $3.3 million for those accepted. IBM customer engineers took 400,000 hours of computer assisted instruction.

A total of 7½ million square feet of new construction was completed or in progress at IBM sites in the U.S. Design work started on an additional four million square feet, and construction began on the 52-story Chicago office building. World Trade Corporation added or completed 3.6 million square feet in its biggest building year. Employment reached 258,000 and stockholders numbered 549,000.

1970. The System/370 was introduced in the company's biggest product announcement year since 1964. Able to run System/370 programs, the system included Model 165, 155 and 145 (the latter being the first general-purpose business computer to use monolithic circuits in all memory and logic functions). The low-cost System/3 Model 6 was introduced, with the ability to process standard ledger cards and switch easily from business applications to complex mathematical problem solving. More than 1,500 low-cost System/3 Model 10s were installed in 1970. The sensor-based System/7 was introduced for process, manufacturing, and laboratory applications.

Advanced peripheral products were announced: the 800-million-character 3330 disk file, 3803/3420 magnetic tape subsystem, 2,000-line-per-minute 3211 printer, 129 card data recorder, and a keypunch with an electronic memory. More than 80 new program products were introduced. The IBM copier was introduced in the U.S. and overseas. IBM computers in Houston assisted flight controllers in the dramatic rescue of Apollo 13's astronauts. A new version of IBM's aerospace computer, the System/4 Pi, Model Ap-101, was introduced. IBM research scientists used an electron beam to make electronic components so small that detail can be seen only through an electron microscope. The College Division was established by SRA.

Close to 10 million square feet of new construction was completed, in process or in design at IBM sites in the U.S. The World Trade Corporation expanded its worldwide manufacturing space by 1.3 million square feet and announced plans to build manufacturing plants in Brazil, Canada, France, West Germany, and Japan. IBM Japan's exhibit at Expo '70 in Osaka attracted more than nine million visitors, a record for any IBM exhibit in a single year. Arthur K. Watson, vice chairman of IBM board and chairman of the board of IBM World Trade Corporation, resigned to become U.S. Ambassador to France.

IBM employment reached 269,000 and stockholders numbered 587,000. Consolidated gross income reached $7.5 billion and gross income from operations outside the U.S. approached $3 billion. At year end, the worldwide backlog of orders for IBM data processing equipment was at a record high.

1971. System/370 Models 135 and 195 were announced, the latter being the most powerful computer to date in IBM's product line. The first customer installations of System/370 were made seven months ahead of schedule. By year end, more than 1,300 System/370 deliveries were made worldwide.

New peripheral products were announced: the 3270 information display system, which let users choose from a family of displays, printers and control units; 3410 magnetic tape subsystem; 3735 programmable buffered terminal, 3670 brokerage communications system; 2798 guidance display unit for manufacturing environments; 2730 transaction validation terminal for checking credit at point of sale. New program products included a securities order matching and communications control system and more than 125 new application program.

More than 4,400 IBM marketing representatives went back to school to study new ways to help customers use IBM equipment more effectively. The IBM "Selectric" II Typewriter with dual pitch was introduced, enabling users to vary the number of characters types per inch. The model IBM "Executary" portable dictating unit and Communicating Mag Card "Selectric" Typewriter were introduced. The IBM credit card service provided embossing, encoding, and addressing under high-security conditions.

IBM computers helped guide Apollo 14 and Apollo 15 moon landings and enhance photos taken by Mariner 9, the first spacecraft to orbit Mars. The Zurich laboratory built transistor amplifiers and oscillators operating at 18 billion cycles per second, the highest transistor circuit frequency to date. The first IBM fare collection system was installed for the San Francisco rapid-transit system.

SRA published 36 educational products in such fields as reading, language arts, mathematics, testing and guidance. IBM's first operational application of speech recognition enabled customer engineers servicing equipment to "talk" to and receive "spoken" answers from a computer. The San Jose laboratory developed an experimental terminal for the blind that printed computer responses in raised dot characters of Braille.

A total of seven million square feet of new construction was completed or in process at IBM sites in the U.S. Office Products Division headquarters moved to Franklin Lakes, New Jersey. Manufacturing plants opened in Bromont, Canada; Sumare, Brazil; and Yasu, Japan. IBM held its first annual meeting outside the U.S. in Toronto, Canada. More than 100 IBM employees were on leave, contributing their talents to the education and solution of social problems.

T. Vincent Learson was elected IBM chairman of the board, Frank T. Cary was elected president, and Thomas J. Watson, Jr. became chairman of the executive committee. IBM employees numbered 265,000, stockholders numbered 580,000, and consolidated gross income reached $8.3 billion.

1972. System/370 Models 125, 158 and 168 were announced; Advanced Function gives virtual storage capability to System/370 users, permitting easier and more economical development of new applications.

New peripheral products were introduced: 3705 communications controller, 2976 mobile terminal system, 3881 optical mark reader, 2922 programmable terminal, 3780 data communications terminal, 2984 cash issue terminal, and the 3886 optical character reader.

The Mag Card "Executive" Typewriter was introduced, combining proportional spacing, interchangeable type elements, and the ability to store typed material on magnetic cards. Five new models of input word-processing equipment were announced. The IBM Copier II, featuring higher speeds and an advanced documentfeed mechanism, was announced, along with the 2991 Blood Cell Processor.

IBM's lunar orbital experiments team received a NASA award for outstanding contributions to lunar science during Apollo 15. IBM Skylab units were accepted by NASA for a mission in 1973. Apollo 16 and Apollo 17, final missions in the moon-landing series, were supported by IBM personnel and products.

IBM received a patent on a way of sensing magnetic bubbles and an experimental approach for storing and processing vast amounts of data. IBM scientists developed the shortest wavelength laser.

Construction was completed on the new headquarters building for IBM West Germany and IBM Mexico. World Trade Corporation was reorganized into two operating groups: IBM Europe and the Americas/Far East Group. SRA announced "Our Working World", a social science program for elementary schools, and opened a subsidiary in France. More than 200,000 customers and customer executives attended IBM classes throughout the U.S. IBM received one of five Business Week awards for business citizenship in recognition of corporate social responsibility for its Bedford-Stuyvesant manufacturing plant in Brooklyn, New York. The Adoption Assistance Plan and Fund for Community Service Program were announced.

The first System/370 Model 135 was installed at a customer site. IBM Chairman T. Vincent Learson, the keynote speaker at the Spring Join. Computer Conference, said data security challenges must be met.

IBM realigned the Data Processing Product Group forming Systems Development,

System Products and General Products Divisions. A total of three million square feet of construction was completed, and two million square feet was in progress at IBM sites in the U.S. IBM's 52-story Chicago office building, the company's largest, was dedicated.

Chairman T. Vincent Learson retired, and Frank T. Cary was elected chairman of the board. IBM employees numbered 262,000, stockholders numbered 558,000, and consolidated gross income reached $9.5 billion.

1973. System/370 Model 115 was announced, as well as System/3 Model 15. Main storage was increased for System/370 Models 115, 125, 135, 158 and 168. Larger Model 145 processors were announced. A larger-capacity of the IBM System/7 was introduced, plus several new industry-specialized products: the 3650 Retail Store System, 3660 Supermarket System, 3600 Finance Communication System, 3890 document processor, 5275 direct numerical control station, and the Energy Management System for utilities.

Other products included: 3704 communications controller; 3740 data entry system using the IBM Disk, a new storage medium; 3340 direct access storage facility; 3336 disk pack; and the 3790 communication system.

Dr. Leo Esaki, IBM Fellow, shared the 1973 Nobel Prize in physics. IBM scientists fabricated a Josephson junction, an experimental electronic device that can be switched in about 10 trillionths of a second, holding promise for ultrafast computers of the future. IBM researchers developed an amorphous film that increased the versatility of magnetic bubble circuits for storing and processing information in future computers.

The new IBM "Selective" typewriter element permitted recording of dance steps and movements. The IBM Correcting "Selectric" Typewriter had a correctable film ribbon and tape that lifts typing errors off paper. IBM introduced the Mag Card II Typewriter with an electronic memory.

NASA's Skylab mission was supported by IBM personnel and products through three trips into earth orbit. NASA awarded IBM a contract to support the Apollo-Soyuz, joint American-Russian space venture scheduled for 1975, as well as contracts to provide computers, displays and programs for NASA's space shuttle, scheduled for operation in the 1980s.

The IBM Model 96 single-element typewriter, designed to meet the Japanese Katakana alphabet requirements, was introduced by IBM World Trade Corporation. Completed were an Office Products plant in West Berlin, the Zurich headquarters of IBM Switzerland, the headquarters of IBM Denmark, and the new development laboratory in Fujisawa, Japan. A Family Dental Plan was announced, and the Advanced Systems Development Division reorganized.

Gilbert E. Jones, chairman of IBM World Trade Corporation, testified at hearings before the U.S. Senate Subcommittee on International Trade. Litigation between Control Data Corporation and IBM in the Federal District Court was dismissed pursuant to an out-of-court settlement that included the sale of Service Bureau Corporation to Control Data Corporation.

IBM employees numbered 274,000 stockholders numbered 574,000, consolidated gross income reached $11 billion, and stock split five for four.

1974. IBM restructured its World Trade business into two new operating units: IBM World Trade Europe/Middle East/Africa Corporation, and IBM World Trade Americas/Far East Corporation. The Data Processing Division announced Advanced Function for Communications using the new 3767 terminal and the 3770 Data Communications System with

System/370 for a unified teleprocessing network; and announced the 3850 Mass Storage System and main storage enhancements for System/370 Models 115 and 145.

The Data Processing Division realigned into 14 regions to move marketing resources closer to branch offices and customers. The General Systems Division became responsible for marketing and servicing the products it developed and manufactured and announced a serial matrix printer.

An IBM mathematician developed a new computer technique for fast, high-resolution structural analysis of large molecules. IBM scientists developed a new concept, called Bubble Lattice Storage, which appeared capable of increasing the storage capacity of bubble memories to more than one billion bits per square inch.

The Office Products Division introduced a new desktop IBM Memory Typewriter that stored typed information and recalled previously typed material for revision. IBM signed a contract with NASA to develop a telemetry online processing system (TELOPS) that accepted satellite experiment data, processed it, and stored up to one trillion bits of information for use by scientists. IBM equipment helped NASA's Applications Technology Satellite (ATS) maintain orbital attitude and receive and decode commands from ground stations.

An energy conservation program produced fuel savings of 31.7 percent at IBM; and electricity use for 1974 is 22.8 percent below the preconservation level. The Field Engineering Division celebrated its tenth anniversary. SRA marked its tenth anniversary as part of IBM and announced the Mathematics Learning System. IBM and Comsat asked the FCC for permission to join in a domestic satellite venture.

A two-year IBM-funded data security study, done in cooperation with MIT, TRW Systems and the state of Illinois, resulted in guidelines for users and for future data security research.

John R. Opel was elected president of IBM; Corporate Management Committee replaced the Management Review Committee and the Management Committee, and Arthur K. Watson, former Ambassador to France and former chairman of the IBM World Trade Corporation, died.

The Fund for Community Service Program was extended to retirees. IBM employees numbered 292,000, stockholders numbered 589,000, and consolidated gross income reached $12.7 billion.

1975. The Systems Development Division was redesignated the System Communications Division. Advanced Systems Development Division's responsibilities were assigned to the System Communications Division, the Data Processing Product Group staff and the Data Processing Marketing Group staff. Some General Systems and Office Products responsibilities were restructured within the General Business Group. A new division, General Business Group/International was established with marketing, service, manufacturing and overall performance responsibility for General Systems and Office Products operations in 17 countries outside the U.S.

An antitrust case brought against IBM by Telex and IBM's counterclaim against Telex was settled without payment by either side. The trial of the Justice Department's antitrust suit against IBM began.

IBM sponsored an Institute of Internal Auditors research project to strengthen control for computer users. It announced plans to build a new plant in Bedford Stuyvesant in Brooklyn to replace the present leased facility. Aetna Life & Casualty was to be the third partner with Comsat General and IBM in a domestic satellite partnership named Satellite Business Systems, which awaited FCC approval. Enhanced versions of System/370 Models 168, 158, 125, and 115 were announced. The 3800 Printing Subsystem was announced, which used laser and electrophotographic technologies with print speeds up to 13,360 lines per minute; and the 3350 direct access storage device was announced. New data communications product announcements included the 3606 and 3608 financial services terminals, 3760 dual key entry station, key entry version of the 3660 Supermarket System, and additions and enhancements to the 3770 Data Communications System.

The Office Products Division announced Mag Card/A Typewriter; Electronic "Selectric" Composer; 6:5 Cartridge System, and a new line of dictation equipment. The General Systems Division announced System/32 and the 5100 Portable Computer.

The IBM Research Division fabricated an 8,000-bit semiconductor memory chip with a storage density of five million bits per square inch, seven times denser than previous chips of similar capacity. It also discovered the first polymer to become superconducting and lose all resistance to electric current flow. The 1,000th patent was issued to inventors at General Products Division's San Jose site. A successful Apollo-Soyuz mission, supported by IBM equipment, concluded NASA's Apollo series of space flights.

The System Communications Division announced a new facility completed for Fujisawa, Japan's development laboratory. Arthur K. Watson International Educational Center was dedicated at La Julpe, Belgium; Americas/Far East Corporation moved into new headquarters in Mount Pleasant, New York; an Office Products manufacturing plant began operations in Guadalajara, Mexico; and

plans were announced for construction of an Office Products plant in Wangaratta, Australia.

IBM employees now numbered 288,000, stockholders numbered 586,000, and consolidated gross income reached $14.4 billion.

1976. IBM helped celebrate the nation's Bicentennial with sponsorship of the exhibition "America on Stage: 200 Years of Performing Arts", at The John F. Kennedy Center for the Performing Arts, Washington, D.C.; a grant to the traveling exhibition, "The World of Franklin and Jefferson"; and a grant to "Operation Sail", an international regatta involving some 150 historic and contemporary sailing vessels from 30 countries.

The Data Processing Division announced System/370 Models 138 and 148, an attached processor for Model 168-3, Model 158 attached processor system, 3838 array processor designed to help pinpoint oil deposits, and the 5937 industrial terminal for plant floor communications. The General System Division introduced the 5230 Data Collection system designed primarily for experienced data processing users. The Office Products Division announced the Series III Copier/Duplicators, the 6440 Document Printer and Word Processor/32. The Information Records Division announced the 2991 Model 2 Blood Cell Processor.

Presentation of the government's case in the Justice Department suit against IBM continued through the year. Several private antitrust suits against IBM (Data Research Corporation, Memory Technology, Inc., Reynolds Computer Corporation and VIP Systems Corporation) were settled. Judgment of dismissal in favor of IBM was entered by the trial judge in Symbolic Control, Inc. antitrust case.

"Enterprise," the first vehicle in America's Space Shuttle program, made its debut at Palmdale, California, carrying flight computers and special hardware built by the Federal Systems Division. Energy usage at U.S. locations was reduced 36 percent from 1972 preconservation levels, for savings of more than $58 million.

Research scientists fabricated the world's narrowest circuit lines, only a few tens of atoms wide; announced a multiplier circuit using ultra-fast Josephson junction; and announced a technique for identifying signatures by their acceleration patterns. A Retirement Education Assistance Plan for employees was announced.

Responsibility for the U.S. central programming service was transferred from the System Communications Division to the Field Engineering Division. General Products Division's Santa Teresa programming development laboratory in San Jose was completed. General Business Group/International Division consolidated headquarters operations at leased facilities in White Plains; established office systems marketing support to GBG country organizations in Europe; and began typewriter production at Wangaratta, Australia.

IBM Brazil dedicated Gavea Residential Educational Center, the first such center in South America. IBM Columbia dedicated a new Office Products plant in Bogota, and a Latin America Advisory Board was formed to advise Americas/Far East management on regional issues.

SRA opened a Consumer Division, adapting educational products for home use with children, and produced its first fully instructional school supplemental programs, the SRA Skills Series kits.

IBM employees numbered 292,000, stockholders numbered 577,000 and consolidated gross income reached $16.3 billion.

1977. The General Technology Division was formed to meet technology requirements of other divisions within the General Business Group. Facilities in Burlington, Vermont and Manassas, Virginia were transferred from the Systems Products Division to the General Technology Division. The new General Systems Division headquarters building in Atlanta, Georgia was dedicated; demolition of a building at 590 Madison Avenue was dedicated; plans for an office tower on the site were evaluated; construction was begun on a corporate Management Development Center in Armonk, New York; and plans were announced to build a plant and laboratory in Tucson, Arizona for the General Products Division.

IBM changed its mode of business operations in India due to equity requirements of the Indian government. The Indonesian government accepted in principle an IBM reorganization plan, enabling the company to continue offering its products and services there. IBM Mexico celebrated its fiftieth anniversary. General Business Group organizations were formed in Columbia, Finland and Norway. General Business Group/International Division line organization was restructured, with country organizations divided into five areas.

The Data Processing Division announced the 3033 processor, a top-of-the-line, high-capacity computer for customers requiring large-scale systems. The 3031 and 3032 processors were announced for those intermediate- and large-system users who needed increased computing power but not the capacity and performance of the 3033. The 3895 Deposit Processing System for banks was introduced; the 3250 graphics display system was offered to help shorten product design and manufacturing time; and two data encryption devices and Cryptographic Subsystem programming were introduced to safeguard information stored and sent by computer.

General Systems Division introduced System/34, a low-cost data processing system with multiple workstations, designed for both experienced and first-time data processing users. The Office Products Division announced Office System 6 Information Processors, Models 6/450, 6/440 and 6/430; the IBM Mag Card II Typewriter-Communication; the Memory 100 Typewriter and the 6240 Mag Card Typewriter. The Information Records Division announced the 2997 Blood Cell Separator.

The first Space Shuttle vehicle successfully completed the approach and landing phase, demonstrating on-board computers and programming provided by the Federal Systems Division. An encipherment/decipherment algorithm, developed by the IBM Research Division and System Communications Division, was accepted as standard by the National Bureau of Standards. Research scientists achieved a major increase in solar cell efficiency.

SRA established a division to publish materials in the health sciences. Its Distar Program was recognized in a major government study as being most effective, among programs studied, in producing gains in basic skills, cognitive and self concept areas.

Presentation of the government's case in the Justice Department's antitrust suit against IBM consumed its second year. The trial judge dismissed a California Computer Products, Inc. antitrust suit against IBM. The trial judge dismissed a Forro Precision, Inc. antitrust claim against IBM; the jury finds Forro misappropriated IBM's trade secrets and IBM interfered with Forro's prospective business advantage; both sides appeal. A new trial was ordered in a Greyhound Corporation, Inc. antitrust suit against IBM.

The FCC approved Satellite Business Systems' applications. U.S. locations surpassed the goal of an additional 5 percent reduction in energy use; value of energy savings from preconservation levels is approximately $90 million. A stock tender offer resulted in the repurchase of 2.6 million shares of IBM stock for $721 million. The board of directors authorized an occasional purchase of additional large blocks of capital stock. A Dividend Reinvestment Plan, providing for optional additional investments by stockholders, was announced.

IBM employees numbered 310,000, stockholders numbered 582,000, and consolidated gross income reached $18.1 billion.

1978. IBM began construction of a 43-story, five-sided office building at 590 Madison Avenue in New York City; a plant and laboratory near Charlotte, North Carolina, for the System Communications Division; a development laboratory and materials distribution center in Austin, Texas, for the Office Products Division; and an automated materials distribution center for worldwide supply of parts in Greencastle, Indiana, for the Office Products Division.

IBM and Xerox Corporation agreed to end all litigation between the two companies, terminating 12 separate lawsuits in the U.S. and Canada. In August, Federal Judge Samuel Conti granted IBM's motion for a directed verdict in the Memorex vs IBM trial, in effect ruling for IBM, after declaring a mistrial when the jury could not reach a verdict. Memorex filed a notice of appeal.

The System Products Division was reorganized into two divisions: the Data Systems Division with responsibility for large, complex systems, and the System Products Division with responsibility for intermediate performance products.

New products included: the 8100 Information System, designed for a wide range of distributed processing needs and incorporating new high-density memory chips that store 64,000 and 18,000 bits of information; the 3730 Distributed Office Communication System;

the 3630 Plant Communication System; the 3033 Multiprocessor Complex; the 3031 Attached Processor Complex; and programmable supermarket terminals that could be tailored to the needs of an individual supermarket or a store within a chain.

General Systems Division announced the 5110, a small computer for a wide variety of business users; System/38, a general-purpose computer that incorporates new semiconductor technology, including a dense random access memory chip storing 32,000 bits of information, high-density 64,000- and 18,000-bit memory chips and large-scale integrated (LSI) logic chips, each logic chip contained up to 704 circuits.

The Office Products Division announced the Electronic Typewriter Model 50 and Model 60, both using microprocessors to provide electronic control of certain typing tasks; the Mag Card Composer, which can use magnetic cards to prepare camera ready copy for publication; and the Office System 6/420, a low-cost, processor.

The Information Records Division announced the 5880 electrocardiograph system, which can be wheeled to a patient's bedside and record and interpret an electrocardiogram within minutes, as an aid in the physician's diagnostic decisions. SRA announced Mark II: Reading Laboratory, a new version of a reading development kit used by more than half of America's elementary schools. Customer deliveries began on the 3033, 3032 and 3031 processors. Order backlog for the new machines exceeded any previous customer demand for IBM processors.

The Federal Systems Division shipped an initial set of computer flight programs for the U.S. Space Shuttle's first orbital test to NASA's Johnson Space Flight Center. The programming automated spacecraft functions from prelaunch through entry and landing. The first digital submarine sonar system, developed by IBM, was formally approved by the U.S. Navy for service use. Its advantages over analog systems were greater speed, increased detection capability and improved reliability.

SRA celebrated its fortieth year of publishing and released a revision of the SRA Achievement Series, a widely used testing instrument designed to measure educational achievement in grades 11 and 12. The Research Division reported on an experimental silicon microcircuit technology that achieved a nearly tenfold increase in circuit density over existing silicon circuits. Experiments show 1/16-inch square chips could contain up to 10,000 logic switches or 250,000 bits of memory.

A block stock repurchase was completed, with a total purchase of 2.4 million shares of stock for $624 million.

1979. More than 11 million square feet of new space (some 8 million for manufacturing and product development) was under construction worldwide which included plants and laboratories in Austin, Texas; Charlotte and Raleigh, North Carolina; Tucson, Arizona; Hannover, West Germany; and Wangaratta, Australia. Also included were materials distribution centers in Greencastle, Indiana and Montpellier, France and a Management Development Center in Armonk, New York.

The Justice Department suit entered its second decade; the jury cannot reach a verdict in Transamerica vs IBM; and on October 18, Federal Judge Robert H. Schnacke decided the case for IBM. Cal/Comp lost its appeal from the 1977 loss in District Court, and IBM's untarnished record of successful defenses in private antitrust suits remained intact.

IBM improved its energy efficiency with conservation measures that amount to a 5 percent saving per square foot at major U.S. locations compared with 1978, bringing the company's total U.S. saving from the 1973 pre-conservation level to 45 percent. In the past six years, IBM had conserved enough electricity in the U.S. to meet the needs of 380,000 homes for a year. Enough oil had been saved to serve 160,000 homes in northern states. In IBM World Trade countries where conservation had been practiced for many years, the energy savings per square foot at major IBM locations from 1973 through 1979 had come to 40 percent. IBM's experience with the use of computers for energy management at its facilities showed typical savings of 10 percent to 15 percent through control of electrical, heating and cooling equipment.

DiscoVision Associates, a joint venture of IBM and MCA, Inc., was formed to develop, manufacture and market video disks and video disk players. By blending complementary technical and marketing skills, this venture provided an opportunity to broaden the use of the video disk technology in home entertainment, industrial education and information fields.

The Data Processing Division announced and shipped the 4300 processors, featuring the densest packaging of memory and logic circuits available on intermediate-size IBM systems and using a disk storage device that offers up to twice the storage capacity of similar devices used with System/370 Model 138 systems. DPD also announced the 3279 color display terminal and 3287 color printer; the low-cost, easy-to-use 3101 display terminal and 3102 printer, marketing through a national sales and information telephone center; major enhancements to SNA; new IBM 3863, 3864 and 3865 modems; the 3033N and 3033 Attached Processor; the 3680 programmable store system; and the 3604 Model 7 administrative terminal for financial institutions. DPD opened the IBM Support Center, which offered around-the-clock telephone assistance for customer

software service and a third headquarters facility in Dallas, Texas.

General Systems Division announced the 5260 retail, point-of-sale terminal and the 5520 Administrative System, which combines text processing and electronic document distribution.

The Office Products Division announced the 6670 Information Distributor that prints with a laser, sends documents electronically and links word and data processing; the 6640 Dual-Speed Document Printer, an ink jet printer that can operate at two speeds; the Executive Recorder and 6:5 Dual Media Transcriber, a pocketsize dictation recorder and transcriber that accepts both minicassettes and 6.5 magnetic disks; the Electronic Typewriter 75, a microprocessor-driven desktop typewriter permitting typists to store and retrieve words, phrases and pages of typing; and the Audio Typing Unit that produces synthetic speech with an unlimited vocabulary, helping blind typists to independently produce error-free copy.

The Federal Systems Division delivered the flight and ground software for NASA's first Space Shuttle orbital mission, scheduled for 1980; delivered the command and control system for the U.S. Navy's first Trident submarine; and began full-scale tests of the U.S. Navy's new ship-air system for defense against submarines and detection of surface vessels.

The Field Engineering Division established software support centers for customers who telephone for help with programming problems, information on preventive service, or assistance in program installation. Toll-free calls could be made at any hour, seven days a week.

SRA published Corrective Spelling Through Morphographs, a one-year spelling program for grades four through adult for those students who had experienced difficulty with learning how to spell.

The Research Division fabricated and tested an experimental magnetic bubble memory device with bubbles 2 to 3 times smaller than any previously announced and also announced the invention of the fastest experimental computer circuits ever reported, an advance in ultra-high speed Josephson computing technology.

The General Business Group announced the IBM System/34 Ideographic (Kanji language) feature, which enabled the system to process more than 11,000 Japanese and Chinese Characters in IBM Japan; opened twenty Business Computer Centers specializing in marketing entry-level systems in 12 countries; and opened Product Centers in London and Buenos Aires. The IBM 1750 Telephone Switching System was announced and marketed in five European countries.

IBM employees numbered 337,000, stockholders number 696,918, and consolidated gross income reached $22.9 billion.

1980. IBM President John R. Opel was elected chief executive officer effective January 1, 1980, with Frank T. Cary continuing as chairman of the board and chairman of the board's executive committee.

The full U.S. Court of Appeals in Washington, D.C. upheld the FCC's 1977 authorization for Satellite Business Systems to construct and operate a domestic satellite communications system. The U.S. Court of Appeals for the Ninth Circuit upheld Federal District Judge Samuel Conti's verdict in favor of IBM over Memorex.

IBM's Management Development Center in Armonk and 1.7 million square feet of space at the Tucson facility were dedicated. IBM completed more than 3.5 million square feet of plant and laboratory space in 1980, with an additional 7 million square feet remaining under construction at year end to meet worldwide product demand.

The Series/1 Energy Conservation System, a programming system that enabled users of the IBM Series/1 computer to conserve energy while performing business applications was announced by the General Systems Division. Computer operation is cost effective, since the same Series/1 that performs commercial processing during business hours can conserve fuel and electricity around the clock. Customers had now installed more than 1,000 IBM energy management systems, with dollar savings ranging from 10 to 25 percent.

IBM Japan commemorated the fifty-fifth anniversary of IBM's business in Japan and the thirtieth anniversary of resumption of operations after World War II.

A word processing center for job training of disadvantaged persons, made possible in part through IBM's loan of equipment and personnel, was dedicated in Washington, D.C. IBM scientists used a computer to transcribe human speech drawn from a 1,000-word vocabulary. The text is read at a normal speaking pace and converted to printed form with 91 percent accuracy, the best yet reported in complex speech-conversion efforts.

Realignment of the General Business Group, including formation of the Information Systems Division, was announced. General Technology Division was realigned and became part of the Data Processing Product Group.

The Data Processing Division announced new models of the IBM 4331 processor, offering about twice the internal performance and up to four times the main memory capacity of earlier models; additional models of the IBM 3850 Mass Storage System that enable users to expand existing storage capacity at a price under two cents a month per million added characters; the new IBM 3848 cryptographic unit, fastest in the family of IBM cryptographic products, which permits high-speed encryption of information to be stored and transmitted; and a new attached processor that expands the system capacity and versatility of the IBM 3033 Attached Processor Complex. DPD also announced two new processors and improvements that extend the power and range of its largest computer system. The 3081 offered up to twice the internal performance of the 3033 processor and significantly reduces space, cooling and power requirements. It featured a thermal conduction module and contained more than three quarters of a million logic circuits in about four cubic feet IBM's densest logic circuit packaging to date. The second processor, the IBM 3033 Model Group S, was more than twice that of a 3031, and was available with four and eight megabyte storage and six channels.

Other announcements included the IBM Distributed Office System which expanded the information processing capability of the IBM 8100 to include text and word processing; two new advanced-technology disk storage files, the larger able to store over 2.5 billion characters of information; a new equipment switching unit that improved operating efficiency within a large computing system; enhancements of IBM's primary large-system control program, Multiple Virtual Storage, that provide more efficient management of data within the processor and overall system; and five program products to improve data management in various IBM storage files.

The General Systems Division announced the IBM 5120, a new desktop computer; the IBM 5280 low-cost distributed data system consisting of "intelligent" terminals; and began shipment of the new IBM System/38.

The Office Products Division announced five new models of the IBM "Selectric" Typewriter; a Displaywriter System, a desktop text processing system; two microprocessor-equipped models of the Series III Copier/Duplicator; and opened Product Centers selling typewriters and supplies in Philadelphia, Pennsylvania and Baltimore, Maryland.

The General Business Group opened seven IBM Product Centers, where typewriters and supplies are sold in Paris, Lyons, Oslo, Stockholm, Brussels, Barcelona and Cordoba (Argentina). The Federal Systems Division established a laboratory at Manassas, Virginia to apply the cost and performance improvements made in mass-produced commercial computer circuits to the needs of U.S. space and defense agencies.

IBM Instruments, Inc., a subsidiary formed this year, announced two lines of analytical instruments: the NR/80 Series of nuclear magnetic resonance spectrometers and the IR/90 Series of Fourier Transform infrared spectrometers. Such products are used primarily by scientists in industry, government and educational institutions to identify and analyze the chemical and physical properties of substances. SRA announced educational courseware for use with personal computers in schools. Consolidated gross income reached $26.2 billion.

1981. In August of that year, IBM announced its smallest, lowest-priced computer system, the IBM Personal Computer. Designed for business, school and home, the easy-to-use system sells for as little as $1600. It offers many advanced features and with optional software, may use hundreds of popular application programs. The IBM Personal Computer is sold through participating ComputerLand dealers and Sears, Roebuck and Company's new business machine stores beginning in the fall. It is also sold through IBM Product Centers and a special sales unit in the company's Data Processing Division.

With such a varied history behind this corporation, it was no wonder that the IBM Personal Computer was the subject of many conversations among personal computer users. This marked IBM's first major marketing effort of a computer system to the more or less private sector. Even before the machine was formally presented and actually seen by the public, expectations were running high based upon IBM's reputation in the computer industry.

IBM retail systems provide service at department store sales counters. Hand-held sensors connected to terminals read magnetically encoded merchandise tags containing price, stock and descriptive data.

Shoppers at a number of major supermarkets are having their purchases tallied by an automated IBM checkout system that eliminates manual keying of many items. The system, which features a high-speed scanner that reads the grocery industry's Universal Product Code, can make checkout faster for shoppers and easier for checkers, while it records the sales data needed to manage a modern, complex supermarket.

An IBM signature validation system is helping a major eastern bank provide better customer service and greater security in making withdrawals and in cashing personal checks. The system flashes a depositor's signature on a screen for verification.

A department store chain is saving as much as 20 percent of its annual energy bill through use of the IBM Series/1 computer for facilities control and power management. At just one location, the chain is saving up to 35,000 kilowatts per month.

IBM is not new to the production of small computers. I am not speaking of the IBM Personal Computer, which to date is the smallest system offered. Rather, IBM offered a small business computer, the System/3, in the early seventies. The System/3 was introduced as a basic card or disk machine and grew by the middle seventies into a compatible family of six processors with a broad range of capabilities. Thousands of these machines were installed due to overall size, performance vs cost figures, and to the availability of diverse program packages. Prior to this, IBM was a major government and big business supplier. The System/3 brought their computer line to the smaller firms, many of which were taking advantage of computerized data processing for the first time. The System/3 was also applicable to some big business uses, so at this time, IBM was not selling completely out of their accustomed realm.

DATA PROCESSING MARKETING GROUP

The Data Processing Marketing Group is divided into three divisions. The *Data Processing Division* (DPD) has marketing responsibility within the U.S. and its territories for IBM's information-handling systems, equipment, computer programming, systems engineering, education, and other related services to customers who require larger systems DPD is headquartered in White Plains, New York, and has sales offices throughout the country.

The Federal Systems Division provides specialized information handling and control systems to the Federal government for seaborne, spaceborne, airborne, and ground-based environments. It also participates in applied research and exploratory development. This division is headquartered in Bethesda, Maryland. Its major facilities are in Gaithersburg, Maryland; Oswego, New York; Manassas, Virginia; and Houston, Texas.

The Field Engineering Division (DP) provides maintenance and related services for products developed and manufactured by or for the DP Product Group and marketed by the

Data Processing Division and support for specified IBM program offerings. It also provides maintenance marketing support and central programming service for assigned products. The Field Engineering division is headquartered in White Plains, New York, and has service offices throughout the United States.

DATA PROCESSING PRODUCT GROUP

The Data Processing Product Group is also divided into separate divisions which treat various aspects of data processing on a more or less specialty basis. The General Products Division (GPD) has worldwide development and U.S. manufacturing responsibility for storage systems, including tape units, disk files and mass storage systems, as well as system printers, program products, programming languages, and related programming. GPD is headquartered in San Jose, California. It operates manufacturing facilities in Tucson, Arizona, and San Jose. Development activities are conducted in San Jose and Santa Teresa, California, and in Tucson, Arizona.

The General Technology Division (GTD) has worldwide development and U.S. manufacturing responsibility for IBM semiconductor components used in IBM's small, medium, and large computers and office products. GTD is headquartered in White Plains, New York. It operates manufacturing and development facilities in East Fishkill, New York; Burlington, Vermont; and Manassas, Virginia. GTD also provides technological leadership and guidance to semiconductor manufacturing functions at Essonnes, France; Sindelfinger, West Germany; and Yasu, Japan.

The System Communications Division (SCD) has worldwide development and U.S. manufacturing responsibility for information-handling systems and products that serve a wide range of end-users. These include distributed data processing systems, industry systems for retail stores and supermarkets, display terminal products, telecommunications systems and related technologies and programming. SCD is headquartered in Harrison, New York. It operates a manufacturing facility at Raleigh, North Carolina; and a development facility at Kingston, New York; has development activities at Gaithersburg, Maryland; Raleigh, North Carolina; Yorktown Heights, New York; is supported by development units at La Gaude, France; Hursley, England; and Fujisawa, Japan.

The System Products Division (SPD) has worldwide development and U.S. manufacturing responsibilities for intermediate-range processors and related programming, finance and manufacturing industry products, impact printer products, and semiconductor packaging. SPD is headquartered in White Plains, New York. It operates a manufacturing and development facility in Endicott, New York and Charlotte, North Carolina, and is supported by development units in Boeblingen, West Germany, and Essones, France.

The Data Systems Division (DSD) has worldwide responsibility for the development of large, complex systems (with primary emphasis on high-performance products) and for associated programming, and U.S. responsibility for manufacturing those systems. DSD is headquartered in White Plains, New York. It operates a manufacturing facility and development laboratory in Poughkeepsie, New York. It also conducts manufacturing test operations in Kingston and Brooklyn, New York, and is supported by operations at Yorktown Heights, New York, and Dayton, New Jersey.

GENERAL BUSINESS GROUP

Four divisions make up the General Business Group, which is responsible for the worldwide marketing of all IBM products. The General Systems Division (GSD) has worldwide market requirements responsibility and U.S. marketing and service responsibility for low-to-moderate-price information-handling systems, including related programming. GSD is headquartered in Atlanta, Georgia. It operates application development centers in Georgia and California, and has sales and service offices throughout the U.S.

The Information Records Division (IRD) has U.S. marketing responsibility for magnetic tape, disk, data modules and disk packs, as well as U.S. manufacturing and marketing responsibility for data processing cards, business forms, ribbons, other consumable products used in information-handling systems, and biomedical devices and supplies. IRD is headquartered in Princeton, New Jersey. It operates production facilities in Dayton, New Jersey and Washington, D.C., and has manufacturing activities in Boca Raton, Florida. IRD has sales offices throughout the U.S.

The Information Systems Division (ISD) has responsibility for worldwide development and U.S. manufacturing of products, including low-to-moderate-price information handling systems, typewriters, electronic typewriters, office systems and copiers. ISD is headquartered in White Plains, New York. Development and manufacturing facilities are located in Austin, Texas; Boca Raton, Florida; Boulder, Colorado; Lexington, Kentucky; and Rochester, Minnesota.

The Office Products Division (OPD) has worldwide and U.S. marketing responsibilities and, service and field administration responsibility for electronic, electric and magnetic media typewriters, text processors, copiers, dictation equipment, direct impression composing products and related supplies. OPD is headquartered in Franklin Lakes, New Jersey. It operates a field service distribution center in Greencastle, Indiana. OPD has sales and service offices throughout the U.S.

To market the IBM Personal Computer, a special System Products Division has been established in Boca Raton, Florida. All inquiries are channeled through this office. While the IBM Personal Computer was announced over a year ago, it is still too early to come up with accurate predictions on the role IBM will play in the personal microcomputer field. Presently, the personal computer industry is a relatively small one (money-wise), in comparison with the larger computer market. However, while this field may be small, the rate of growth is increasing, possibly by leaps and bounds. It is obvious that IBM is looking more at this growth potential than at its present marketing attributes. To be successful, IBM must carry over to their Personal Computer line the service, technical improvements and customer attention which has been expected and received in their other product lines. To me, this is a main buying point and is the reason the IBM Personal Computer has had such a great impact in the personal computer field.

Chapter 2

The IBM Personal Computer

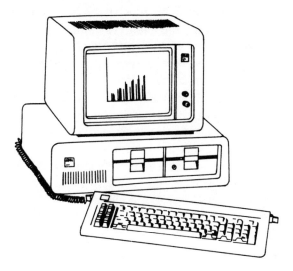

August 12, 1981, will be remembered by many as a red letter day for the microcomputer enthusiast. On this date, IBM Corporation announced its smallest, lowest-priced computer system, the IBM Personal Computer.

Designed for business, school, and home, this computer sells for as little as $1,600, offers advanced features, and may be used with hundreds of popular application programs already available. With the introduction of this machine, IBM broke a long-standing position by moving into the personal computer field and continued the trend by announcing that their personal computer would be sold through participating ComputerLand dealers and Sears, Roebuck and Company business machine stores. These outlets are in addition to IBM Product Centers and a special sales unit within IBM's Data Processing Division.

According to IBM, its personal computer is designed for both the first-time and the advanced user. It is as applicable to the businessman in need of accounting help as it is to a student preparing a term paper. With the help of excellent operation manuals, which are included with this system, it is possible to begin using the computer within hours and to develop programs quite easily, even without previous microcomputer experience.

Shown in Fig. 2-1, the IBM Personal Computer is available with an 83-key adjustable keyboard, up to 262,144 characters of user memory (16,384 is standard), a printer that can print in two directions at 80 characters per second, selftesting capabilities that automatically check the system components and a 16-bit microprocessor.

The IBM Personal Computer uses the Intel 8088 microprocessor chip, which has 16-bit computing capability, rather than the 8-bit chips offered by most other personal computers. Since the entire industry is presently geared toward 8-bit microprocessors, the 8088 chip is able to communicate through an 8-bit bus instead of a 16-bit bus. The 16-bit microprocessor is certainly the coming thing in microcomputers. The memory limitations of 8-bit chips were no problem during the first generation phase of microcomputers, but present use and technology have pretty much exhausted this type of processor. The Intel 8088 is discussed fully in a later chapter.

The IBM Personal Computer can generate and display charts, graphs, text, and numerical information. Business applications such as accounts receivable and word processing can be run on the system. A color graphics option can provide the user with a text system capable of displaying 256 characters in any of sixteen foreground and eight background colors. Graphics may be displayed in four colors. The system's keyboard comes with a six-foot,

coiled cable for flexibility. It can be used in the lap or positioned across a desktop without moving the computer itself.

The optional IBM screen display and printer are attachable units. The display has an antiglare screen, green phosphor characters for reading comfort and controls for brightness and contrast. Automatic flashing and underlining can be used to call attention to important information on the screen. The printer provides twelve type styles. Both printer and system unit can run self-diagnostic checks so that users can verify that components are functioning properly.

The availability of software has been a subject of some concern to potential buyers. At present, the software library for this machine is growing steadily. In a statement made on August 12, 1981, C.B. Rogers, Jr., IBM Vice

Fig. 2-1. The IBM Personal Computer system (courtesy IBM).

President and Group Executive, General Business Group, said "We intend the IBM Personal Computer to be the most useful system of its kind. Besides making it easy to set up and operate, we are offering a program library that we expect will grow with the creativity of the Personal Computer users."

Mr. Rogers was saying that the individual users of this machine were being asked to submit program ideas to IBM based upon their own experiences with the machine. Apparently, this concept has paid off, because a wide range of programs are now available and the library is growing. IBM then established the Personal Computer Software Publishing Department, which publishes programs written by IBM employees and those accepted from independent software companies and outside authors.

The Personal Computer can be tailored to fit the user's needs. A basic system with color graphics for home use attached to an audio tape cassette player and a television set would sell for approximately $1,600, while a more typical system for home or school with color graphics, a memory of 64,000 bytes (a byte is equal to one letter, number, space, or special character), a single disk drive, and the IBM Disk Operating System is priced at about $2,700. An expanded system for business with two disk drives, an IBM display, and a printer costs about $4,500.

Chapter 3 discusses the various portions of the IBM Personal Computer system in detail, but at this point, a brief overview is appropriate. The basic configuration consists of a system unit and keyboard. The former is the heart of the computer, and with its companion keyboard, controls a variety of input/output devices. Each System Unit comes with at least 16K bytes (16,384) of memory for user programs. Each System Unit includes in the 40K byte ROM (read only memory) an enhanced version of the popular Microsoft BASIC-80 Interpreter, and a jack for attachment of a cassette recorder for loading or saving programs and data. A speaker is also standard. The System Unit can be expanded through options that are customer installed in five system expansion slots (one of which is used for a display or monitor adapter).

Memory may be incremented from 16K to 64K bytes on the system board of the System Unit and then up to a System Unit total of 256K. One or two 5¼-inch drives may be added for rapid access to programs and data.

The keyboard, with an adjustable typing angle, offers commonly used data- and word-processing functions in a design that combines the familiar typewriter and calculator pad layouts. All noncontrol keys are repeating. Ten program-supported function keys (total of 40 possible functions using keyboard shift keys) are standard. Special symbols, such as those to draw lines, may be accessed with a combination of keys. Depending on the program, from ten to forty special function keys may be supported. Other keys, like those used to print the current screen contents, correct a typing error, or "scroll" a long document, are clearly labeled. Access to all 256 characters (ASCII and special) is provided by use of the ATL key.

The approximate dimensions of the keyboard are: 200mm (8″) depth, 500mm (20″) length, 57mm (2.5″) height. The approximate weight is 2.8 kg (6 lbs.).

For video output, the user has a choice of the IBM Monochrome Display, a color or black-and-white monitor, or, a color or black-and-white television set. Computer-generated video output may vary from a simple 40 by 25 character alphabetic display, to 80 character-per-line "text" applications, to high-resolution graphics.

The keyboard and customer-supplied cassette recorder are plugged directly into the

Fig. 2-2. The IBM Monochrome Display is a high resolution (80 by 25) black-and-white Monitor.

System Unit. The displays and printer are connected via optional adapters installed inside the System Unit.

When turned on, the System Unit automatically runs a power-on self test to verify system readiness. If the validation is successfully completed, the BASIC ROM Interpreter (cassette level) is made ready and identified on the display screen. The user may then enter a program from the keyboard or load it from a cassette recorder. If a failure is found, an identifying number will appear on the screen.

If a disk drive is installed, the System Unit automatically loads from the disk in drive "A." This is typically the Disk Operating System (DOS) or an application program. The DOS may in turn invoke Disk or Advanced BASIC, followed by the manual or automatic execution of one or more BASIC programs.

The IBM Monochrome Display shown in Fig. 2-2 is a high-resolution device with an 11½-inch diagonal, green phosphor screen. The screen area provides for 25 rows of 80 characters. Characters are 7 by 9 dots in a 9 by 14 dot box. Both upper- and lowercase letters can be displayed. The character attributes provide underline, blinking, high intensity, reverse image, and nondisplay. In addition to the normal alphanumeric characters, a large number of special characters are provided. A set of line graphic characters is supported for display drawings.

The Monochrome Display is supplied with signal and power cables. The signal cable is plugged into the Monochrome Display and Printer Adapter, which is inserted into the second system expansion slot on the left as viewed from the front of the System Unit. The power cable is plugged into the System Unit.

The approximate display dimensions are 350mm (14″) depth, 380mm (15″) length, 280-mm (11″) height, 7.9kg (17 pounds).

The printer, which is shown in Fig. 2-3, is an 80-character-per-second bidirectional matrix printer. It uses pin-feed continuous form (4 inch to 10 inch width), multipart paper. The pitch can be selected for 40-, 66-, 80- or 132-character lines. Horizontal and vertical tabs are supported. Twelve character styles are available. When first turned on, it runs a self test. A bell sounds when it is out of paper. Paper is simple to load and adjust. The ribbon cartridge can be quickly changed, and the print head is a low-cost item that can be replaced by the user. Also, the printer is made by Epson, a Japanese Company.

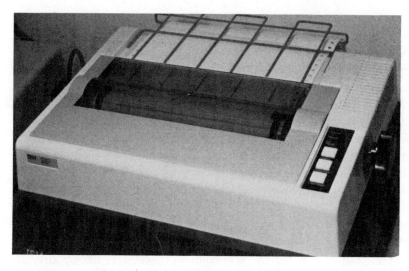

Fig. 2-3. The IBM 80 CPS Bidirectional Matrix Printer (courtesy IBM).

The printer responds to a variety of commands from the System Unit to control page spacing, select the desired character style, or skip to a specified row or column. It requires a signal cable for connection to either the Monochrome Display and Printer Adapter or the IBM Printer Adapter. A six-foot signal cable may be purchased from IBM. The printer comes with a six-foot power cable and requires a 120-volt, 60-Hertz source. The approximate printer dimensions are 400mm (16") length, 370mm (15") deep, and 110mm (4.5") height. It weighs approximately 5.9kg (13 lbs.).

There are several options which can be added to the System Unit. The IBM Monochrome Display and Printer Adapter is an adapter which provides for attachment of both the IBM Monochrome Display and the IBM 80 CPS Matrix Printer. The adapter provides cable connectors for attachment of the printer and the display at the rear of the System Unit. The adapter should be plugged into the second system expansion slot on the left, as viewed from the front of the system unit.

The Color/Graphics Monitor Adapter provides for the attachment of a television frequency display to the IBM Personal Computer. Either a "direct-drive RGB" signal or a "composite" video signal can be selected. The display can be a monitor or a standard television set. Sixteen foreground and eight background colors are supported in text (character) mode. This attachment also provides support for four-color medium resolution graphics (320 dots horizontal, 200 dots vertical) and black-and-white high-resolution graphics (640 dots horizontal, 200 vertical). There are 256 characters available in "text" mode and 128 in medium or high-resolution graphics. The adapter provides 16K bytes of built-in memory to store multiple display screen contents and supports a light pen.

A Printer Adapter provides for attachment of the IBM 80 CPS Matrix Printer. This option is used when the Color/Graphics Monitor Adapter is selected instead of the IBM Monochrome Display and Printer Adapter.

A 16K byte Memory Expansion Kit allows up to 64K bytes of memory to be plugged into the system board. A 32K Memory Expansion Option is also available. The system board must first contain 64K bytes of memory before this option can be used. Each option requires a system expansion slot. Finally, the 64K bytes Memory Expansion Option is used to increase the memory beyond the 64K bytes of the system board by installing one or more of these boards. The system board must first contain 64K before this option can be used. Each option requires a system expansion slot.

The 5¼-inch Disk Drive Adapter and disk drive allow up to two 5¼-inch-160K byte disk drives to be installed inside the System Unit. The user-installable drive allows the Personal Computer to read, write, and store data on 5¼-inch disks. Storage capacity is approximately 160K bytes per disk. The disk drive has the following characteristics: 48 tracks/inch, 40 tracks/disk, 300 revolutions/minute, 80 ms track-to-track access time, and 20,480 bytes/second transfer rate. Two may be installed in a System Unit.

The Asynchronous Communications Adapter provides the computer user with a channel to data processing or input/output devices outside the system. These can be connected by telephone using a modem or directly by cable when the device is nearby. The communication target may be a large computer, a Series/1, another IBM Personal Computer, a paper tape reader, a communicating typewriter, a laboratory instrument, or other machines providing the RS-232-C asynchronous interface. The adapter is flexible enough to match most of the computers and related products available in the microcomputer marketplace. The user's program selects the appropriate speed (50-9600 bps), format (5-, 6-, 7-, or 8-bit characters), parity, and stop bits to reflect the attached device. The adapter can communicate with an IBM Series/1 with feature #1610, 2091/2092 attachment card using a sample program provided on the DOS disk, and an application program running on Real-time Programming System Version 5 (5719-PC5) and Event Driven Executive Version 3 (5719-XS3).

The Asynchronous Communications Adapter provides an RS-232-C Interface. One 25-pin "D" shell, male-type connector is provided to attach various peripheral devices. In addition, a current-loop interface is located in the same connector. A jumper block is provided to manually select either the RS-232-C or the current loop interface.

BASIC language application programs supporting communications will require a disk-based, minimum 32K byte system containing DOS and the BASIC language extensions which include communications support.

The Game Control Adapter supports two customer-supplied joysticks for video game interaction, allowing the user to move an object on the screen in any direction, or supports up to four game "paddles" for horizontal or vertical movement.

WARRANTY AND MAINTENANCE

When considering any piece of electronic equipment, a major factor is the warranty and the maintenance program which has been established by the manufacturer. The IBM Personal Computer has a warranty period of three months, and service may be obtained by delivering the malfunctioning machine element (System Unit, keyboard) to an IBM Product/Service Center, an IBM Customer Service Division (CSD) designated Service Location, or to an authorized IBM Personal Computer dealer. Warranty service is also available by mailing the malfunctioning unit to the IBM National Support Center, Greencastle, Indiana. Proof of purchase from IBM or an authorized IBM Personal Computer dealer is required to obtain warranty service.

Warranty service by IBM is the repair of the System Unit and the replacement of the Monochrome Display, the Matrix Printer, or the Keyboard. The replacement unit will be a similarly configured unit in good working order. The malfunctioning unit becomes the property of IBM.

Customers desiring warranty service from IBM must call the toll-free number for the National Support Center and provide information, including the results of the problem determination Diagnostic Aid program, machine serial number, and location, and whether the malfunctioning unit will be carried to a service location or mailed to the National Support Center. Units taken to a service location are picked up by the customer. For units mailed to the National Support Center, the customer must pay shipping charges to the center and insure or assume risk of loss or damage in transit. IBM will pay these charges for return shipment to the customer's location. It is IBM's objective to repair the customer's System Unit in one or two days. If the repair is performed at the National Support Center, shipping time should be added to the repair time. If the malfunctioning unit is the Monochrome Display, the Matrix Printer or the Keyboard, IBM will try to have a replacement unit available at a service location within 24 hours of notification to IBM. If the customer ships the malfunctioning unit to the National Support Center, they will try to ship a replacement unit within 24 hours of receipt.

If a customer requests warranty service on a unit IBM would ordinarily elect to replace instead of repair, the customer may choose to have the unit repaired at the National Support Center, instead of exchanged, at an additional charge. IBM will try to repair the unit in one or two days. Shipping time should be added to the repair time.

Maintenance service is offered by IBM and is available under the terms and conditions of the IBM Personal Computer Service Agreement, Warranty Extension Option and Annual Option. The Warranty Extension Option is available only if selected prior to or during the warranty period. The agreement commencement date is concurrent with the start of warranty and continues for twelve months. At the end of the twelve months, the service agreement will be renewed automatically under the Annual Option, which is discussed later in this section. Written notice of any applicable price changes are provided prior to renewal. Customers not wishing to renew must withdraw their machines from the agreement.

The Warranty Extension Option provides for IBM-arranged pickup of the malfunctioning unit and replacement with a similarly configured unit in good working order at a location designated by the customer. Pickup and delivery is available if the unit is located within a designated service area, nominally within a 30-mile radius of a service location. Service continues to be available by carry-in to a service location or mail-in to the National Support Center. IBM will try to have a replacement unit available at a service location for pickup or for delivery to the customer if within the designated service area within 24 hours of notification to IBM. If the customer ships the unit to the National Support Center, IBM will ship a replacement within 24 hours of receipt of the unit.

The Annual Option may be selected during the warranty period and if accepted by IBM, the commencement date will be the day after the end of warranty. If this agreement is selected after the end of the warranty period, IBM must inspect the machine at the National Support Center. There is a charge for this inspection. If repairs are required to qualify for this agreement, IBM will provide an estimate and upon the customer's authorization, the work will be performed. The customer will be billed at the time and material rates in effect at that time. The service provided by the Annual Option is the same as that provided by the Warranty Extension Option. The term of this option is twelve months and it is automatically renewed annually. Written notice of any price changes will be provided prior to renewal. Customers not wishing to renew must remove their machines from the agreement.

Under both options, the customer may choose to have a unit repaired rather than replaced at the National Support Center. In that case, IBM will try to repair the unit in one or two days. Shipping time is added to the repair time.

The following customer responsibilities apply during warranty and under the Service Agreements:

1. Identifying the malfunctioning unit through problem determination using the Diagnostic Aid program.

2. Notifying IBM, through the National Support Center toll-free number, of the malfunctioning unit and providing all required information, including results of the Diagnostic Aid program, machine serial number and location.

3. Preparing the malfunctioning unit for shipment in the original or equivalent container. IBM will provide shipping containers for purchase by the customer.

4. Removing all non-IBM devices or features prior to delivery to IBM.

5. Accepting, unpacking and checkout of the replacement (or repaired) units.

The National Support Center is accessible via a toll-free number to receive notification of hardware problems and to assist the customer in isolating a problem to a specific unit. The Center will obtain certain customer information, provide advice on equipment disposition related to the customer's agreement, assist in isolation of the malfunctioning unit and coordinate pickup and delivery when required.

Agreements are not transferable in the event of the loss or sale of a unit. Agreements are purchased for a period of twelve months, payable through a one-time annual charge at time of purchase. This charge is not refundable.

Time and materials service is only available via mail-in to the National Support Center, Greencastle, Indiana. Labor, service parts, and all transportation costs are billable to the customer. The customer's responsibilities are to perform problem determination using the Diagnostic Aid program, telephone the National Support Center, remove all non-IBM devices and features, insure or assume risk of loss or damage in transit and accept, unpack, and check out the repair unit.

In addition to the CSD service offerings, the customer may purchase Advanced Service Aids which will enable the customer to isolate a problem to an under-the-cover field replaceable unit (FRU). Personnel using this diagnostic package must have completed the service training requirements for the IBM Personal Computer. If the customer has the technical ability to follow written service procedures, the customer will be able to perform many of the necessary repairs.

The Personal Computer is a customer setup (CSU) machine. The allowance for setup is one day. Detailed setup instructions are included with each machine. The customer is responsible for unpacking the system components, attaching them correctly, and running the diagnostic program. Customers using the DOS disk and any software which requires the use of disks are responsible for producing back-up copies of the original disks, when copying is permitted, and according to the terms and conditions of the IBM Program License Agreement.

TECHNICAL ASSISTANCE

A newly formed Personal Computer Assistance Center will provide telephone assistance to customers installing IBM-marketed software for the Personal Computer for a period of three months after the date of installation of each system. In addition, customers who have signed a VPA may designate a coordinator at one location who may call the center. Assistance for this coordinator will be available during the VPA period and for three months after the date of installation of the last system shipped under the VPA. If it appears that a problem is related to a code defect in the software, the center will document the problem and submit it to the Information Systems Division (ISD). Additional details on the Personal Computer Assistance Center are available at the time of first-customer shipment.

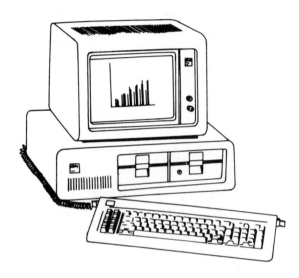

Chapter 3

IBM Personal Computer Hardware

The IBM Personal Computer can be broken down into two major elements, a keyboard and the System Unit. The keyboard consists of 83 keys and offers commonly used data and word-processing functions in a design which combines the familiar typewriter and calculator pad layout. It is attached to the system unit by means of a coiled cable. The System Unit houses the microprocessor, read-only memory (ROM), read/write memory (RWM) power supply, and system expansion slots for the attachment of up to five options.

In addition to these two basic elements, IBM offers a variety of options, shown in Fig. 3-1.

POWER SUPPLY

The power supply included with the com-

puter supplies power for the system unit, the keyboard, and all possible options. It is capable of a continuous output of 63.5 watts. Figure 3-2 illustrates the power supply unit and its output connectors and pin voltages.

The power supply is designed to deliver four discrete outputs and incorporates a switching regulator to hold the output voltages to very close tolerance. The supply provides an output of +5 volt dc at a maximum drain of 7 amperes, 2 amperes at +12 volt dc, 300 milliamperes at −5 volt dc, and 250 milliamperes at −12 volt dc. All positive voltage outputs are held to within a tolerance of ± 5 percent; the negative outputs are held to within ± 10 percent. All outputs are regulated with overvoltage and overcurrent circuits. Input to the power supply is a 120 volts ac. A 2 ampere fuse

Portions reprinted from "The IBM Personal Computer" by David J. Bradley and Lewis C. Eggebrecht, IBM Corp., Boca Raton, FL 33432. (c) Copyright International Business Machines Corp. 1981. Reprinted with permission.

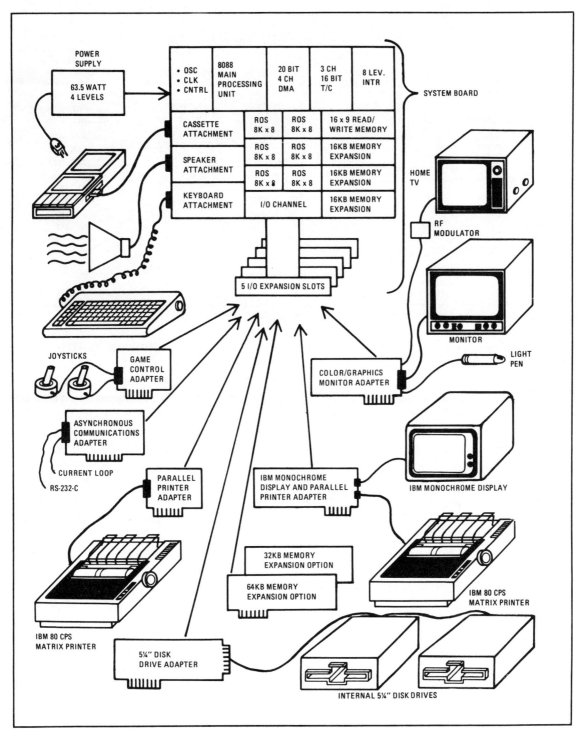

Fig. 3-1. System block diagram for the IBM Personal Computer (courtesy IBM).

37

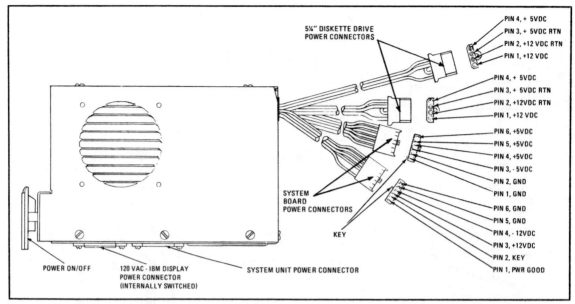

Fig. 3-2. The IBM power supply is a multi-output unit (courtesy IBM).

protects the unit. When a dc overload or over-voltage condition occurs, the supply circuitry automatically shuts down.

The system board draws approximately 3 amperes at 5 volts dc. This allows approximately 4 amperes of current for powering optional equipment. The +12 volt dc supply powers the two internal 5¼-inch disk drives, along with the system's dynamic memory. This part of the supply is set up to drive only one motor at a time. This is the normal mode of operation, even though two disk drives are provided.

The −5 volt dc supply is used for memory bias voltage and analog circuits in the disk adapter. The positive and negative 12 volt dc portions power the serial interface card EIA drivers and receivers for the Asynchronous Communications Adapter. All four power levels are bussed across the five system expansion slots.

When the IBM Monochrome Display is used, the high resolution display receives ac power from the system unit power system. This display contains its own power supply but receives input power through the system unit, allowing the entire system to be switched on and off with the main power switch. The ac output for the display is a nonstandard connector, so only the ac high-resolution display can use this outlet.

The power supply, located in the right rear section of the system unit, provides two connections for powering the disk drive when included. Figure 3-3 shows the nominal power requirements and output voltages for this unit.

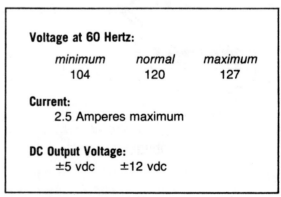

Voltage at 60 Hertz:

minimum	*normal*	*maximum*
104	120	127

Current:
2.5 Amperes maximum

DC Output Voltage:
±5 vdc   ±12 vdc

Fig. 3-3. Power supply specifications.

In their Personal Computer, IBM has included what they call a "power good signal." This is an indication that there is adequate power to continue processing. If power falls below a certain preset level, the power good signal triggers a system shutdown. The power supply provides a power good signal output to indicate that the + and − 5 and + and − 12 volt dc outputs are above the sense level, which is shown in Fig. 3-4. This serves to protect the stored data within the system.

Output	Nominal Sense Voltage
+5 vdc	+4.0 vdc
−5 vdc	−4.0 vdc
+12 vdc	+9.6 vdc
−12 vdc	−9.6 vdc

Fig. 3-4. Power supply sense level specifications.

SYSTEM BOARD

The IBM Personal Computer system board fits horizontally in the base of the System Unit and is approximately 8½ by 12 inches. Dc power and a power-good signal are connected to the board from the power supply. Other connectors on the board attach the keyboard, audio cassette, and the speaker. Five sockets are also mounted on the system board for the attachment of option cards. The system I/O channel is bussed to each of these slots, so that they may be used interchangeably. There are 13 switches on the board which can be read by software to indicate the system state on power up. This includes the amount of installed storage, both on the system board and in the I/O channel, the type of display adapter installed, and the desired operating mode.

The major elements of the system board are divided into five major functional areas. They are the processor and its support elements, ROM, RAM, integrated I/O adapters, and I/O channel. The processor for the IBM Personal Computer is Intel's 8088 microprocessor, which is an 8-bit bus version of the 16-bit 8086 microprocessor, also by Intel. The 8088 is software compatible with the 8086 and thus supports 16-bit internal arithmetic, including multiply and divide. The 8088 can address up to one megabyte of storage with its 20 address lines. It is wired in maximum mode so that coprocessors may be added at a later time. The processor is operated at 4.77 MHz, derived by dividing the 14.31818 MHz crystal by three. This gives a bus cycle of four 210 ns clocks, or 840 ns per cycle. The crystal frequency is also divided by four to provide the 3.58 MHz color burst frequency required for color television.

The processor is supported by a set of high function devices providing four channels of 20-bit direct memory access (DMA), three 16-bit timer/counter channels, and eight prioritized interrupt levels.

Three of the four DMA channels are available on the I/O bus to support high-speed data transfers between I/O devices and memory without processor intervention. The fourth DMA channel is programmed to refresh the system dynamic memory. A channel of the timer/counter requests dummy DMA memory reads at the rate necessary to maintain the dynamic storage.

Channel 0 of the timer/counter is used to time and request refresh cycles from the DMA channel. Channel 1 is used by the system as a general-purpose timer to provide a constant time base for implementing a time-of-day clock. Channel 2 generates tone for the audio speaker and the cassette write operations. Each channel has a minimum timing resolution of 1.05 microseconds.

Of the nine prioritized levels of interrupt, seven are available for use by option cards. The Non-Maskable Interrupt (NMI) of the 8088 is used to report system error conditions, primarily parity errors in the memory. The next two highest levels are used by the integrated I/O on the system board. One is attached to the timer/counter for timer interrupts; the other is attached to the keyboard adapter circuits to interrupt for each scan code received from the keyboard. The remaining six interrupts are used solely by option cards.

The system board is designed to support both read-only memory (ROM) and read/write memory (RWM). Six module sockets are available for ROM, each containing an 8K byte device. The IBM Personal Computer uses five of these sockets for the BASIC Interpreter and the ROM BIOS.

The system board may also contain from 16K by 9 to 64K by 9 bits of RWM. The minimum system would have 16KB of RWM with module sockets for an additional 48KB. Additional RWM beyond the system board's maximum of 64KB is obtainable by adding storage cards in the I/O channel. All user RWM is parity-checked to detect storage errors on reads.

Contained in the system board are circuits for attaching an audio cassette, serial keyboard, and speaker. The cassette adapter allows any good quality audio cassette recorder to be connected through either the microphone or auxiliary inputs, jumper selectable. A cassette motor control line allows program control of motor operation. The cassette interface reads and writes at a date rate between 1000 and 2000 baud, depending on the data content. For diagnostic purposes, the tape interface can loop write output to read input in order to test the interface circuitry. The ROM BIOS device handler for the cassette handles the blocking of cassette data. A cyclic redundancy check (CRC) value is calculated for and tagged onto every block of data during the write operation and checked when read back.

The system board has the adapter circuitry for attaching the serial keyboard unit to the system. This adapter deserializes the scan codes from the keyboard and generates an interrupt to the processor when a complete scan code has been received. The serial interface is bidirectional so that the processor can request the execution of the keyboard diagnostic and prevent additional scan codes from being transmitted into the present one has been handled. The keyboard unit itself contains an Intel 8048 microcomputer to scan the capacitive keyboard array and determine the scan code for each of the 83 keys. In addition to the normal typewriter layout, there is a set of ten function keys to the left and a combination numeric keypad and cursor control area to the right. Every key is typematic in action and reports scan codes for both the depression ("make") and release ("break") of every key. This feature allows the user to configure the keyboard in any manner desired, allowing any key to be used as a shift key, for example. The ROM BIOS routine for the keyboard performs a normal translation of the keyboard, maintaining the current shift state and reporting ASCII character codes to the caller. All 256 character codes may be entered through the keyboard and ROM BIOS, in addition to special function codes for the special keys.

A 2¼ inch audio speaker is mounted inside the System Unit. The system board contains the control circuits and driver for the speaker, which connects by cable to the system board. The drive circuit can provide up to ½ watt of power to the speaker. The controls allow the speaker to be modulated in several methods. First, a direct program control bit may be toggled to generate a pulse train; second, the output of one channel of the timer/counter may be programmed to generate a waveform to the speaker; third, the clock input to the counter can be modulated with a program controlled I/O bit. All three forms of control may be applied simultaneously.

INPUT/OUTPUT CHANNEL

The I/O channel is an extension of the 8088 microprocessor bus. It is demultiplexed, repowered, and enhanced by the addition of interrupts and Direct Memory Access (DMA) functions.

The I/O channel contains an 8-bit directional data bus, 20 address lines, 6 levels of interrupt, control lines for memory and I/O read or write, clock and timing lines, 3 channels of DMA control lines, memory refresh timing control lines, a channel check line, and power and ground for the adapters. Four voltage levels are provided for the I/O card: +5 vdc, −5 vdc, +12 vdc, and −12 vdc. These functions are provided in a 62-pin connector with 100 mil card tab spacing.

A ready line is available on the I/O channel to allow operation with slow I/O or memory devices. If the channel's ready line is not activated by an addressed device, all processor-generated memory read and write cycles take four 210 ns clock or 840 ns/byte. All processor-generated I/O read and write cycles require five 210 ns clocks or 1.05 ms per byte. DMA transfers require five clocks for a cycle time of 1.05 ms per byte. Refresh cycles are present once every 72 clocks or approximately 15 ms and require five clocks or approximately 7 percent of the bus bandwidth.

I/O devices are addressed using I/O mapped address space. The channel is designed so that 512 I/O device addresses are available to the I/O channel cards. A channel check line exists for reporting error conditions to the processor. Activating this line results in a NMI (nonmaskable interrupt) to the 8088 processor. Memory expansion options use this line to report parity errors.

The I/O channel is repowered so there is sufficient drive to power all five system expansion slots, assuming two loads per slot. The optional I/O adapters typically use only one load. An illustration of the system I/O is shown in Fig. 3-6.

The oscillator output signal (+OSC) is a 14-31818 MHz clock with a 50 percent duty cycle and a 70 ns period. The system clock output (CLK) is a divide-by-three circuit of the oscillator and produces an output at 4.77 MHz. The reset driver (RESET DRV) is used to reset or initialize system logic upon applying power or during a low-line voltage outage.

Address bit outputs are labeled A0-A19 and are used to address memory and input/output devices within the system. These twenty address lines allow access of up to 1 megabyte of memory. A0 is the least significant bit (LSB), while A19 is the most significant bit (MSB). These lines are generated by either the processor or the DMA controller and are active high. D0-D7 designate data bits 0 to 7. These input/output lines provide data bus bits for the processor, memory, and I/O devices. They are active high and D0 is the least significant bit, while D7 is the most significant bit.

The Address Latch Enable (ALE) is a part of the 8288 bus controller on the System Board to latch valid addresses from the processor. It is an indicator to the I/O channel of a valid address within the processor. This is used in conjunction with the Address Enable Output, which is used to indicate the processor and other devices from the I/O channel to allow direct memory access to transfer to take place.

The I/O Channel Check ($\overline{I/O\ CH\ CK}$) is an input line that provides the central processing unit with error information on memory or devices in the I/O channel. When this signal is active low, an error is indicated.

The I/O Channel Ready (I/O CH RDY) is an input line which is normally high (when in the ready state). It is pulled low (not ready) by a memory or I/O device to lengthen an I/O or

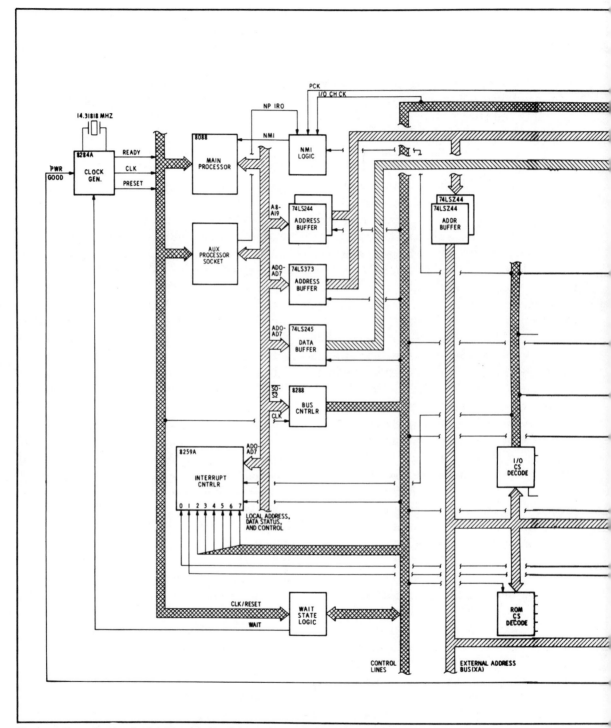

Fig. 3-5. Chart showing the functional areas of the system board (courtesy IBM).

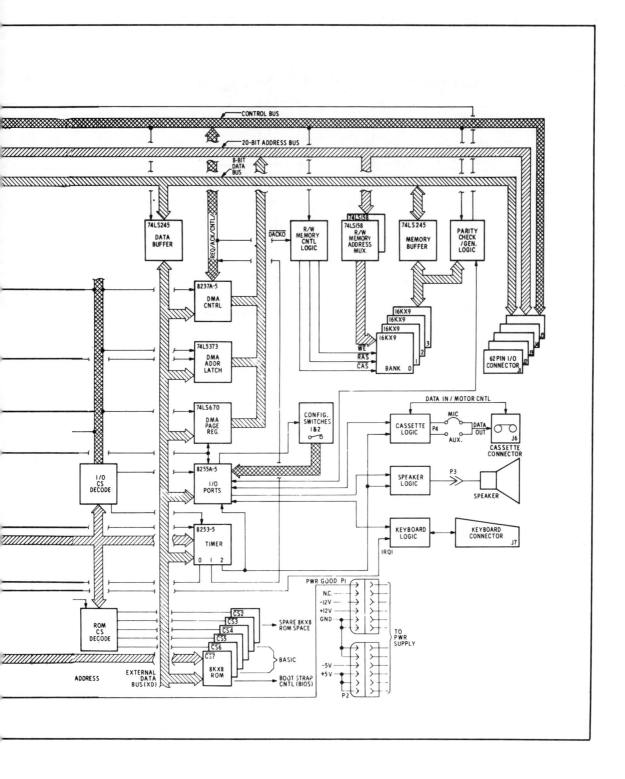

CONTROL BUS

20-BIT ADDRESS BUS

8-BIT DATA BUS

74LS245 DATA BUFFER

REQ/ACK/CNTL.

DACKO

R/W MEMORY CNTL LOGIC

74LS158 R/W MEMORY ADDRESS MUX.

74LS245 MEMORY BUFFER

PARITY CHECK /GEN. LOGIC

8237A-5 DMA CNTRL

74LS373 DMA ADDR LATCH

74LS670 DMA PAGE REG.

16KX9
16KX9
16KX9
16KX9

WE
RAS
CAS

BANK 0

62 PIN I/O CONNECTOR

CONFIG. SWITCHES 1 & 2

DATA IN / MOTOR CNTL

CASSETTE LOGIC

MIC
P4
AUX.

DATA OUT

J6
CASSETTE CONNECTOR

8255A-5 I/O PORTS

SPEAKER LOGIC

P3

SPEAKER

8253-5 TIMER

0 1 2

KEYBOARD LOGIC

KEYBOARD CONNECTOR

J7

IRQ1

I/O CS DECODE

PWR GOOD P1

N.C.
-12V
+12V
GND

TO PWR SUPPLY

ROM CS DECODE

CS2
CS3
CS4
CS5
CS6
CS7

SPARE 8KX8 ROM SPACE

BASIC

8KX8 ROM

BOOT STRAP CNTL (BIOS)

-5V
+5V

P2

ADDRESS

EXTERNAL DATA BUS (XD)

43

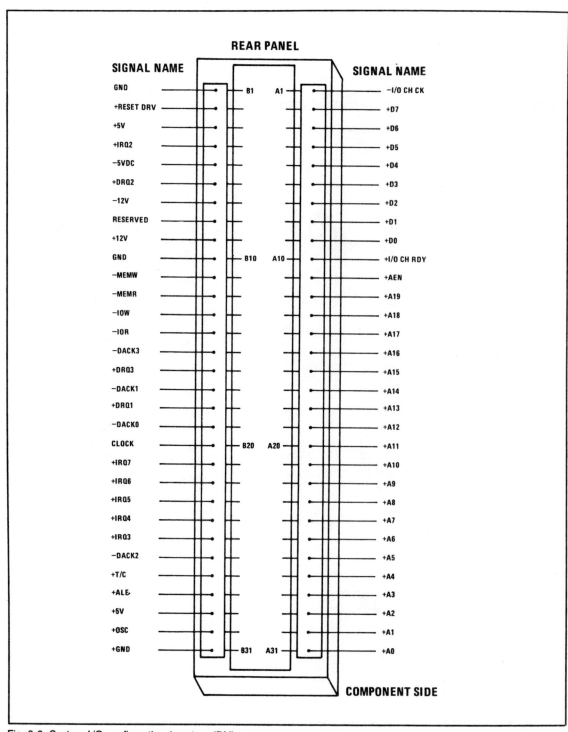

Fig. 3-6. System I/O configuration (courtesy IBM).

memory cycle. This line should never be held low for any period in excess of 10 clock cycles (2.1 microseconds).

IRQ2-IRQ7 are the interrupt request lines and are used to signal the processor that an I/O device requires attention. IRQ2 has the highest priority, while IRQ7 has the lowest. An interrupt request is generated by raising an IRQ line from a normally low state to a high one and holding it in the latter mode until acknowledgement is received from the processor.

The I/O Read Command ($\overline{\text{IOR}}$) is an output command line which instructs an I/O device to drive its data on to the data bus. This signal is active low and may be driven by the processor or the direct memory access controller. The I/O Write Command ($\overline{\text{IOW}}$) instructs an I/O device to read the data on the data bus. This signal is also active low.

The Memory Read Command ($\overline{\text{MEMR}}$) instructs the memory to put its data onto the data bus. The signal is an active low and may be driven by the processor or the controller.

The Memory Write Command line ($\overline{\text{MEMW}}$) is an output which instructs the memory to store the data present on the data bus. This is also driven by the processor or controller and its signal is active low. The DMA request lines (DRQ1-DRQ3) are inputs that are asynchronous channel requests used by any peripheral devices to gain direct memory access service. DRQ1 has the highest priority and DRQ3 is the lowest. A request is generated by bringing a DRQ line to an active level (high). This line must be held high until the corresponding DACK line goes active. The latter is the Direct memory access Acknowledge and consists of three lines (matching the DMA request lines). These acknowledge DMA requests and refresh the system dynamic memory. They are active low.

The Terminal Count line (T/C) provides a pulse when the terminal count for *any* DMA channel is reached. This signal is active high.

KEYBOARD

The IBM Personal Computer keyboard is a real joy to use and, as was pointed out earlier, is not a part of the major processing unit (System Unit), as is the case with many microcomputers. This provides a definite operational advantage, especially with the IBM system, since it is rather large. It is often not possible to mount the System Unit and monitor screen on smaller desks, so the alternative is to mount them on a nearby table and locate the keyboard only on the desk or in any other operating position. The keyboard is connected to the System Unit by a six-foot flexible coiled cord which will allow it to be mounted this same distance from the rear of the System Unit. The System Unit provides power to the keyboard through a 5-volt line and a ground. There are two bidirectional signal lines within the same cord for inputting information. The cable is permanently attached at the keyboard end. A DIN connector accesses the rear of the System Unit at the appropriate receptacle. Note: The keyboard receptacle is mounted to one side of the cassette receptacle. The proper connection point is clearly marked on the rear of the System Unit, so make certain you access the correct one for keyboard connection. The keyboard is enclosed in a low-profile, metal container, and there is a tilt adjustment which will allow it to be raised or lowered.

The heart of the keyboard is an Intel 8048 chip which is a microcomputer in itself, using capacitive technology to perform the keyboard scan functions. The keyboard unit contains 83 keys in three groupings. The center portion contains a standard typewriter keyboard layout. The soft keys (F1 to F10) are located on the left side and can be programmed to perform many different operating functions. These keys are user-defined by software, and when

Fig. 3-7. Keyboard .

operating in DOS, are already assigned. The right-hand grouping of keys is a numeric pad in lowercase mode. When in uppercase, this grouping functions as a cursor control for screen editing. In most cases, the latter mode of operation will be used on an almost full-time basis.

Figure 3-7 shows the IBM Personal Computer keyboard. You can clearly see the three major groupings. The space bar is very sensitive in later-model machines, although earlier models often require a strike at dead center to function properly. In using an earlier model keyboard and then a later model, I found this improvement to be quite significant in reducing programming time.

The internal "computer on a chip," the Intel 8048, performs a power-on self-test function when requested to do so by the System Unit. This is part of the Diagnostic Routine which is sold with each IBM Personal Computer and allows the keyboard to check itself for proper operation. Figure 3-8 provides a table

of scan codes for the keyboard. Figure 3-9 shows a block diagram of the keyboard interface on the system board. Again, when interfacing the keyboard with the System Unit, it is possible to access the wrong receptacle. Figure 3-10 shows the rear of the System Unit and the keyboard receptacle. This is located on the left side as you face the rear of the unit. It must be properly identified, since either of the two receptacles will accept the DIN plug. Apparently, no damage will result to either the keyboard or System Unit if you accidentally access the wrong receptacle, but of course, the system will not operate either.

CASSETTE USER INTERFACE

Although most persons will select the Diskette Drive Adapter and at least one diskette drive for storage, some may still opt for the older, cassette tape medium. This was quite popular during the early stages of microcomputer usage, but is fast falling by the wayside due to the higher efficiency offered by

Key Position	Scan Code in Hex	Key Position	Scan Code in Hex
1	01	43	2B
2	02	44	2C
3	03	45	2D
4	04	46	2E
5	05	47	2F
6	06	48	30
7	07	49	31
8	08	50	32
9	09	51	33
10	0A	52	34
11	0B	53	35
12	0C	54	36
13	0D	55	37
14	0E	56	38
15	0F	57	39
16	10	58	3A
17	11	59	3B
18	12	60	3C
19	13	61	3D
20	14	62	3E
21	15	63	3F
22	16	64	40
23	17	65	41
24	18	66	42
25	19	67	43
26	1A	68	44
27	1B	69	45
28	1C	70	46
29	1D	71	47
30	1E	72	48
31	1F	73	49
32	20	74	4A
33	21	75	4B
34	22	76	4C
35	23	77	4D
36	24	78	4E
37	25	79	4F
38	26	80	50
39	27	81	51
40	28	82	52
41	29	83	53
42	2A		

Fig. 3-8. Scan codes of the system board keyboard interface (courtesy IBM).

diskette storage. The IBM Personal Computer does contain cassette interface control, which is implemented in software. Data to the cassette recorder is controlled by an 8253 timer output. A DIN connector at the rear of the System Unit (next to the keyboard connector) is used to interface the recorder/player. Data from the cassette recorder is read by an 8255 programmable peripheral interface input port bit. Incoming data from the cassette player is fed to pin 4 of the cassette connector. The cassette drive motor is controlled through pins 1 and 3 of this same connector. The motor on/off is controlled by an 8255 output port bit.

In BASIC, the MOTOR statement is used to activate the cassette drive. The statement MOTOR 1 turns it on; the statement MOTOR 0 turns it off. Actually, if the numerical designator following the statement is non-zero, the motor is automatically turned on. This statement may also be used without a designator, and the motor will automatically reverse states. The MOTOR statement, when used alone, will turn the motor on if it is off, and vice versa.

The 8255 A-5 programmable peripheral

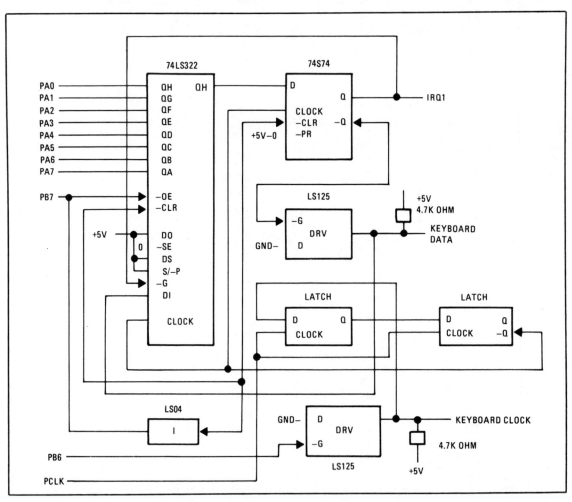

Fig. 3-9. Block diagram of keyboard interface (courtesy IBM).

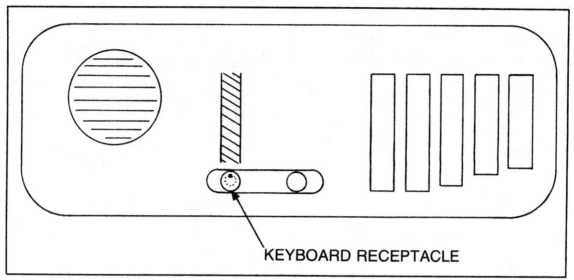

KEYBOARD RECEPTACLE

Fig. 3-10. Rear of System Unit showing location of keyboard receptacle.

interface offers 24 programmable I/O pins, has direct bit set/reset capability, and is fully TTL compatible. Figure 3-11 shows this chip in pictorial form.

A Berg-pin and jumper are used on the cassette data out line. The pin/jumper combination will allow the data line to be used as a microphone input when the jumper is placed across the pins as shown on the left. When the jumper is placed on the right-hand set of pins, this makes an auxiliary input available which provides a 0.68-volt input to the recorder.

SPEAKER INTERFACE

The IBM Personal Computer contains a built-in 2¼-inch permanent magnet speaker at the left front of the System Unit. The speaker is capable of being driven by an 8255 A-5 PPI output bit or by a timer channel clock output. Figure 3-12 shows the speaker drive system in block diagram form and accesses to its two drive sources.

The speaker is used during initial system activation to indicate that the power supply and self test functions are operational. Approxi-

mately 15 to 45 seconds after the System Unit has been switched on (total time being dependent upon memory), the speaker will emit a short beep, which indicates proper operation. Outputs are fed to the speaker when programming in BASIC by using the SOUND, PLAY, and BEEP statements. The audio output may be used as a prompt or as an integral part of a program run which may output music or a fixed series of audio tones.

IBM MONOCHROME DISPLAY AND PARALLEL PRINTER ADAPTER

The IBM Monochrome Display and Parallel Printer Adapter is a dual-function system expansion card. It mounts in one slot on the IBM system board and is contained within the System Unit. This card interfaces the system board with the IBM Monochrome Display and also functions as a parallel interface for the IBM 80 CPS Matrix Printer. The latter capability is also available from a separate parallel interface board and is available to those individuals who might choose to use a television receiver as a monitor, which would be driven

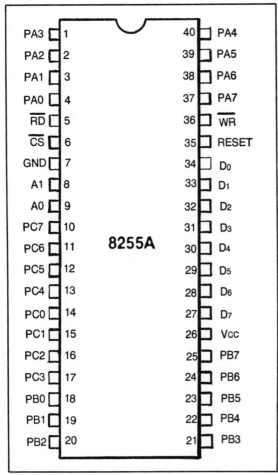

PA3	1	40	PA4
PA2	2	39	PA5
PA1	3	38	PA6
PA0	4	37	PA7
$\overline{RD}$	5	36	$\overline{WR}$
$\overline{CS}$	6	35	RESET
GND	7	34	D0
A1	8	33	D1
A0	9	32	D2
PC7	10	31	D3
PC6	11	30	D4
PC5	12	29	D5
PC4	13	28	D6
PC0	14	27	D7
PC1	15	26	Vcc
PC2	16	25	PB7
PC3	17	24	PB6
PB0	18	23	PB5
PB1	19	22	PB4
PB2	20	21	PB3

8255A

Fig. 3-11. Functional pin description for the 8255 PPI (courtesy IBM).

by the color/graphics board. In such a situation, if a printer were to be used, the separate parallel interface board would be opted for because its price is lower than that for the dual-function card.

The monitor interface portion of the Monochrome Display and Parallel Printer Adapter is built around the Motorola 6845 CRT controller module. The card contains 4000 bytes of static memory used for the display buffer. A dual-ported memory is also provided and is accessed directly by the central processor unit. Figure 3-13 shows a block diagram of the monochrome display function found on this board.

This card supports 256 character codes, which include alphanumeric and block figures for low-level graphics work. The character code must be an even address; the attribute code is an odd address in the display buffer. This is shown in Fig. 3-14.

The display adapter function supports an alphanumeric-only, 80-character-by-25-line screen format. Characters are 7 by 9 dots formed within a 9-by-14-dot box. Characters may have one line of ascender and two lines for descenders. The character font is double dotted for good readability in reverse video mode. The display buffer provides character attributes, with each character represented by two 8-bit bytes. The first byte is the character code (one of 256), and the second byte contains the attribute information for that character. Character attributes include reverse video, highlighting, underscore, nondisplay, and blinking. The adapter contains 4K bytes of RWM which contains the display buffer and the attribute buffer. This memory is dual-ported such that the process may access it at any time without causing display interference. Like the Color/Graphics Monitor Adapter, the display buffer is directly addressable by the processor for ease of software access to the buffer.

The Monochrome Display Adapter character set is compatible with the color/graphics character set, with the exception of a different font style for the larger character box size. The ROM BIOS provides a display interface which treats the two displays identically whenever the special attributes of the color/graphics display are not in use. This allows the application programmer to write code that is compatible with either of the display attachments without being concerned with the differences in the two.

The ROM BIOS provides the ability to set

the mode of operation for either of the cards. The BIOS also provides the interface to set the cursor position, read or write a character at that location, scroll a selected window of the display either up or down, and even provides an entry point to make the display act as a simple teletypewriter simulator. This latter mode of operation greatly simplifies the display interface for simple applications.

A particularly convenient feature of the ROM BIOS is the ability to read and write text information in the APA modes of the color graphics card. Using this feature, alphanumeric information may be written to the display in addition to the graphic material. This

allows the user to edit programs while in the graphics mode.

MONOCHROME DISPLAY

The IBM Monochrome Display (Fig. 3-15) is a high-resolution monitor. It attaches to the System Unit by two cables. One is a power cable, which is in parallel with the 115-vac input to the System Unit and is active when the System Unit switch is in the on position. The other is a signal cable, which provides the signal interface between the two units. The fact that the power cable attaches to the System Unit is quite advantageous, since the monitor will normally rest atop the System

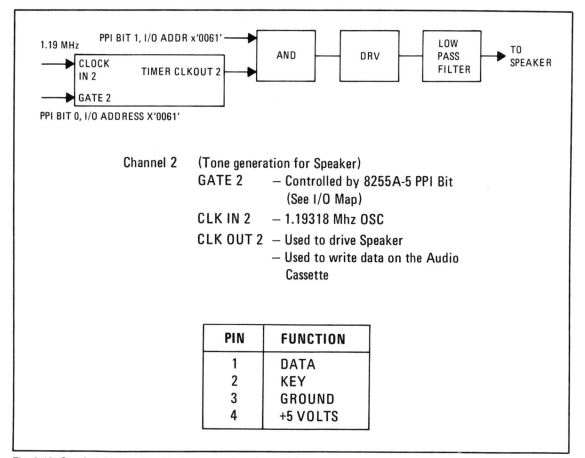

Fig. 3-12. Speaker drive system block diagram (courtesy IBM).

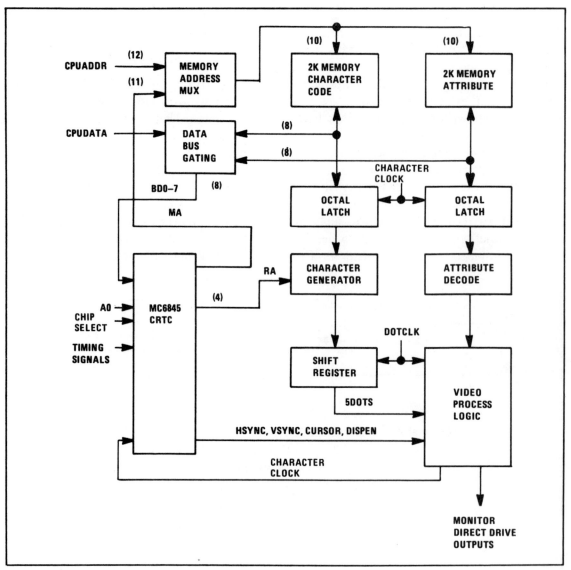

Fig. 3-13. Monochrome display functions (courtesy IBM).

Unit. This cuts down on the number of wall outlets that need to be accessed by the entire system.

The display has a long-persistence green phosphor (P39) with an etched viewing surface to reduce glare. Two controls are provided on the lower right-hand side of the enclosure to vary the brightness and the contrast of the characters and viewing screen, respectively. The monitor contains its own built-in power supply, which provides high voltage for the CRT, which is operated at a scan rate of over 18 kHz to minimize the audio interference of the internal flyback transformer.

The signal cable is terminated in a nine-pin DIN connector, which attaches to the back

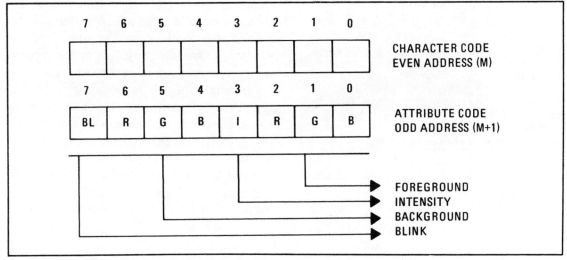

Fig. 3-14. The character code must be an even address and the attribute code must be odd (courtesy IBM).

of the Monochrome Display/Printer Adapter Board. The screen is capable of displaying 80 characters horizontally and 25 vertically. Each character box is 14 dots high and 9 dots wide.

COLOR/GRAPHICS MONITOR ADAPTER

The Color/Graphics Monitor Adapter is designed to attach a wide variety of TV frequency monitors and TV sets (with user-supplied rf modulator) to the IBM Personal Computer. It is capable of operating in black and white or color and provides three video interfaces: a composite video port, a direct drive port for RGB monitors; and a connection for driving an rf modulator. In addition, a light pen may be connected.

The card has two basic modes of operation: alphanumeric (A/N), or text mode; and all points addressable (APA) or graphics mode. Within each of these, there are several methods of displaying the data. In A/N mode, the display may be 40 characters by 25 lines for low-resolution monitors and TVs, or 80 characters by 25 lines for high-resolution monitors. In both cases, characters are defined in an 8-by-8 box and are 5 by 7, with one line of

descender for lowercase (both upper- and lowercase characters are supported in all modes). In black and white displays, the character attributes of reverse video, blinking, highlighting, and nondisplay are available. For color displays, there are 16 foreground colors and 8 background colors available per character. Additionally, each character may be blinked. Also, the screen border may be any of 16 colors. The adapter card contains 16K bytes of storage; thus, for a 40-by-25 screen, 1000

Fig. 3-15. IBM Monochrome display.

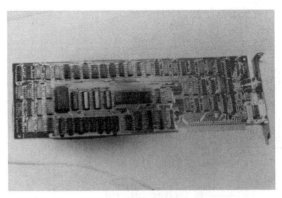

Fig. 3-16. The Color/Graphics Monitor adapter board.

bytes are used to store character information and 1000 bytes are used for attribute/color information. This means that up to 8 different display screens may be kept in the adapter simultaneously. Similarly, in the 80 by 25 mode, four pages may be stored. The full 16K bytes of storage on the display adapter is directly addressable by the processor, allowing maximum software flexibility in managing the screen. Note that this storage is independent of the storage on the system board or in the memory expansion cards on the I/O channel. Thus, a minimum system with 16K bytes of storage and a Color/Graphics Monitor Adapter really has 32K bytes of read/write storage attached.

In text mode, characters are formed with a ROM character generator on the adapter. The character generator contains dot patterns for all 256 possible characters. The character set includes the 96 ASCII characters, as well as graphics for games, word processing, international uses, business line graphics, scientific and commonly used Greek letters.

In APA mode, there are two resolutions available: 320 horizontal by 200 vertical points, or 640 horizontal by 200 vertical points. In 320-by-200 mode, each picture element (pel) may have one of four colors. The background color may be any of the 15 possible colors. The

remaining three colors come from one of the two software selectable palettes. One palette contains green/red/brown; the other contains cyan/magenta/white. By judicious use of color mixing (different colors next to each other on a horizontal line), it is possible to create graphics displays with more than four apparent colors. The 640 by 200 mode is black and white only, since the full 16K bytes of storage is used to define the pels with one bit each.

The Color/Graphics Monitor Adapter is contained on a single circuit card and is fitted into one of the five system expansion slots on the system board. This is a long card and will span the entire depth of the System Unit enclosure. Normally, a snap-in plastic retainer is sold with this card, which is fitted to the inside front of the System Unit enclosure in order to hold the card firmly in place.

The display adapter is implemented by the Motorola 6845 CRT controller device, making the combination highly programmable regarding raster and character parameters. By reprogramming the adapter, many additional modes of color/graphics operation are possible.

PARALLEL PRINTER ADAPTER

The Printer Adapter card is specifically designed to attach the IBM wire matrix printer to the system, but it may be used to attach any printers using an appropriate parallel port interface. Likewise, the attachments may be used as a general-purpose parallel port with 12 TTL level outputs and 5 TTL level inputs. The outputs are latched and may be read or written under program control. The inputs may be read in a similar fashion. In addition, one of the inputs can also be used to create a processor interrupt. This interrupt can be enabled and disabled under program control. The same function is also part of the Monochrome Display and Printer Adapter card.

The ROM BIOS provides the ability to print a single character. The character is latched into the output buffer, the program waits for the printer to be ready, then strobes the character to the printer. Any errors are reported to the caller on the return.

When a printer is attached to the adapter's output, all data are loaded into an 8-bit latched output port and the strobe line is activated, which writes data directly to the printer. The program may be set up to check on printer status by reading the input port. This forms an indication as to when the next character may be written in.

As was previously mentioned, the full capability of the Parallel Printer Adapter is also found on the Monochrome Display and Printer Adapter card. The separate parallel interface card is provided for those individuals who do not wish to use the monochrome display, but who still have need of a printer interface.

IBM 80 CPS MATRIX PRINTER

The wire matrix printer is a self-powered tabletop unit. It attaches to the System Unit with a parallel signal cable six feet in length from either the Printer Adapter card, or the Monochrome Display and Printer Adapter. The printer operates at 80 characters per second and prints bidirectionally. It can print in a compressed mode of 132 characters per line, a standard font of 80 characters per line, and a large font of 66 characters per line. Also available are double-size characters and double-dotted characters.

Shown in Fig. 3-17, the printer prints the standard 96 character ASCII set of upper- and lowercase letters. A set of 64 special block graphic characters are also available. Most form parameters such as line spacing, and lines per page are programmable.

The printer interfaces with the Parallel

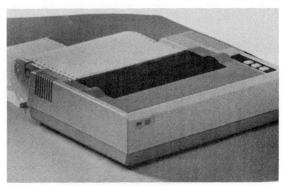

Fig. 3-17. IBM 80 CPS matrix printer.

Printer Adapter (or dual adapter card) at the rear of the System Unit by means of a very bulky cable, owing to the fact that it must contain the 25 signal leads along with a shield. The cable is terminated in a 25-pin "D" type connector at the System Unit end and a 36-pin connector which attaches to the printer. In certain configurations, the cable may interfere with paper feed to the tractor unit, but the IBM printer stand comes equipped with a plastic, friction-fitting clamp which can hold this cable out of the way. When connecting the 36-pin plug to the printer, a separate ground wire is attached to a screw-in terminal. While the printer will work without this connection being made, the effect of the shield is wholly or partially eliminated, and interference can result. Figure 3-18 provides a table of specifications for the IBM 80 CPS Matrix Printer.

DISKETTE DRIVE ADAPTER

The System Unit allows space and power for the installation of up to two 5¼-inch diskette drives. Two types of drives are available. The single-sided type allows for storage of up to 160,000 bytes; the double-sided drive can store up to 320,000 bytes on a double-sided diskette. There is a track-to-track access time of 6 milliseconds and a motor start time of 500 milliseconds. Both types of drives require the Diskette Drive Adapter board, which normally

Size: Width - 15.7 in., depth - 14.5 in., height - 4.3 in.

Weight: 12.5 lb

Electrical requirements: 120 volts AC, 100 watts

Features:
    Bi-directional printing
    80-characters-per-second rated speed
    Continuous feed, multipart paper
    Self-diagnostic checks for proper operation
    12 types tyles to suit various printing needs
    9 × 9 character dot matrix
    Page spacing and column skip for word processing
    40, 66, 80 or 132 characters-per-line formats
    Out-of-paper alarm
    Replaceable ribbon cartridge and print head

Fig. 3-18. Printer (80 CPS matrix printer) specifications.

fits in the far right-hand system expansion slot when facing the front of the unit. The board may be placed in other slots. However, it is necessary to route a ribbon cable to its output, and this can interfere with other cards when the far right-hand slot is not used.

Whether your computer comes equipped with one or two drives, the daisy-chained flat cable, which connects to the end of the drive card, contains two diskette drive connectors. In single-drive systems, one connector is not used and simply lays within the chassis. The diskette adapter card also contains a second connector at the rear of the System Unit, allowing for the connection of two additional drives. The adapter card, then, is capable of attaching up to four single- or double-sided diskette drives to the System Unit (internally and externally).

The adapter is designed for MFM-coded drives and uses write precompensation with an analog phase locked loop for clock and data recovery. The attachment uses the NEC uPD765 diskette controller for the data channel control of the diskettes. All I/O connections are buffered on the I/O bus and use direct memory access for data transfers. An interrupt level is used to indicate operation complete and status conditions requiring processor attention.

The ROM BIOS provides a physical record level interface for the user program. The calling program requests a read/write operation on a specific track and sector. The operation is performed, with the data being placed (or taken from) the user specified area. Upon completion of the operation, control is returned to the caller, with the status of the result set in the registers. The user need not be aware of any of the physical parameters of the system other than the actual track and sector on which the data resides. Figure 3-19 shows a block diagram of the Diskette Drive Adapter.

DISKETTE DRIVE ASSEMBLY

The IBM Diskette Drive is available in single-sided and double-sided versions and up to two may be installed within the System Unit. Two outboard drives may also be connected, and all will attach to the diskette drive adapter board. Each unit is self-contained and an electronics card is mounted atop each. Connectors from the power supply are attached to this board and a ribbon cable interfaces between the drive and the adapter.

These assemblies incorporate a spindle drive system, a read/write/erase system, and a positioning system. The slotted openings for the diskettes are horizontally mounted when the drive is a part of the System Unit. A front latch is opened to insert the diskette. When the latch is closed, the drive engages the diskette. The disk is positioned by plastic guides and the front latch.

When the front latch is closed, this activates a cone/clamp system which automatically centers the disk and clamps it to the drive hub. The latter rotates at a constant speed of

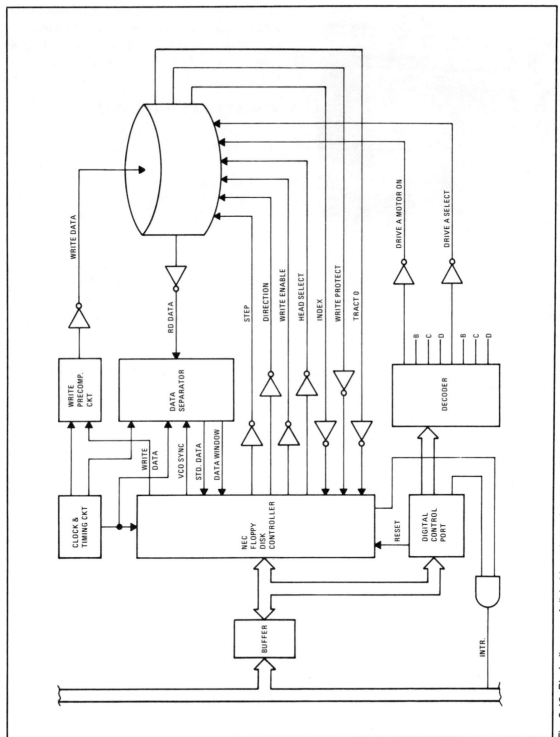

Fig. 3-19. Block diagram of disk drive adapter (courtesy IBM).

Fig. 3-20. A typical 5¼-inch diskette.

300 revolutions per minute and is powered by a servo-controlled dc motor. The magnetic head(s) is loaded into contact with the diskette as soon as the latch is closed.

The drive system incorporates a four-phase stepper motor/band assembly. One-step rotations cause one-track linear movements. The drive also contains a write-protect sensor which disables the recording mode when a write-protect tab is applied to the diskette. When this situation is sensed, a signal is applied to the interface and the computer monitor screen will indicate that an attempt has been made to write onto a protected diskette.

Each drive uses a standard 5¼-inch diskette. Single-sided or double-sided diskettes may be used interchangeably with either drive unit, but, of course, the single-sided drive can read only one side at a time. Figure 3-20 shows a typical 5¼-inch diskette used with the IBM drives. This is a flexible disk that has been treated with magnetic particles and is completely enclosed in a paper jacket. The disk rotates within the jacket, which contains a soft fabric inner lining. A slotted opening near the bottom of the diskette allows for read/write

access. There are two other openings in the diskette. The center one allows for the magnetic diskette to engage the drive hub. A small hole to the right of center serves as the disk index.

MEMORY EXPANSION OPTIONS

Memory expansion refers to the insertion of one or more memory cards into the system expansion slots to improve on the quantity of memory contained on the system board proper. The IBM Personal Computer is available with 16K, 32K, 48K, and 64K contained on the system board and without using the expansion slots. If you want to expand the memory to more than 64K, you can purchase one of two memory cards. One card offered by IBM adds 32K to the 64K already contained on the system board. The other board adds 64K memory. Several boards may be used to provide a memory of up to 256K. This maximum configuration would be arrived at using three 64K boards in three of the system expansion slots. A memory card may be configured to reside in any 32K boundary within the system one megabyte of address space by setting switches on the card. These switches are contained in a DIP package and are set to the on or off positions through the aid of a chart supplied by IBM. The actual settings are dependent upon the total amount of memory contained. Switches on the System Unit board must also be set to reflect total memory.

Both the 32K and 64K memory expansion cards are parity checked. If a parity error occurs, the I/O channel check line is activated. The process will respond immediately and prevent the error from propagating further into the system.

In addition to extra memory, the expansion boards contain dynamic memory timing generation, address multiplexing, bus buffering, and card select decode logic. While dynamic memory refresh timing and address generation are not performed on the expansion boards proper, these are done one on the system board and made available on the I/O channel for all devices.

GAME CONTROL ADAPTER

The Game Control Adapter is used for programming video action games in which players manually activate or control on-screen functions, especially graphics animation. The Game Control Adapter allows for the connection of two joysticks or up to four paddles to the System Unit. The joysticks and paddles are not provided by IBM, but many, available from other manufacturers, are compatible with the Game Control Adapter. In addition to these devices, four switch inputs are provided. Often, at least one switch will be provided with each joystick and is typically used to activate a single on-screen function such as the firing of a missile in a video war game.

Joysticks may be thought of as variable resistors and the changing resistance as the stick controls are moved as read by the computer. This, in turn, varies the motion of an on-screen character. In conjunction with system software, the adapter converts the resistance value to a relative joystick position.

The Game Control Adapter is inserted into one of the five system expansion slots and provides an output connector at the rear of the unit. The game control interface cable attaches here. The BASIC Interpreter contained within the system ROM allows direct interrogation of all four paddle positions. The Advanced BASIC allows the switch input to cause "on" conditions to be executed within the BASIC program, allowing immediate reaction to switch input. All four one-shots are fired at once by an OUT to address X'201'. The four one-shot outputs will go positive or high after the fire pulse and will remain in this state for a varying

period of time, depending upon where each potentiometer is set.

ASYNCHRONOUS COMMUNICATIONS ADAPTER

The Asynchronous Communications Adapter is designed to support serial communication with any device using the RS232-C electrical interface and a start/stop line protocol. An alternate current loop electrical interface is also provided. The attachment supports asynchronous communications with 5-, 6-, 7-, or 8-bit data, using 1, 1½, or 2 stop bits, and even or odd or no parity. Baud rates from 50 to 9600 are supported in half and full duplex mode.

The attachment supports the RS232-C interface lines of Transmit Data, Receive Data, Request to Send, Clear to Send, Data Terminal Ready, Data Set Ready, Ring Indicator, and Carrier Detect. The adapter is designed so that data may be looped through the attachment for diagnostic purposes.

Both Disk BASIC and Advanced BASIC, available on the DOS diskette, provide software support for asynchronous communications. In both cases, the BASIC interpreter will provide input and output buffers for the asynchronous communications, which will transmit and receive data without direct program intervention. Data is transmitted from BASIC using the PRINT statement and read from the communications line using the INPUT statement. In Advanced BASIC, the receipt of communications may generate an on condition for "interrupt" processing within BASIC.

The Asynchronous Communications Adapter plugs into the system expansion slot and is about 4 inches high and 5 inches long. A jumper module is provided to select current loop or RS-232-C operation. This adapter is programmable, supports asynchronous communications only, and is built around the Ins

Fig. 3-21. The IBM asynchronous communications adapter board.

8250 LSI chip. In some cases, IBM may use a functional equivalent. The chips offers full prioritized interrupt system controls and false start bit detection. IBM does not offer a telephone modem for phone line communications between two computers, but these are commonly available from many different manufacturers. The adapter is often used to drive serial printers and such devices as speech synthesizers. In testing the performance of this adapter, I used a Votrax speech synthesizer set up to receive data at the 9600 baud rate. This synthesizer was fully compatible with the asynchronous interface and made for an excellent combination. Figure 3-21 shows the Asynchronous Communications Adapter, which contains an on-card, highly stable oscillator operating at 1.8432 MHz. The output from the card is a 25-pin D-shell connector, which is pretty much standard in the industry.

Chapter 4

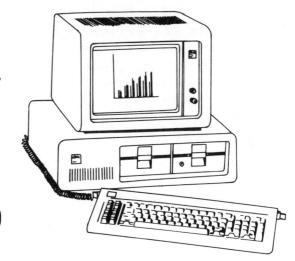

Equipment Setup

The IBM Personal Computer is quite easy to set up if you use the IBM Guide To Operations manual, which is included. IBM advertises that the Personal Computer is a very versatile piece of equipment that can be set up and used by the neophyte as well as by the experienced programmer. This is true based upon my initial setup.

When the equipment arrived, I had already decided to handle the initial setup and operation in strict accordance with the manufacturer's directions. All previous computer training was forgotten for the time being, and I tried to proceed like a rank newcomer to this field. IBM's Guide to Operations manual is an excellent text and eliminates nearly every chance of an improper initial setup. In my opinion, a good installation manual does not neglect the obvious. The reason for this is that what is obvious to you and me may not be obvious to others. The manual starts at the

beginning by instructing the owner on removal of packaging tape and even the cardboard inserts which protect the disk drive(s).

The first setup procedure involves the System Unit, which is placed on a work area, Next, the keyboard is unpacked and connected to the System Unit. The keyboard is equipped with a flexible coiled cord which will later allow it to be operated up to about six feet away from the System Unit. It is terminated in a 5-pin octal plug which is inserted into the rear of the System Unit. There are two 5-pin receptacles closely spaced at the rear of the System Unit, either of which will accept this plug, although only one is designed for keyboard input. The other accepts the input from a cassette recorder. The instructions are very explicit as to which receptacle is to be used for keyboard input. Apparently, the first System Units produced by IBM did not contain placards above the proper receptacles. This was corrected in later models, as some persons were plugging the keyboard output into the cassette input and probably vice versa. In addition to the excellent instructions found in the installation manual, the keyboard input is now labeled to avoid any chance of error.

Attachment of the keyboard to the System Unit is done before power is connected. The next step involves making sure the on/off switch located on the right rear side of the System Unit is in the off position. The removable power cord is then inserted into its receptacle at the right rear of the System Unit and the plug inserted in the wall. IBM has supplied a six-foot cord for these purposes, which is standard, although I prefer ten-foot cords for increased versatility when mounting locations are located some distance from the nearest wall outlet.

At this point, the initial basic installation is complete and the machine can be switched to the on position. Here, the internal Self-Test routine takes over. Within fifteen seconds after

activation, a short beep should be heard from the speaker at the left front of the System Unit. In their manual, IBM states "If you heard other than one short beep, return your IBM Personal Computer to place of purchase." This initial test beep is activated by the main 12-volt source in the internal power supply of the System Unit. An IBM technician who provided a great deal of assistance explained that the power supply is an "intelligent" type which will automatically shut down if circuit parameters are not what they should be. If the main 12-volt source is not operational, then the beep will not be heard. This is an indication that either the power supply is defective or there are other circuit problems causing the power supply to shut down.

Figure 4-1 shows the back of the System Unit with its various receptacles. The power supply is cooled by a whisper-quiet fan that cannot really be heard in a normal operating environment. Placing your hand at the fan outlet, you will note an almost imperceptible

Fig. 4-1. View of the back panel of the system unit.

Fig. 4-2. The IBM Monochrome display may sit atop the system unit.

breeze. While you can't hear this fan, you can probably feel its vibration by placing your hand on the side of the cabinet. On the right side of the back of the System Unit are the card inputs and outputs. Their internal connections are parallelled. The unit supplied to me by IBM contained a 64K byte memory card which is mounted in the far right-hand slot, while the disk drive card is mounted on the far left.

Once you have ascertained that the System Unit is operational, the options may be connected. I was supplied with the IBM Monochrome Display, which can sit atop the System Unit, as shown in Fig. 4-2. It receives its power from the video power outlet on the left rear of the System Unit. A 9-pin connector interfaces the display with the System Unit.

Once the monitor has been connected, a

Fig. 4-3. Self-Test functions.

further test or mini-test, as IBM calls it, is internally generated. IBM advises that the monitor or television contrast and brightness controls be turned to maximum gain. When you first position the System Unit switch to on, it again performs the Power-On Self-Test, which is evidenced by the beep. With the monitor connected, a further self-test function takes place. The time it takes to complete this test will be determined by the amount of memory contained in the System Unit. Total time can range from 3 to 45 seconds.

When the System Unit is switched to on, there will normally be three responses:

1. A cursor will appear on the screen in approximately 4 seconds.

2. One short beep will be heard after the memory is tested (45 seconds maximum).

3. "IBM Personal Computer" will appear on the monitor screen.

Figure 4-3 shows the three self-test functions. IBM makes note of the fact that the three aforementioned responses indicate that the self-test has been completed successfully. Other information may appear on the screen but is not important at this stage in the testing. Now, the contrast and brightness controls may be adjusted for eye comfort.

DISK TEST

In their Guide to Operations manual, IBM has provided a disk labeled "Diagnostic" which is used for test purposes. Loading this disk is very simple and is always done with the System Unit in the off mode. At this point, the disk load lever is lifted and the disk inserted until the rear stop is felt. The lever is then pushed to the down position and the System Unit switched on (Fig. 4-4). With the disk in place, the monitor screen should match (Fig. 4-5).

This completes the system minitest. IBM

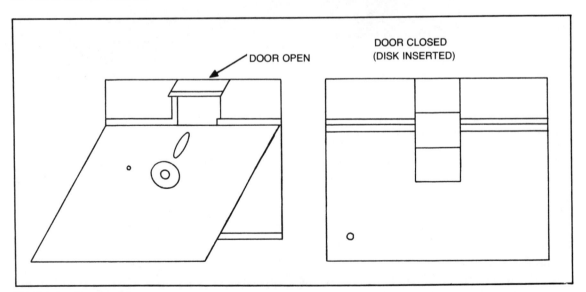

Fig. 4-4. Loading the disk.

```
Version 1.02 (C)Copyright IBM Corp 1981, 1982

SELECT AN OPTION

0 - RUN DIAGNOSTIC ROUTINES
1 - FORMAT DISKETTE
2 - COPY DISKETTE
9 - EXIT TO SYSTEM DISKETTE
```

Fig. 4-5. Screen printout when diagnostics disk is loaded.

recommends that you perform a complete system checkout whenever the machine is recabled or an option is installed. They provide a problem determination procedures section in their operations guide which will allow the user to possibly determine a minor problem which is associated with an incorrect installation. I have found that IBM service personnel in Boca Raton, Florida, are also quite willing to provide service information via telephone. Chapter 9 provides further test procedure information using the Diagnostic Aids disk.

CASSETTE TEST

IBM may also supply a Diagnostic Aids cassette when a cassette recorder is to be attached. A cassette user's manual is also included. If you have elected to go with this option, the cassette is inserted into the recorder and the tape rewound to the beginning. The System Unit switch is placed in the on position and you must wait for the Self-Test to be completed (45 seconds maximum). The playback volume of the cassette recorder is turned to maximum, and the Play button is depressed. At this point, you will type *load"ldcass* on the keyboard. Then, the Enter button on the keyboard is depressed. Now, you must look to verify that your cassette is turning.

If everything is operational so far, *.B found* will appear on the monitor screen. A few

seconds later, *Ok* will also appear. Then, type RUN on the keyboard and press Enter. In a minute or two, the option frame will appear on the monitor and will be similar to that shown in Fig. 4-6. The actual printout will be determined by the options attached to the System Unit. If, for some reason, the cassette data will not load into the machine, IBM states the most likely causes are:

1. Faulty cassette recorder.
2. Wrong or damaged cassette.
3. Keyboard failure.

KEYBOARD

The keyboard contains an internal adjustment stand to allow it to be raised to a position similar to that of a standard typewriter keyboard, with the back being a few inches

```
THE INSTALLED DEVICES ARE

SYSTEM BOARD
 64KB MEMORY
KEYBOARD
MONOCHROME & PRINTER ADAPTER
COLOR/GRAPHICS ADAPTER
1 DISKETTE DRIVE(S) & ADAPTER
ASYNC COMMUNICATIONS ADAPTER
MATRIX PRINTER

IS THE LIST CORRECT (Y/N) ?
```

Fig. 4-6. Option frame screen printout.

higher than the front. The stand is brought into play by rotating the two end tabs 90° (Fig. 4-7). Alternately, the keyboard may be operated in the flat configuration. Even here, the back of the unit is a bit higher than the front. The internal stand is used to make adjustments for the operator's most comfortable typing position.

The keyboard is illustrated in Fig. 4-8. Note that the number and letter keys are identical to the configuration used on a standard typewriter. Additional keys are included to aid the operator in writing, updating, and running programs. A total of seven keys are used specifically for this purpose and are explained in Fig. 4-9.

At the far left of the keyboard are the program function keys. These are identified by the "F" designation, followed by a number from 1 to 10. The function keys are used to make the system perform the following commands:

F1 This is the LIST key. When pressed, it lists the lines of the program currently in memory.

F2 This is the RUN key, which begins execution of a program from the beginning.

F3 This is the LOAD key. It is followed by the filespec of a program you wish to load into memory. When the program is accessed by this key, it is stored in main memory.

F4 This is the SAVE key and is followed by the name of a program which is to be committed to diskette, cassette, or other form of auxiliary storage.

F5 This is the CONT key, which stands for continue. It restarts the program in memory after it has been interrupted by a CTRL BREAK or STOP command.

F6 This is the LPT1: key and is used to transfer information to the printer. When

pressed in conjunction with F1, the program lines of the program in memory will be printed.

F7 This is the TRON key, which is an abbreviation for Trace On. It causes the display screen to print the line numbers of the program as the lines are executed.

F8 This is the TROFF key, meaning trace off. It simply negates the function brought on by F7.

F9 This is known as the "KEY" key. It's used to change the specific functions of the other keys on this board section.

F10 This is the SCREEN key and outputs a "SCREEN 0,0,0" command, which returns the system to text mode from graphics mode and turns off all color.

Note that on the right-hand side of the

Fig. 4-7. The IBM Personal Computer keyboard can be raised and lowered by rotating the end tabs.

Fig. 4-8. Keyboard.

keyboard there is a numeric key pad. At the top center of this pad is a key labeled "Num Lock." This means number lock and is a toggle key. When this key is depressed once, the numeric key pad is activated. A second press cancels the numeric pad. With the "Num Lock" acti- vated, keys 1 through 9 will be operative. At the bottom right of the pad is a wide key that is labeled with a decimal point and the letters "Del". You will also find a 0 key as well as plus (+) and minus (−) keys which are designated only with their appropriate symbols.

ALT   This is the alternate key and is used in conjunction with al- phabetic keys to enter BASIC keywords. For example, when you press the ALT key and simultaneously press the key for the letter P, the keyword PRINT will be entered.

CTRL   This is the control key and is used with other keys simultane- ously to bring about a specific function. By pressing the CTRL and the SCROLL-LOCK key simultaneously, a scrolling screen print will stop.

ESC   This is the escape key and is used for editing. When it is depressed, the computer line that the cursor is on is removed, but it is not deleted from memory.

This is the tab key, which advances the cursor eight spaces forward.

This is the shift key and changes lowercase letters to upper- case or vice versa when the keyboard is operating in the uppercase mode.

This is the backspace key and moves the cursor toward the left. It will remove any characters it passes over and erase them from the program.

This is the enter key and returns the cursor to the left-hand side of the keyboard, down one line from its previous position. When a program line is typed in, pressing enter commits it to memory.

Fig. 4-9. The seven program editor keys and their functions.

When the "Num Lock" is pressed for the second time to cancel the numeric key pad, the bottom designation of each of the keys on the numeric pad becomes operative. "HOME" moves the cursor the first character position of the top line of the screen. The key marked with an 8 and a vertical arrow moves the cursor one line up for each keystroke. Another key labeled with a 4 at the top position and a horizontal arrow pointing to the left at the bottom moves the cursor to the left one character for each key stroke, while the "6" key with a horizontal arrow pointing to the right moves the cursor to the right one character for each keystroke. The cursor may be moved down one line for each keystroke of the key marked "2" at the top and a vertical arrow pointing downward below. Again, all of these operations are accomplished after "Num Lock" is pressed a second time to cancel the numeric key pad. Additional key operations include "END," which moves the cursor to the last character on that line. The "Del" key deletes the character where the cursor is positioned. Finally, the "Ins" key sets the keyboard to the Insert mode so that characters will be entered at the cursor position and all data to the right will move to the right. By pressing the Ins keys a second time, the keyboard exits the Insert mode.

Other key functions include "Caps Lock," which causes letters to type in uppercase (capitals) and, of course, the symbols above the standard typewriter numeral keys will be operative as well. Pressing the key again returns the letter portion of the keyboard to lowercase mode. Above and to the right of the "Caps Lock" key is one marked "PrtSc." This is an abbreviation for "Print Screen" and will cause an asterisk to be printed. When this key is pressed with the "Shift" key, it will print all data on the screen. Another key marked "Scroll Lock" is an inactive key.

Figure 4-10 shows some examples of

CTRL + NUM LOCK	This combination temporarily stops the program from running. You can press any key on the keyboard to continue.
CTRL + HOME	This clears the screen and returns the cursor to the upper left-hand corner, or home position.
CTRL + DEL + ALT	This is the system reset combination and accomplishes the same purpose as turning off the power at the System Unit and then flipping it back on again. For example, if you wish to load another operating system into memory to replace one that is currently there, you would insert the new diskette and then execute this combination to have the new diskette information read into memory.

Fig. 4-10. Examples of control key functions.

"Control" and "Alternate" functions. The Control key is labeled "CTRL" and is located to the immediate left of the key marked "A." The Alternate key is located two keys below the Control key.

You will find the keyboard to be a versatile input device, one which allows you to easily perform many input functions and offers excellent expansion capabilities. The coiled cord arrangement is especially nice when compared with computers that include the keyboard as a part of the system unit. In many applications, it is not convenient to place the entire system in one position. I used the Personal Computer with the System Unit mounted at knee level, the display mounted at standing eye level, and the keyboard at the normal typing level. The name "Personal" is not just manufacturer's hype; it is a practical reality.

IBM 80 CPS PRINTER

Figure 4-11 shows the printer with paper rack attached. The power switch is located on the right side of the device just in back of the platen knob. When this switch is activated, the "power" light on the control panel will come on. Below the power light is an identical one marked "ready." This will light when the printer is ready to receive data. Additionally, there is a "paper out" light which is activated

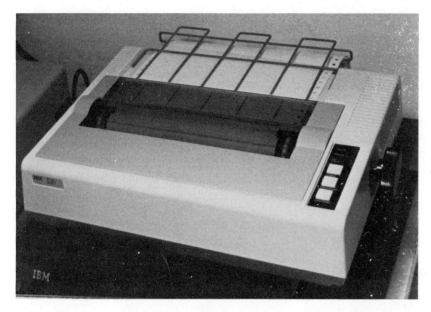

Fig. 4-11. IBM 80 CPS matrix printer with paper rack attached (courtesy IBM).

when the paper supply is near the end. When this comes on, an audible beep is also heard, alerting the operator that it's time to refresh the paper supply.

The control panel to the right front of the 80 CPS Printer contains three pushbutton switches. The one marked "On Line" is a multifunction type. When depressed once, the printer is switched off line and will not receive data from the computer. When pressed a second time, the printer is returned to the on-line mode and is ready to receive data from the host computer.

The switch marked Form Feed allows you to feed paper a form at a time. This is used to advance the tractor assembly in order to move any text past the plastic lid so that it may be torn off. This switch is active only when the printer is off line.

The Line Feed switch is also active only when the printer is off line and advances paper one line at a time. You may hold the switch down, and the forms will continue to advance a line at a time until the switch is released.

The printer is an impact type which uses a replaceable ribbon cartridge. It is inserted into the top section of the unit and contains a knob which allows the operator to take up any ribbon slack. Using a pencil or other cylindrical object, the ribbon is inserted into the slot between the print head and the ribbon shield (Fig. 4-12). The overall installation of the ribbon is very simple due to the plastic fin which IBM

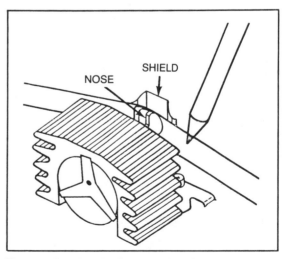

Fig. 4-12. Inserting the ribbon cartridge into its appropriate slot in the 80 CPS printout (courtesy IBM).

69

has installed on the top of its case. Just hold the fin and drop the cartridge into place. Many cartridges do not contain this feature, as is evidenced by the many stained hands which are seen immediately after a ribbon-changing maneuver.

Insertion of the printing forms is equally as easy. The plastic cover is raised and the paper positioned behind and below the printer (Fig. 4-13). A printer stand supplied by IBM adequately contains the two stacks of paper, but the floor also works well. Once the paper has been inserted, the print scale is moved forward and the form's guide roller is centered.

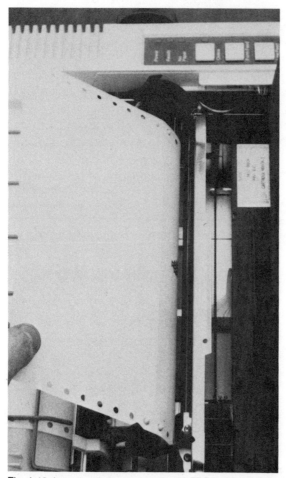

Fig. 4-13. Inserting the paper into the 80 CPS matrix printer.

Two covers are provided for the two tractors, the plastic parts whose pins fit the form perforations and guide the paper through the machine. These covers open outward and allow for the ends of the forms to be mated with the plastic rollers. The tractor covers are then closed and adjusted with the tractor lock levers for proper centering.

On the left side of the machine near the print head is the form's "Thickness" lever. This is used to adjust the position of the print head to allow adequate space for single or multi-part forms. For single forms, the level is moved toward the rear. Multi-part forms are accepted by advancing the lever toward the front. There are seven slotted positions for thickness control.

The printer has a built-in Self-Test. This test is conducted *before* the printer is interfaced with the System Unit. First, the printer is plugged into a 110-volt wall outlet. The power switch is placed in the On position *while* you simultaneously press and hold the Line Feed switch. The printing operation should start almost immediately. When this happens, you may release your hold on the Line Feed switch. It will take a little over ten minutes to complete the full test, which is a cycling procedure. To stop the test turn the power off. Figure 4-14 shows the test printout. Your machine should produce similar results.

Attaching the printer to the System Unit is done with both pieces of equipment in the off position. A double-ended 25-pin connector-equipped cable is used. The end which attaches to the System Unit is equipped with two side screws which are tightened after insertion at the rear of the unit. The other end is attached to the rear of the printer and is held in place with spring retainers. This plug does contain a ground wire and a connector which is screw-fitted to the back of the printer. Figure 4-15 provides pin identification for interfacing the

```
 !"#$%&'()*+,-./0123456789:;<=>?@ABCDEFGHIJKLMNOPQRSTUVWXYZ[\]^_`abcdefghijklmno
!"#$%&'()*+,-./0123456789:;<=>?@ABCDEFGHIJKLMNOPQRSTUVWXYZ[\]^_`abcdefghijklmnop
"#$%&'()*+,-./0123456789:;<=>?@ABCDEFGHIJKLMNOPQRSTUVWXYZ[\]^_`abcdefghijklmnopq
#$%&'()*+,-./0123456789:;<=>?@ABCDEFGHIJKLMNOPQRSTUVWXYZ[\]^_`abcdefghijklmnopqr
$%&'()*+,-./0123456789:;<=>?@ABCDEFGHIJKLMNOPQRSTUVWXYZ[\]^_`abcdefghijklmnopqrs
%&'()*+,-./0123456789:;<=>?@ABCDEFGHIJKLMNOPQRSTUVWXYZ[\]^_`abcdefghijklmnopqrst
&'()*+,-./0123456789:;<=>?@ABCDEFGHIJKLMNOPQRSTUVWXYZ[\]^_`abcdefghijklmnopqrstu
'()*+,-./0123456789:;<=>?@ABCDEFGHIJKLMNOPQRSTUVWXYZ[\]^_`abcdefghijklmnopqrstuv
()*+,-./0123456789:;<=>?@ABCDEFGHIJKLMNOPQRSTUVWXYZ[\]^_`abcdefghijklmnopqrstuvw
)*+,-./0123456789:;<=>?@ABCDEFGHIJKLMNOPQRSTUVWXYZ[\]^_`abcdefghijklmnopqrstuvwx
*+,-./0123456789:;<=>?@ABCDEFGHIJKLMNOPQRSTUVWXYZ[\]^_`abcdefghijklmnopqrstuvwxy
+,-./0123456789:;<=>?@ABCDEFGHIJKLMNOPQRSTUVWXYZ[\]^_`abcdefghijklmnopqrstuvwxyz
,-./0123456789:;<=>?@ABCDEFGHIJKLMNOPQRSTUVWXYZ[\]^_`abcdefghijklmnopqrstuvwxyz{
-./0123456789:;<=>?@ABCDEFGHIJKLMNOPQRSTUVWXYZ[\]^_`abcdefghijklmnopqrstuvwxyz{|
./0123456789:;<=>?@ABCDEFGHIJKLMNOPQRSTUVWXYZ[\]^_`abcdefghijklmnopqrstuvwxyz{|}
/0123456789:;<=>?@ABCDEFGHIJKLMNOPQRSTUVWXYZ[\]^_`abcdefghijklmnopqrstuvwxyz{|}~
0123456789:;<=>?@ABCDEFGHIJKLMNOPQRSTUVWXYZ[\]^_`abcdefghijklmnopqrstuvwxyz{|}~
123456789:;<=>?@ABCDEFGHIJKLMNOPQRSTUVWXYZ[\]^_`abcdefghijklmnopqrstuvwxyz{|}~
23456789:;<=>?@ABCDEFGHIJKLMNOPQRSTUVWXYZ[\]^_`abcdefghijklmnopqrstuvwxyz{|}~
3456789:;<=>?@ABCDEFGHIJKLMNOPQRSTUVWXYZ[\]^_`abcdefghijklmnopqrstuvwxyz{|}~
456789:;<=>?@ABCDEFGHIJKLMNOPQRSTUVWXYZ[\]^_`abcdefghijklmnopqrstuvwxyz{|}~
56789:;<=>?@ABCDEFGHIJKLMNOPQRSTUVWXYZ[\]^_`abcdefghijklmnopqrstuvwxyz{|}~
6789:;<=>?@ABCDEFGHIJKLMNOPQRSTUVWXYZ[\]^_`abcdefghijklmnopqrstuvwxyz{|}~
789:;<=>?@ABCDEFGHIJKLMNOPQRSTUVWXYZ[\]^_`abcdefghijklmnopqrstuvwxyz{|}~
89:;<=>?@ABCDEFGHIJKLMNOPQRSTUVWXYZ[\]^_`abcdefghijklmnopqrstuvwxyz{|}~
9:;<=>?@ABCDEFGHIJKLMNOPQRSTUVWXYZ[\]^_`abcdefghijklmnopqrstuvwxyz{|}~
:;<=>?@ABCDEFGHIJKLMNOPQRSTUVWXYZ[\]^_`abcdefghijklmnopqrstuvwxyz{|}~
;<=>?@ABCDEFGHIJKLMNOPQRSTUVWXYZ[\]^_`abcdefghijklmnopqrstuvwxyz{|}~
<=>?@ABCDEFGHIJKLMNOPQRSTUVWXYZ[\]^_`abcdefghijklmnopqrstuvwxyz{|}~
=>?@ABCDEFGHIJKLMNOPQRSTUVWXYZ[\]^_`abcdefghijklmnopqrstuvwxyz{|}~
```

Fig. 4-14. Printout or 80 CPS printer self-test.

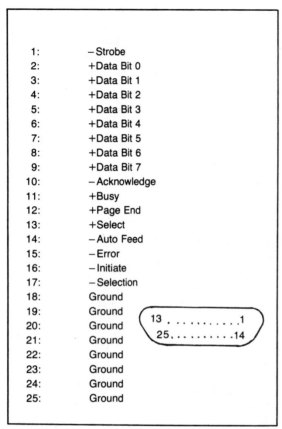

1:	– Strobe
2:	+Data Bit 0
3:	+Data Bit 1
4:	+Data Bit 2
5:	+Data Bit 3
6:	+Data Bit 4
7:	+Data Bit 5
8:	+Data Bit 6
9:	+Data Bit 7
10:	– Acknowledge
11:	+Busy
12:	+Page End
13:	+Select
14:	– Auto Feed
15:	– Error
16:	– Initiate
17:	– Selection
18:	Ground
19:	Ground
20:	Ground
21:	Ground
22:	Ground
23:	Ground
24:	Ground
25:	Ground

Fig. 4-15. Pin identification for interfacing other printers to the IBM computer.

printer with the Personal Computer or other microcomputers with parallel interface.

The basic setup of the IBM Personal Computer system is very simple and should give no one any real problems. Setup and checkout took me approximately one hour, but this included unpacking and overviewing each procedure very closely in order to spot any possible vague areas that might bear mentioning in this book. Of course, you have to add another hour for reading of the setup portion of the Guide to Operations manual. This is mandatory with any computer system.

The only instruction that gave me problems was the printer testing procedure (Self-Test). Instead of depressing the Line Feed switch *before* activating power, I reversed this procedure. In their Guide to Operations, IBM did not include the time it required for the printing operation to begin. I held the Line Feed button down until several sheets of paper were run through the machine, none of which was printed on, before returning to the manual. The exact instruction read, "Position the power switch to On while you press and hold the Line Feed switch." This was a relatively clear instruction, but if the while had been underlined, I might have gotten it the first time. The printing process should begin within one second after this step is initiated.

When one thinks of IBM and the computer products they make, extreme complexity comes to mind. It is fair to state that the IBM Personal Computer is a highly sophisticated and complex piece of equipment, but concentrating on the word "personal," IBM has built in the self-test functions needed for anyone to test this complex system through very simple steps. When backed up by their excellent Guide to Operations manual, the simplicity of operating this machine is enhanced. While the Personal Computer may contain complex circuitry, it is user-designed for operating simplicity. Once you become accustomed to operating your machine, you will find that nearly every procedure is common-sense oriented. It benefits no one to offer a piece of equipment whose operation is so complex as to not be practical to the average user.

Chapter 5

Installation of Options

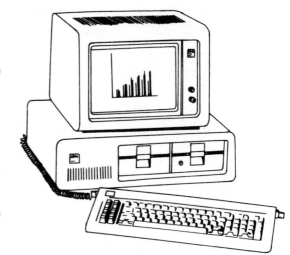

Some options are user-installed inside the IBM System Unit. For the sake of this discussion, we shall consider the basic IBM Personal Computer to include only the System Unit and keyboard. This is available without expanded memory and without the disk drive(s).

MEMORY OPTIONS

The standard IBM Personal Computer comes equipped with 40K of permanent memory. The optional 16K bytes Memory Expansion Kit consists of 9 modules (boards) that are plugged into the System Board. Three kits may be installed to give the System Board a total of 64K bytes of memory. Additional memory is added by installing the 32K or 64K bytes Expansion Options.

To install the nine memory modules you need a medium-sized flat-blade screwdriver, medium screw starter, module insertion tool, a 3/16-inch nutdriver or wrench, and a module puller. IBM can supply most of these tools, but you can also purchase them from a local electronics hobby store.

Before installing options, the System Unit should be switched off, and the entire system unplugged from the wall. If your system has already been set up, disassemble it by removing the keyboard, monitor and printer cable hookups. You should be left with the System Unit alone, in which all system installation will take place.

Turn the System Unit so the rear faces out. Loosen the mounting screws located on the far left and right bottom of the cabinet back (Fig. 5-1).

Once the mounting screws have been removed, insert a fingernail under the upper lip of the case while pulling forward on the cabinet. With a little patience, carefully slide the cover away from the rear and toward the front (Fig. 5-2). When the cover will go no

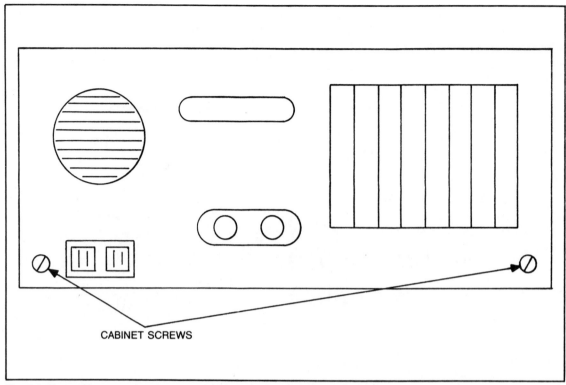

Fig. 5-1. Two cabinet mounting screws must be removed to gain access to the interior of the system unit.

further, tilt the front upward and remove it completely from the base (Fig. 5-3). Set the cover aside, until reassembly. Figure 5-4 shows the internal circuitry of the IBM System Unit.

Looking at the inside left rear of the circuitry, you will see five system expansion slots. Figure 5-4 shows four of these slots filled. Depending upon the options ordered from the factory, one to five slots may be in use. In any event, remove all of these boards to install the memory.

The option boards are held in place by a set screw mounted at the top of each card (board) connector, where it mates with the back of the System Unit's cabinet. Using a flathead screwdriver, remove the screw that holds each option in place. Then, grasp the card by the top corner and lift straight up. When

removing the cards from my computer, I was concerned about breakage, so I accomplished the removal procedure through a series of gentle tugs. I found it helpful to loosen the board just a bit and then insert the head of a screwdriver beneath the attachment lip through which the set screw was originally located. This allowed me to gingerly pry up the board from one end and then raise it by hand at the other end. Make note of which card fills which space for reassembly. Figure 5-5 shows the same left rear portion of the System Unit with all option boards removed.

There are nine modules for each memory kit. Figure 5-6 shows the System Board as it should appear in your machine. Note that it is not necessary nor desirable to remove the System Board from the unit. The factory-installed memory kit will be located in the fourth row up

Fig. 5-2. Once the screws are removed, the enclosure may be slid forward.

Fig. 5-3. When the cover will slide no further, the front is tilted upward for complete removal.

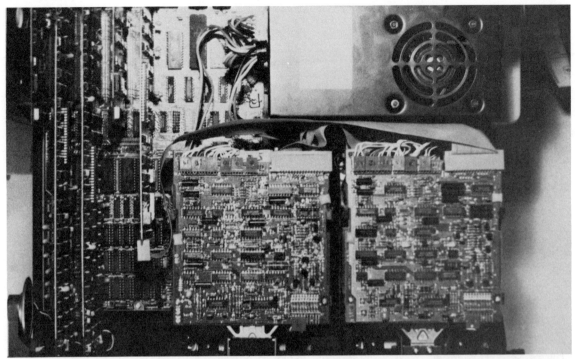
Fig. 5-4. Internal circuitry of the IBM System Unit.

Fig. 5-5. System Unit with all option boards removed.

from the front of the System Board. If you are installing only one 16K kit, insert the modules in the row directly in front of this one.

It is now time to install the nine memory circuits. Handle these delicate integrated circuits with care, as the pins are easily bent and must be aligned with the connector before they are pressed in place. Each circuit has a notch. This must always face toward the rear of the unit. *Caution:* They can be reversed 180° and fit perfectly, but they will not operate. Make certain each of the pins is in alignment with all others and then insert the first IC in the far left-hand socket. It's a good idea to use a bench lamp here in order to make certain that all of the pins mate with their appropriate holes in the socket. Do not press down on the module yet. Once you are sure that everything lines up, firmly press the module in place by pressing the thumb flush against the center of the IC. Once the circuit snaps in place, give the installation a close examination to make certain that no pins have been bent under the package or have been allowed to slip past the connector notch and bend to the outside. If you make a mistake, you can remove the module with the module puller specified in the tool complement. Repeat this process with the remaining eight ICs.

Once your modules are in, reset the two DIP switches. Figure 5-7 shows the switch locations, which are to the right of the fifth options socket at the left rear of the System Unit. The System Board switches must be set to reflect the addition of memory and other options installed. You will find a ballpoint pen comes in handy in setting the slide contacts. This can be done with the index finger, but it's tricky. Figure 5-8 shows the correct positions of switches 1 and 2 for the various amounts of memory options installed. The top four sets involve the installation of the memory circuits on the System Board. The bottom six pairs indicate the setting when memory options are installed by means of single cards.

The latter options are installed in option slots. These go in in reverse order to the method used for removing the option boards to make the installation on the System Board just outlined.

After setting the switches, reassemble. Noting the charts you made for the originally installed options, align each board in its proper slot, temporarily mating it with the connector found on the System Board. When you are sure all pins are aligned, firmly press the board downward until it snaps into place. Incidentally, if you didn't take my advice and make a chart, don't worry, because all five positions are interchangeable and any option will work properly in any of the five expansion slots. While aligning these boards, note the set screw hole in the option retaining bracket. Adjust the board until the hole is properly aligned with the flange slot. Then reinsert the set screw and tighten it. Repeat these steps for each option board to be installed.

Now, look over your installation, making certain that everything is in place. If all appears well, push the cover over the System Unit base by reversing the steps for removal. Initially, the front of the case should be slanted upward until it slides over the front panel. It may then be lowered and pushed toward the back of the unit until the cabinet holes align with the base holes at the left and right rear positions. Reinsert the cabinet set screws and tighten them. Your installation is now complete, and you may go through the system setup procedure.

5¼-INCH DISK DRIVE

While many IBM Personal Computers are ordered with one or two disk drives already installed, some are not. The System Unit can contain two of these drives, which may be customer-installed.

Fig. 5-6. IBM Personal Computer system board.

The tools that will be required to install your 5¼-inch disk drive include a medium-size flat-blade screwdriver, a medium screw starter and a 3/16-inch nut driver.

As before, the System Unit must be completely disconnected from the wall outlet and from the printer, keyboard and monitor. Remove the case. With the back of the base unit facing toward you, remove the drive "A", or "B" (if a drive is in A already), faceplate by prying the retaining clips off and separating the faceplate and the backing plate from the front mounting panel (Fig. 5-9).

Examine the output leads and connectors from the power supply, which is located on the left side of the back panel when the front panel is facing away from you. Two six-pin connectors should already be attached to the System Board and there will be two other four-pin connectors exiting from the same hole in the power supply chassis. These are the power connectors for the "A" and "B" disk drives. Either of these connectors may be used for either drive unit, although IBM calls for the one labeled P10 to be attached to drive "A" and connector P11 to drive "B." Figure 5-10 shows these two connectors.

IBM supplied disk drives comes as a package containing mechanical and electronic portions attached to the frame. Slide the disk drive through the front mounting panel about halfway into the base. At this time, the power supply

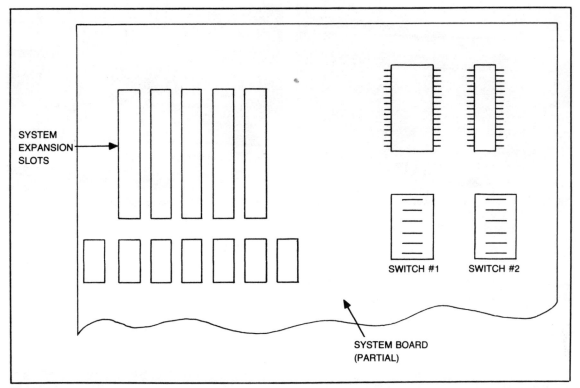

Fig. 5-7. System board switch locations.

connector is attached to the right-hand bottom side of the circuit board on the drive unit. These instructions assume that you are facing the rear panel. The mating connector for the power plug is located beneath the circuit on the bottom right-hand edge, and this may be a tight fit. The plug will fit only with the designation number facing the back panel. Grasp the bottom right-hand edge of the circuit card with your thumb and forefinger to stabilize it. Push the plug into its socket carefully while applying equal pressure with your other hand on the top of the board. Be careful here, because if you become too exuberant, you may actually crack the printed circuit board. Figure 5-11 shows the disk unit and the proper plug attachment point.

Now, slide the drive completely into the base unit until the front panel is flush with the faceplate. Insert the supplied three hex-slotted screws in the proper slots and tighten, making certain the disk drive panel is still flush with the System Unit's face.

Now install the disk adapter card, shown in Fig. 5-12. I have found the ideal mounting

Bytes	Switch 1	Switch 2
16 KB	3,4 On	1,2,3,4 On
32 KB	3 Off, 4 On	1,2,3,4 On
48 KB	3 Off, 4 On	1,2,3,4 On
64 KB	3,4 Off	1,2,3,4, On
96 KB	3,4 Off	1 Off, 2,3,4 On
128 KB	3,4 Off	1,3,4 On; 2 Off
160 KB	3,4 Off	1,2 Off; 3,4 On
196 KB	3,4 Off	1,2,4 On; 3 Off
228 KB	3,4 Off	2,4 On; 1,3 Off
256 KB	3,4 Off	1,4 On; 2,3 Off

Fig. 5-8. Switch settings for the various amounts of memory.

79

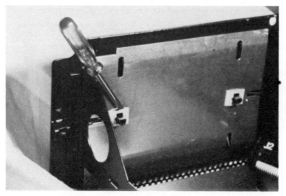

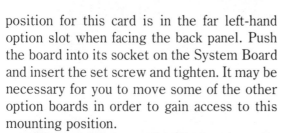

Fig. 5-9.Removal of the disk faceplate for drive installation.　Fig. 5-10. Disk drive power connectors.

position for this card is in the far left-hand option slot when facing the back panel. Push the board into its socket on the System Board and insert the set screw and tighten. It may be necessary for you to move some of the other option boards in order to gain access to this mounting position.

　　Figure 5-13 shows the signal cable, a rib-bon type that is used for connecting the drive to the adapter card. As can be seen, the ribbon cable contains one long section terminated with connectors at either end and then a short section, again terminated in a matching connector. If you have installed one disk drive, attach the connector at the end of the short portion of the cable circuit board on top of the

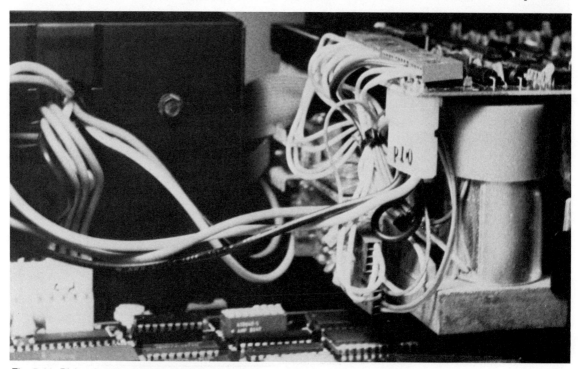

Fig. 5-11. Disk unit and proper plug attachment point.

Fig. 5-12. Disk adapter option card.

drive. The connector will fit only one way, shown in Fig. 5-14. Now, use the other connector (the one at the end of the long ribbon strip) for connection to the back of the disk drive adapter card (Fig. 5-15). The remaining connector is used only when a second disk drive is installed and may be allowed to rest at the bottom of the chassis. Figure 5-16 shows the completed installation of the disk drive, drive adapter and ribbon cable.

Before replacing the chassis cover, adjust switch 1 on the memory board. When only one drive is used, switch 1 must be fixed so that pin 1 is off, pin 2 is on and pins 7 and 8 are on. No other adjustments are necessary. The panel may now be replaced and the system checked for proper operation.

When a second disk drive is installed, the same basic steps outlined above are repeated. Panel B is removed, the second unit slid in place, the second power plug connected, and the remaining ribbon cable connector properly mated. You must change the settings of switch 1. With two disk drives, pins 1 and 7 are in the off position, while pin 8 is on.

While this may sound like a fairly complicated procedure, it is relatively simple. Total installation time should be no more than a half hour, although if you are unaccustomed to working with ribbon cables and circuit boards, it may take you a bit longer. The only tricky part is in getting the power plug to mate with its socket on the bottom of the board without the possibility of causing the board to break. If

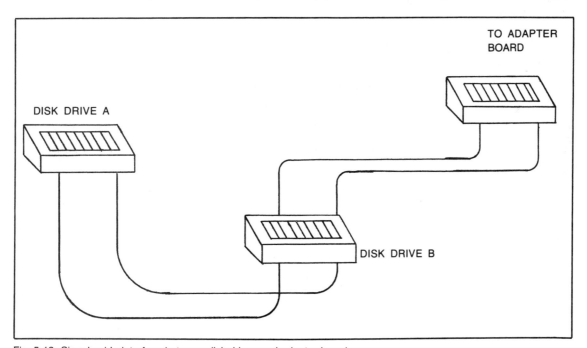

Fig. 5-13. Signal cable interface between disk drives and adapter board.

Fig. 5-14. Connection of ribbon cable to disk drive (A).

Fig. 5-15. Connection of ribbon cable to disk drive (B).

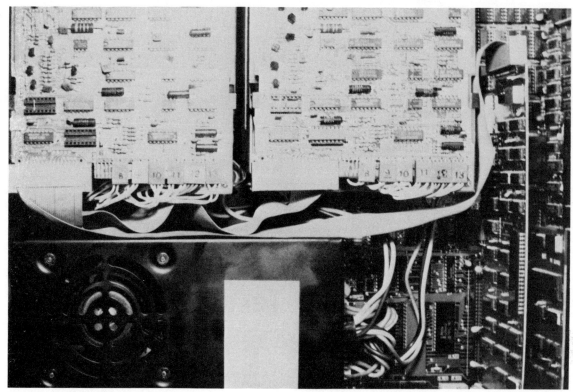

Fig. 5-16. Completed drive installation.

you proceed with caution at this point, you should have no problem. The ribbon cable connectors mate easily with the board, but should you get a fairly tight fit, proceed with caution and rock the connector into place. Make certain that the adapter card is mated with its vertical socket, and that the set screw is tightened in place. It's a good idea to test for proper operation before replacing the cover. Reconnect the System Unit to the keyboard, activate the switch and observe the panel lamp on the disk drive. It should light, and with the faceplate closed, the disk motor should turn. If you experience problems, recheck your power connections after removing the plug from the wall outlet. The Guide to Operations provides an excellent section in problem determination.

At the time of this writing, IBM announced a new 320K byte disk drive that ac-commodates up to 327,680 characters of programs and data on 5¼″ disk drives. The double-sided drive is now pretty much standard, but single-sided units are still available. This enables the user to store and update information on 320K double-sided or 160K byte single-sided disks. This costs about $200 more than the standard 160K disk drive. The installation is handled in a similar manner.

The greater storage capacity and programming flexibility of the new disk drive means that applications currently running on the IBM Personal Computer can take advantage of larger data files, providing for future growth. The 320K disk drive is supported by the new version of the Disk Operating System, as well as by the CP/M-86 and UCSD p-System from Digital Research Inc., Version IV.0 operating systems.

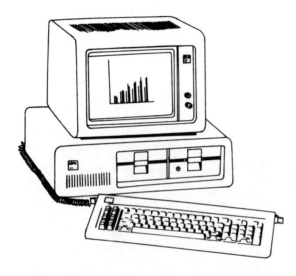

Chapter 6

Software and Programming Techniques

The System Unit has 40K bytes of ROM (read only memory). One 8K byte module contains the ROM BIOS and a power-on self test. These routines initialize and test the system when first powered on and then provide the device level control necessary for the system. The ROM BIOS also has a time of day clock built in. This clock is available to any programmer working at the machine level and is provided for the BASIC programmer when using Disk or Advanced BASIC. A screen print function is available in the ROM, either from the keyboard or through a call to that routine.

The ROM BIOS is accessed through the 8088 software interrupts. Each of the major devices has a software interrupt assigned, and the various functions are indicated by register contents in the calling sequence. To maximize the flexibility of the ROM BIOS, parameter lists are located by RWM vectors whenever possible to allow different devices to be installed. For example, the disk drive parameter table contains track-to-track times, motor start times, and disk format information that needs to be changed for some applications. The ROM BIOS may still be used with a new table installed for those applications. Another parameter table is for the display mode set, allowing monitors and televisions with varying overscan to be attached. The second 128 characters displayed as text while in the APA mode are also set by the user, allowing an unlimited character set while in that mode.

The remaining 32K of ROM contains the Microsoft BASIC interpreter. All of the standard BASIC functions are present, as well as special constructs to manipulate the features of the Personal Computer, such as Line and

Portions of this material are reprinted from *The IBM Personal Computer* by David J. Bradley and Lewis C. Eggebrecht, IBM Corp. © Copyright International Business Machines Corp. 1981. Reprinted with permission.

Sound. Disk BASIC and Advanced BASIC, available on the DOS disk, provide additional capability. Most notable are the communications support and the advanced graphics commands, such as PUT, GET, CIRCLE, PAINT and DRAW, and the PLAY command.

The Disk Operating System (DOS) provides an environment for the execution of many applications. In addition to the BASICs, DOS offers utilities to manipulate the file system. For the programmer at the machine level, the DOS interfaces provide access to a named file system.

Finally, a number of applications are already being used. These include VisiCalc, the popular spread sheet program; EasyWriter, a word processor; a business accounting package from Peachtree Software that includes general ledger, accounts payable and accounts receivable; and Microsoft Adventure.

Programs to assist students and to help business people have also been made available for the Personal Computer. The IBM Personal Computer Education Program Series offers students programs to assist them in learning and building skills at their own pace. The Fact Track program, from Science Research Associates, Inc., helps students learn basic arithmetic skills. Arithmetic Games Set 1 and Set 2, also from S.R.A., develop and refine mathematics and logic skills in game-playing situations. Typing Tutor, from Microsoft, Inc., is a touch-typing instruction and drill program, General Accounting by BPI Systems, Inc., an accounting system designed for the small business or professional user, is part of the Business Program Series. This program requires minimum computer knowledge.

In addition, the Computer Language Series has been expanded to give customers a wide choice of programming languages and operating systems. The new offerings include: a Macro Assembler, which runs under the IBM Personal Computer Disk Operating System; a FORTRAN Compiler, which also runs under the DOS and UCSD p-System (trademark of the Regents of the University of California), an advanced operating system, with UCSD Pascal™ (also a R. of U.C. trademark) and FORTRAN-77 languages.

EDUCATIONAL SERIES

The *Fact Track* program by Science Research Associates, Inc., is a basic arithmetic skill builder organized by level of difficulty which can be used by students of various age levels, as well as by adults who would like arithmetic practice. Mastery of arithmetic facts, the sums and products of 1-digit numbers (390 questions), can be measured in two ways: by the correct answer and the rate of response. Each user sees a different sequence of facts and the program delivers these facts in random order. The program works with the DOS with a single disk drive and 64K of user memory.

Arithmetic Games Set 1 and Set 2 by Science Research Associates, Inc., develop and refine mathematic skills while having fun. Each Set has two games. Set 1 includes the Beano and Rockets games. Beano is a bingo-like game. The object of Beano is to match all the numbers on a game card displayed by the computer either by adding, multiplying, subtracting or dividing numbers the computer randomly selects. In the Rocket game, the screen becomes a field of 225 squares in outer space. Players move their rockets by dividing, multiplying, subtracting or adding numbers randomly selected by the computer. The object is to shoot down your opponent's rocket by skillfully moving your rocket into firing range.

Set 2 includes the Discovery Machine and Number Chase games. In the Discovery Machine game, the computer displays a number. It then performs a secret calculation on it and displays a new number. The object of the game is to discover what mathematical rule the computer used to calculate the new number. Number Chase is a game that develops logic skills. The player must guess a secret number selected by the computer. The player, using mathematical skills, tries to guess the secret number based on clues provided by the computer. Each player sets a goal for the number of guesses it will take to guess the secret number. Arithmetic games work with the DOS a single disk drive and 64K of user memory.

Typing Tutor by Microsoft, Inc., is an interactive, touch-typing instruction and drill program. It creates individualized typing drills for increasing speed and vocabulary. It also memorizes progress by keeping track of the keys you know and the keys you are learning. The program runs with one disk drive, 48K of user memory and the DOS or with a cassette recorder and 32K of user memory.

General Accounting by BPI Systems, Inc., is an accounting system for a small business or professional user. It includes accounts receivable, accounts payable, inventory control and payroll features. Once a company's records are within the General Accounting program, entries are made in the journals selected; then posting of ledgers, financial statement preparation and the closing of books can be accomplished by the program. It can also provide customized balance sheets and profit and loss statements.

General Accounting works with two disk drives, a printer, 64K of user memory and the DOS.

LANGUAGE SERIES

IBM Personal Computer Macro Assembler by MicroSoft, Inc., enables users to develop and produce programs that may run several times faster than equivalent highlevel language routines. Assembler-produced programs may be called from other BASIC programs, as well as from other high-level languages such as Pascal and FORTRAN. The Macro Assembler works with the DOS with a minimum of 96K bytes of user memory (64K if the subset assembler, which does not support Macros, is used) and one disk drive.

IBM Personal Computer Fortran Compiler by MicroSoft, Inc., a language compiler, enables users to write programs in a version of FORTRAN-77, a scientific and engineering computer language. Object files can be linked with files from Macro Assembler programs. This compiler also allows access to formatted and unformatted sequential and direct files. The FORTRAN Compiler contains an augmented OPEN statement that takes additional parameters not included in the subset. This includes runtime file name assignment and a form of the CLOSE statement. In addition, the IBM FORTRAN Compiler features subscript, DO variables, unit number, and Input/Output list expressions. The FORTRAN Compiler works with the DOS, a minimum of 128K and two disk drives to produce the final load module, although the module itself may be executed in a smaller system.

UCSD p-System (Version IV) with UCSD Pascal™ and *FORTRAN-77* by Softech Microsystems Inc., is an advanced operating system for program development. It enables the user to write, assemble, compile, edit, link and execute programs. The file handler integrates all these functions and provides the user with easy access to both system and user created files. With UCSD Pascal and its structured programming approach, users are given operating environments that make it easy to develop Pascal programs with assembler language subroutines on the Personal Computer, as well as extensions for systems development and commercial applications.

With FORTRAN-77, users can take advantage of the power, portability and completeness of the p-System on the computer. FORTRAN and Pascal are compatible, allowing applications to be developed which are part Pascal and part FORTRAN.

The complete UCSD p-System program package for the Personal Computer includes: a screen-oriented editor that runs in a programming and textediting modes; a macro-assembler that provides code that can be linked to FORTRAN or Pascal programs; and advanced turtlegraphics, offering extended capabilities and graphic displays. The UCSD p-System with either FORTRAN-77, UCSD Pascal or both requires a minimum of 64K bytes of user memory and two disk drives.

EASYWRITER

EasyWriter is an easy-to-use word processing program. It is written and designed to accommodate users of varied skills. EasyWriter handles text creation and filing, editing and revisions, formatting, and final printing of documents or correspondence.

With EasyWriter, it is possible to work with 25 lines of 80 characters each in upper and lower case. EasyWriter files are stored on 5¼-inch disk. The documents you create can be viewed on your display screen (in the proper format) for verification before printing. The EasyWriter combination of simple text entry, full screen editing, and simple comands for moving and arranging text offers flexibility in the formatting of printed documents.

All EasyWriter functions (text entry, filing, editing, formatting and printing) are performed by selecting simple commands from multiple-choice menus that are displayed on the computer's screen. EasyWriter provides three special "task" menus to guide you through various word processing jobs:

1. The File Menu lets the user save, retrieve, delete, print, revise and link text or pieces of text that are saved in disk files. This menu also provides reference information such as the name of the file currently being worked on, the number of characters in the file, the percentage of disk space already being used by stored files, and a list of the files stored on that disk. Each Personal Computer disk can hold up to 31 EasyWriter text files.

2. The Editor Menu displays the commands used to enter new text to the files and change existing text. Pressing a single key switches the computer to the edit mode. Here, an operator can look through a "window" into the computer to display any portion of a file on command. Horizontal and vertical movement is provided in the edit mode so information can be entered or deleted anywhere on the screen.

3. The Additional Commands Menu offers capabilities such as searching and replacing information and selective or global replacement of strings of characters. This menu also lets the operator align, center and justify information, as well as set tabs, page numbers or margins.

The EasyWriter software package for the Personal Computer includes a program disk, a users' reference manual and users' reference card. EasyWriter runs on a Personal Computer with a disk drive, printer, 64K of user memory and the DOS. For display purposes, the user has the option of using the IBM Monochrome Display or other 80-character displays.

ACCOUNTS RECEIVABLE

Accounts Receivable is an invoicing and monthly statement generation package. It helps to simplify accounting procedures and improve control over receivables by keeping track of both current and aged accounts. With Accounts Receivable, the computer maintains an accounting record for each of the user's customers. The record includes credit information and account status.

To make receivables processing even easier, each program within the package contains a set of operator prompts and other "help" messages to allow even an inexperienced operator to make productive use of the system in a short time. The foundation of the Accounts Receivable package is the customer file. The system provides a flexible alphanumeric customer numbering scheme for the file, which contains information such as: customer number; address; credit, discount and tax rate; balances; credit, debit, and year-to-date information.

Transactions such as sales, receipts, credits and adjustments can also be entered. Invoices can then be printed, and information from them can be stored with other summary transactions.

Besides generating customer statements, the Accounts Receivable package will also produce an Aged Accounts Receivable Report; Invoice Register; Payment, Credit and Adjustment Register; and Customer Account Status Report. The Accounts Receivable package will also:

1. Handle open item or balance forward accounts.
2. Print invoices automatically, if requested.
3. Assign accounts to any of three aging periods or the current period.
4. Print customer account information on request.
5. Handle overpayment or prepayment on accounts.
6. Consolidate multiple transactions on open accounts, if requested.
7. Post transactions to the general ledger at month-end.

Using the Personal Computer in conjunction with the Accounts Receivable package, it is possible to reduce manual accounting workloads; maintain more up-to-date accounting files; provide customers with business-like payment records; and most importantly, monitor and control cash flow and collection activities.

The Accounts Receivable package is one of several accounting system packages by Peachtree for the IBM Personal Computer. It may be used alone or in conjunction with other program packages to handle business accounting needs. The Accounts Receivable software package includes program disks, a demonstration data disk, a users' reference manual and users' reference card.

GENERAL LEDGER

General Ledger is a versatile software package for the Personal Computer that offers an easy way to automate business accounting and improve the overall effectiveness and accuracy of financial information. It allows the user to maintain a detailed record of financial transactions and generates the balance sheet and income statements to provide information on the financial status of the company. To insure the tightest possible control, General Ledger provides the flexibility to let the user determine how to set up and operate the ledger. It matches the user's way of doing business and provides the answers needed to plan for the future. With this software package, decision makers in business have a powerful and personal management tool to help run the business and sharpen the focus on day-to-day financial control.

The General Ledger package includes a set of sixteen application programs which handle file creation, maintenance, updating and report writing. All General Ledger programs are initiated by selecting simple commands from multiple choice menus that are displayed on the computer's screen. The Personal Computer guides the user through the steps of a task, checking the work and highlighting errors as they are detected. The General Ledger package allows the user to set up a Chart of Accounts, which can be added to, changed or deleted as requirements change.

Transactions are easily entered through one transaction entry task. After performing any required editing of the information, transactions are automatically posted to the appropriate account. If running other IBM accounting system packages by Peachtree on the Personal Computer, such as Accounts Receivable or Accounts Payable, summary transactions from these applications can be automatically passed to the General Ledger at the close of the accounting period. At the end of the accounting period, the General Ledger package generates management reports, including Trial Balance, Transaction Registers, Balance Sheet and Income Statement. This package also provides:

1. Detailed comparison of prior year and budgeted amounts.
2. Password security to limit access to sensitive financial data.
3. Departmental income statements.
4. Subsidiary schedules.
5. Depreciation/amortization schedules.
6. Automatically repeating journal entries.

The General Ledger software package for the IBM Personal Computer includes program disks, a demonstration data disk, a user's reference manual and a users' reference card. General Ledger is copyrighted by Peachtree Software Incorporated.

ACCOUNTS PAYABLE

Accounts Payable is a vendor control and check generation package. It handles office procedures and the ability to manage outgoing cash by keeping track of current and aged accounts payable.

With the Accounts Payable programs, the Personal Computer maintains a computerized record for each vendor. The record provides information on due dates, discount dates, cash requirements and other data to help the user analyze cash position and determine who to pay, when to pay, and how much to pay. To make payables processing even simpler, each program within the package contains a set of operator prompts and other "help" messages.

The Accounts Payable package maintains a vendor file that contains information such as name, address, phone number, year-to-date purchases and payments, and current balances. Any invoices or credits entered into the computer are applied by the system to update this vendor file. To allow the user to examine this information prior to paying vendors, Accounts Payable will produce, Cash Requirements, Aged Payable and Open Voucher reports. After analyzing these reports and considering cash on hand, you may use the Payment Selection program to select the exact vendors and vouchers to be paid. The system will then print the specified chesks and even produce a Check Register as an audit trail.

In addition, the system performs month-end processing, which accumulates the debit and credit transactions for automatic posting to the general ledger. Other features which add to the flexibility and usefulness of the Personal Computer include the:

1. Option to print a Cash Requirements forecast based on either due dates or discount dates.
2. Option to allow voucher deletion.
3. Ability to print checks with detailed stubs for vendors.

With the IBM Personal Computer and Accounts Payable, the user receives an overview of cash requirements, making it possible to plan disbursements ahead of time and review or change payment procedures easily. An accounts payable operation can not only be controlled, but designed and organized to help you gain maximum benefits when dealing with vendors. The Accounts Payable software package includes program disk, a demonstration data disk, a user's reference manual and a user's reference card. Accounts Payable is copyrighted by Peachtree Software, Incorporated.

VISICALC

VisiCalc is a financial spread sheet package for business executives, accountants, analysts and planners of all kinds. With VisiCalc, you can do corporate or family budget planning, financial and statistical analyses, sales projections and business plans, cash flow projections, market analyses, etc., faster, easier, more accurately and more flexibly than by hand or with a calculator.

VisiCalc lets you use the computer's display screen as a "window," through which it is possible to create and manipulate a large "electronic work sheet" of up to 63 columns and 254 rows. Any element in this grid can be an arithmetic operator, numeric value, a label or a formula. These can be modified at will, and VisiCalc will automatically recalculate the entire work sheet using the new values.

The speed and accuracy of the Personal Computer can save hours of tedious recalculation. Also, the system printer can be used to produce reports that display the different "what if" situations created with the simple change of one or more of the data elements.

To use VisiCalc, you create the work sheet at the keyboard by typing the headings for each column and row. Wherever it is desired for the program to perform a calculation, a formula is typed. Formulas can be as simple as comparing one sales figure to another, or as complex as a high-level scientific problem. These formulas allow you to relate grid elements to each other in very flexible ways. The formulas can also use the standard VisiCalc functions, which include summation, net present value, average, integer, and trigonometric functions.

TIME MANAGER

Another program I tested was created by The Image Producers, Inc. and produced by MicroSoft. Time Manager allows you to organize and plan personal and business activities while maintaining records for future reference.

Time Manager is a daily organizer and calendar that lists each day's activities by preestablished priorities. Appointments are listed according to time, and important activities are displayed from day to day until they are completed. This program actually forms a "to-do" list which is constantly displayed day after day until you input the fact that it has taken place. Time Manager is also a data processing tool. When making an entry, you can designate one of 26 categories. Later, you can select any category for review. Time Manager will scan all entries for information which meets your selection criteria. You can quickly access complete files on people, events, companies, projects, etc. These features may be used to determine time and money expended on overall projects and/or activities. This program also provides a number of notepads for maintaining lists of information that are not part of your daily schedule.

Time Manager is also an accounting tool for home and business applications. It may be used to verify expenditures at tax time or to create expense reports, project evaluations, billing records, invoices or internal accounting reports.

MICROSOFT ADVENTURE

Microsoft Adventure is a role-playing game where a single player acts out an adventure with the help of an IBM Personal Computer. The setting for this adventure is a vast network of caves beneath the earth and the land outside in the vicinity of the entrance to the caves. The world created by this program contains 130 rooms or nodes, 15 treasures, 40 useful objects, and 12 problems to solve.

Microsoft Adventure was designed to operate on an IBM Personal Computer with at least 32K bytes of memory, one diskette drive, and one of the following display options:

1. The IBM Monochrome Display and the IBM Monochrome Display and Printer Adapter

2. A customer-supplied color or black-and-white monitor with the Color/Graphics Display Adapter

3. A customer-supplied color or black-and-white TV set with the Color/Graphics Monitor Adapter and a customer-supplied rf modulator.

ASYNCHRONOUS COMMUNICATIONS SUPPORT

This support allows users, with no additional programming support, to use their IBM Personal Computer as a TTY ASR 33/35 terminal. In addition to the interactive terminal support, the package provides for the exchange of program and data files between the IBM Personal Computer and the host system with which it is communicating as well as between two IBM Personal Computers if both have the Asynchronous Communications Support.

The Asynchronous Communications Support Program is designed to allow connection to most host systems which support TTY ASR 33/35 terminals. The following terminal parameters may be stored on the IBM Personal Computer or specified interactively at program initiation:

1. Bit rate (75 bps to 2400 bps)
2. Parity
3. Number of stop bits
4. Line output turnaround characters
5. Half or full duplex
6. XON/XOFF support

If additional parameter settings supported by the Asynchronous Communications Adapter are needed, the user can expand the program using the BASIC language.

The program has operated with VM/370 Release 6 and VM/Systems Product Release 1 on an IBM System/370 Model 158 with an IBM 3705.

The IBM Personal Computer configuration must include 64K bytes of memory, the Disk Operating System (DOS), Disk BASIC language extensions, and the Asynchronous Communications Adapter.

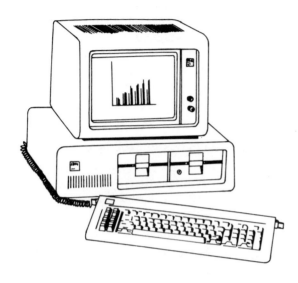

Chapter 7

The Intel 8088 Microprocessor

The 8088 microprocessor chip, manufactured for IBM by the Intel Corporation, is the heart of the System Board in the IBM Personal Computer. It was over ten years ago that the Intel introduced the first microprocessor. Advertised in 1971, Intel announced not just a new product, but a new era of integrated electronics. A microprocessor is a programmable microcomputer on a single chip.

Dr. Marcian E. "Ted" Hoff, Jr., conceived the microprocessor. Given the task of designing a complex set of chips for a customer planning to manufacture a family of programmable calculators. Dr. Hoff suggested a simpler solution. Rather than produce a set of chips dedicated to one function, he suggested Intel design a standard logic chip that could be made to do many things.

Dr. Hoff realized the same architectural principles used to build mainframe and minicomputers could be applied on a very small scale to produce a microcomputer. All computers, whatever their size and power, have four major elements:

1. Arithmetic Logic Unit (ALU): A microprocessor is the ALU of a microcomputer system. It is designed to recognize and execute a predetermined number of instructions. These instructions are presented to it as "data words" that are 4, 8, 16 or 32 bits long, depending on the power of the microprocessor. Each bit is represented as a 1 or 0 that can be understood and manipulated by the microprocessor.

2. Program Memory: The instructions that can be understood by a microprocessor can be stored in various types of read-only memory chips (ROMs, PROMs, EPROMs and E^2PROMs). By creating a sequence of instructions (a software program), programmers direct the microprocessor to perform a given task.

3. Data Memory: The variable data to be processed by a microcomputer is stored in chips called random access memories (RAMs). In the case of a gasoline pump, RAMs would store data such as gasoline flow rate and whether the pump is on or off.

4. Input/Output Devices: To enable a microcomputer to interact with the outside world, there must be ways to enter and access data. Input devices include keyboards and sensors. Output devices include printers, terminals and microfilm devices.

Four considerations determine the power of a microprocessor:

1. How fast can it process data?

2. How many instructions can it understand? (The greater the number of instructions, the easier it is to write programs.)

3. How wide a data word can it handle? (The wider the word, the greater the throughput of data.)

4. How much memory can it address? (Each data word stored in memory has a specific address, and many more addresses are possible with longer data words.)

A comparison of the first microprocessor, Intel's 4004, with the 8086 is provided in Fig. 7-1. This chart shows the rapid progress made in a few short years.

The first commercial microprocessor, the Intel 4004, actually changed the way in which new electronic products were designed. Equipment makers no longer had to develop new circuit designs for every product. They now had a standard block of logic that could be programmed to do a job. Because of their small size, high reliability and low price, microprocessors made possible a whole new class of intelligent machines.

The impact of the microprocessor has been similar to that of the development of the fractional horsepower motor in the nineteenth century. The first fractional horsepower motors gave users the freedom to apply affordable horsepower where it was needed, creating uses never imagined with the large motors that ran entire factories. The microprocessor has done the same thing for man's brain power that the fractional horsepower motor did for muscle power. For the first time, it has become possible to distribute computer intelligence to the fingertips of the user, an impossible task with the big computers of the early 1970s. An example of this can be found in the home. A modern household contains an average of forty motor-driven appliances and other machines. In the next decade, it is possible that the number of microprocessors in the home will overtake the number of motor-driven household items. Already, these chips have found their way into thermostats, automobiles, microwave ovens, sprinkler systems, stereos, toys, videocassette recorders, security systems, dishwashers and many more everyday items.

Intel's 4004 was the first in a series of processors that led to the introduction in 1981 of the Intel iAPX 432, a three-chip set designed specifically for the information-intensive applications of the 1980s. The 4004 had the equivalent of 2,300 transistors and made possible the first intelligent instruments and computer terminals. The iAPX 432 has the equivalent of 225,000 transistors and will open the door to numerous applications.

Between these two milestone processors is a well-coordinated group of products. The essence of Intel's approach is to have a coordi-

	4004	8086
ALU ADD TIME	10.8 MICROSEC	1.1 MICROSEC.
NUMBER OF INSTRUCTIONS	45	133
DATA WORD WIDTH	4 BITS	16 BITS
MAXIMUM MEMORY SIZE	4500 BYTES	1 MILLION BYTES

Fig. 7-1. Comparison of performance and characteristics of Intel 4004 and 8086 microprocessors (courtesy Intel).

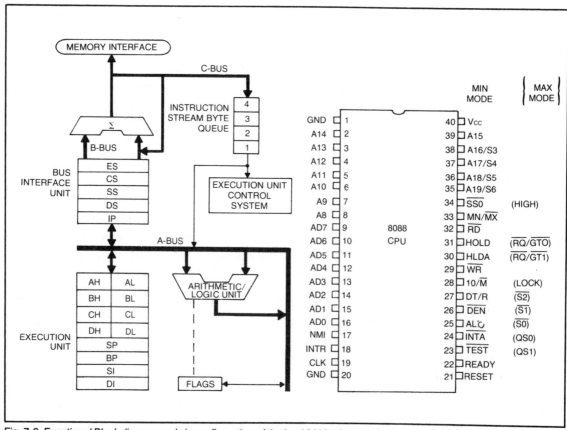

Fig. 7-2. Functional Block diagram and pin configuration of the Intel 8088 microprocessor used in the IBM Personal Computer (courtesy Intel).

nated series of processors so each customer can select the right unit for his system needs. The 432, 8086 and 8088 represent the top end of this continuum. The 8086 family, introduced in 1978, has been designed into about 5,000 products.

In the middle of the series are the 8080A and 8085 8-bit microprocessors. The 8048 and 8051 families of single-chip microcomputers are at the lower end. These single-chip units integrate not only the central processing unit of a computer, but also the input/output circuitry and data and program memory needed. In all, Intel offers 18 microprocessors and microcomputers.

We have referred to the 8088 as a 16-bit microprocessor. Actually, it does not operate like a true 16-bit processor such as the Intel 8086. The 8088 contains an 8-bit data bus interface which allows it to communicate at an 8-bit level. However, it contains a 16-bit internal architecture, allowing processing at the 16-bit rate. The processor has the attributes of both 8- and 16-bit microprocessors. For this reason, it is directly compatible with software designed for their 8086 microprocessor (16-bit) *and* their 8080/8085 (8-bit) hardware and peripherals. Use of the 8088 chip allows the IBM Personal Computer to be compatible with the more standard 8-bit hardware and software currently in use.

Shown in Fig. 7-2, the 8088 microprocessor is implemented in N-channel, depletion-load, silicon gate technology (HMOS) and packaged in a 40-pin CerDIP housing. The 8088 address/data bus is broken into three parts. The lower eight address/data bits (AD0-AD7), the middle eight address bits (AD16-AD19) make up these three parts.

The address/data bits and the highest four address bits are time multiplexed. This techniques provides the most efficient use of pins on the processor and permits the use of the standard 40-lead package. The middle eight address bits are not multiplexed. They remain valid throughout each bus cycle. Additionally, the bus can be demultiplexed at the processor with single address latch if a standard, nonmultiplex bus is desired for system operation.

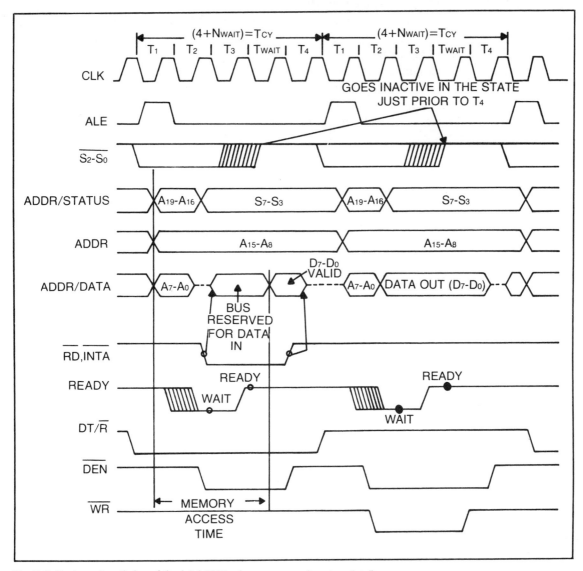

Fig. 7-3. Basic system timing of the Intel 8088 microprocessor (courtesy Intel).

Basic system timing is illustrated in Fig. 7-3. Each processor bus cycle consists of at least four clock cycles (CLK). In the diagram, these are referred to as T1, T2, T3, and T4. The address is emitted from the processor during T1 and data transfer occurs on the bus during the T3 and T4 clock cycles. Clock cycle T2 is used primarily for changing the direction of the bus during read operations. In the event that a "NOT READY" indication is given by the addressed device, "wait" states (Tw) are inserted between cycles T3 and T4.

It is not the purpose of this book to go into great detail on every circuit within the IBM Personal Computer. It is hoped that this discussion of the 8088 chip will help clear up the questions some persons have had regarding the 16-bit versus 8-bit operation of microprocessors in general. The 8088 allows direct addressing capability to one megabyte of memory. It also provides 24 operand addressing modes, 14-word by 16-bit register set with symmetrical operations, as well as byte, word and block operations. The 8088 is capable of 8-bit *and* 16-bit signed and unsigned arithmetic in binary or decimal, including multiply and divide.

In the microprocessor world, most of us are accustomed to chips which are either designated as 4-bit, 8-bit, 16-bit and even 32-bit types. The 8088 is unusual, in that it combines the increased capabilities of a 16-bit processor in a package which can communicate with an 8-bit world.

Chapter 8

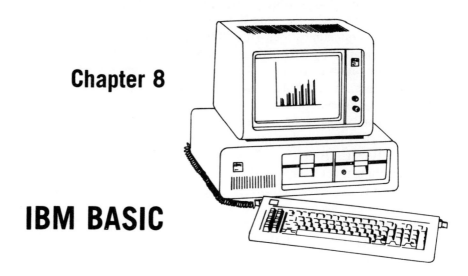

IBM BASIC

IBM Personal Computer BASIC is a powerful and versatile language and is not too different from other BASIC dialects. There are differences, however, and many programs written in BASIC for other machines cannot be run directly. In these instances, some modifications will be required. This is not unusual, since dialect modifications are often required for different machines. Fortunately, the BASIC language is quite easy to master and dialect modifications come with equal ease.

The IBM Personal Computer offers three versions of the BASIC interpreter. There are Cassette, Disk, and Advanced BASIC. IBM points out that the three versions are upward-compatible, meaning that Disk BASIC does everything that Cassette BASIC does and a little more. Likewise, Advanced BASIC does everything that Disk BASIC does and offers some additional features.

I have found Disk BASIC (operating within the IBM Disk Operating System program) to be highly useful. This program also contains the Advanced BASIC feature, which is mandatory for graphics applications.

The nucleus of BASIC is the Cassette version, which is built into the IBM Personal Computer in 32K bytes of read-only storage. You can use Cassette BASIC on an IBM Personal Computer with any amount of RAM. In Cassette BASIC, the only storage device is a cassette tape recorder.

In all forms of BASIC, you will find an extended character set consisting of 256 different characters. If you have the Color/Graphics Monitor Adapter, you can draw points, lines, and even entire pictures. The screen is all points addressable in either medium or high resolution.

IBM Disk BASIC is a part of IBM DOS, a 5¼-inch diskette program. You load Disk BASIC into memory using the disk drive. This requires a diskette-based machine with at least 32K bytes of random access storage.

Disk BASIC has all of the features of Cassette BASIC, but it also offers input/output to diskette in addition to cassette. An internal clock keeps track of the date and time, and an asynchronous communications (RS-232) support, in combination with the IBM communications adapter, allows you to talk with other IBM computers. Disk BASIC also offers support for two additional printers.

The most extensive form of BASIC available for the IBM Personal Computer is called Advanced BASIC (BASICA). This language does everything that Cassette and Disk BASIC do, plus a lot more. Advanced BASIC requires a diskette-based machine with at least 48K bytes of random access storage; like Disk BASIC, it is part of the IBM DOS program. Special features found only in Advanced BASIC include event trapping, advanced graphics, and advanced music support. The additional graphics statements include CIRCLE, DRAW, GET, PAINT, and PUT. These operations make it easier to create highly complex graphics with the computer and an optional Color/Graphics Monitor Adapter. From a musical standpoint, the Play statement allows easy usage of the built-in speaker to create musical tones.

BASIC STATEMENTS

You will find that many statements in IBM BASIC are similar to or exactly like the statements in other BASIC dialects; some statements, however, will be completely different.

The following list of commands and statements is not complete, but it is a good overview of IBM BASIC to illustrate the similarities and differences between it and other dialects of BASIC. If you are accustomed to programming in another form of BASIC, I think you will find the transition to the IBM Personal Computer version to be quite easy. As a matter of fact, this form of BASIC is more versatile than some other dialects and will allow you to do many things with greater speed using the specialized commands. Certainly, if you are familiar with another form of BASIC, you can start programming right away and experience little difficulty. However, if you learn in time-saving features of this language before you begin programming you will be able to program faster and more efficiently.

ABS This function returns the absolute value of an expression. The absolute value is always positive or zero. For example, the command ABS (8*(− 7)) will return the number 35. This is the absolute value, which, again, is always zero or a positive number.

ASC This function returns the ASCII code to the screen for the first character on the screen that follows. Let's assume that A$ = "RADAR". The command PRINT ASC (A$) will then return the number 82, which is the ASCII value of the letter R.

ATN This mathematical function returns the arctangent of the value that follows it. For example, ATN (3) will return the arctangent of 3, which is 1.249046.

AUTO AUTO is a highly useful command that speeds along programming. It allows you to avoid having to type in a number for each program line. This command is not part of an actual program; rather it is input prior to programming in order to generate the automatic numbering sequence. The command AUTO is input, and when the Enter button is depressed, a 10 will automatically be printed. You type in the program line; when you hit Enter again, a 20 appears in the next line position, and so forth. When doing intensive programming, it is often necessary to constantly refer to the previous line number in order to obtain the correct number for the next line. The AUTO command does this for you automatically. The AUTO command may also be incorporated after programming has started. For example, if you had inserted program lines numbered from 10 through 110, inputting AUTO 120, 10, the line number generated would automatically enter line number 120 and advance in increments of 10 from that point on (130, 140, etc.). Of course, many programmers insert lines in increments other than 10, for example, 5, 10, 15, 20. The AUTO command can do this as well. Inputting AUTO 5, 5 will cause the first line number to be a 5 and for the succeeding lines to be numbered in increments of 5. Without these additional numbers, the default is automatically the number 10 and increments of 10 result. When the additional numbers are inserted, the one immediately following the command will be the next printed line number. The one following the comma will set the incremental steps.

BEEP   The BEEP statement causes the computer to output an 800-hertz tone to the internal speaker. The tone lasts for approximately one-quarter second and is used as an audible prompt.

BLOAD   The BLOAD command causes a memory image file to be loaded into memory. When a BLOAD command is executed, the file is loaded into memory, starting at a specified location. This command is immediately followed by the string expression for the file and then by an offset number which specifies the address at which loading is to start. The BLOAD statement is usually preceded by a DEF SEG statement, which defines the current segment of storage.

BSAVE   This command saves portions of the computer's memory on a specified device. If the device name is omitted, the machine defaults to the first drive (cassette or diskette). When using a dual-disk system, this statement is quite handy in choosing which drive is to receive the input information.

CALL   The CALL statement calls a machine-language subroutine and is a method of interfacing machine-language programs with BASIC. This statement is followed by the name of a numeric variable whose value indicates the starting memory address.

CD BL   This function converts the numeric expression that follows it to a double-precision number. The value of the number is accurate to the second decimal place after rounding.

CHAIN   The CHAIN statement transfers control of the machine to another program and passes along the variables from the current program to the one which is to be in control. This allows the operator to easily insert previously input variables within one program into the new one and greatly speeds overall run time.

**CHR$**   This function is the opposite of the ASC function previously discussed. It is used to convert an ASCII code into its character equivalent. For example, CHR$(82) will return the letter R. The CHR$ function is used for many purposes, including the writing of some limited graphics using the IBM Monochrome Monitor and Adapter Board. For example, CHR$(219) causes a solid square to be printed on the screen. This is not available by depressing a single keyboard key.

CINT   The CINT function is used to convert a numeric expression to an integer. For example, CINT(37.92) would result in 38. The numeric expression is converted to an integer by rounding its fractional portion.

CLEAR   The CLEAR command frees all memory used for data without erasing the program currently in memory. It sets all numeric values to zero and all string variables to null.

CLOSE   The CLOSE statement is used to end all input/output to a device or file. This statement may be followed by designators that determine which files or devices are to be closed. When used alone, CLOSE causes all open devices and files to be closed.

CLS The CLS statement clears the screen. If the screen is in graphics mode, the entire screen buffer is cleared to the background color. The CLS statement is used within a program to erase all printed information which has been input to the screen to this program point.

COM The COM statement is used in conjunction with a communications adapter and enables or disables trapping of communications activity. The statement COM(n) ON enables the communications adapter. The same statement followed by OFF disables it. Here, no trapping takes place, and no communications activity is remembered. The COM statement followed by STOP disables the adapter. However, any communications activity that does take place is remembered. The variable that immediately follows COM(n) is the number of the communications adapter, of which there may be a maximum of two.

COMMON The COMMON statement passes variables to a chained program. This statement is used in conjunction with the CHAIN statement.

CONT This command stands for continue and is used to resume the running of a program after a break. This avoids the necessity of rerunning an entire program when it has become necessary to stop it during execution.

COS The COS function causes the computer to return the trigonometric cosine function. For example, COS(3.14) will return a −1, which is the cosine of pi radians.

CSNG This function is similar to CDBL, but it converts a numeric expression to a single-precision number.

CSRLIN CSRLIN is a variable that causes the screen to print the vertical coordinate of the screen cursor. This allows the operator to obtain the coordinates of the exact position of a point on the screen. This information may later be used within a program to print a keyboard input at the same location.

CVI,CVS,CVD These functions convert string variable types to numeric variable types. They are available only in Disk BASIC and Advanced BASIC. CVI converts a two-byte string; CVS and CVD convert four- and eight-byte strings, respectively. Using these functions, the actual bytes of data are not changed, but the way BASIC interprets those bytes is.

DATA The DATA statement stores numeric and string constants within a program. These constants are accessed by a READ statement within the same program.

**DATE$** DATE$ is a variable and a statement and is used to set or retrieve the date. The year must be in the range of 1980 to 2099. As an example, if DATE$ ‡ "7/19/83", the printout will be 08-29-1983.

DEF FN This statement defines and names a function written into a program. The statement is followed immediately by the written name of the function and then by an argument or formula for determining when the function is to be named during the execution.

DEF SEG This statement defines the current segment of storage and is followed by an address which is a numeric expression in the range of 0 to 65,535.

DELETE The DELETE command erases program lines. For example, DELETE 30 would erase program line 30. Using this command, you can erase whole sections of programs. DELETE 30-200 would erase all program lines between and including 30 and 200.

DIM This statement specifies the maximum values for array variable subscripts and allocates appropriate storage. This command is common to all dialects of BASIC.

EDIT   The EDIT command is used to display a particular program line for editing purposes. The cursor is then moved to the faulty part of the line, where new information may be input. EDIT 40 recalls line 40 for editing purposes. The same line could also be recalled and edited by inputting LIST 40. (See LIST.)

END   The END statement is used within a computer program to stop program execution. It closes all files and returns the machine to the command level.

ERASE   The ERASE statement is followed by the name of a specific array and erases it from storage.

FILES   The FILES command causes the names of all files residing on a diskette to be displayed on the screen. This command is available only in IBM DOS.

FOR and NEXT   This statement does not differ from other dialects of BASIC and is used to perform a series of instructions within a loop a number of times. The FOR statement is followed by a variable and then by two numeric expressions, one being the initial value and the other the final value. For example, the program line FOR X = 1 TO 10 would set the starting value of X at 1 and the final value at 10. A NEXT statement must follow in order to allow the loop to be repeated the set number of times.

GOSUB and RETURN   These are common statements within any dialect of BASIC. They allow branching to a subroutine and returning from it. GOSUB 130 causes a branch to line 130 during program execution. At some point past 130, a RETURN statement is required to cause BASIC to branch back to the program line immediately following the one containing the GOSUB statement.

GOTO   GOTO is similar to GOSUB, but the branch is unconditional. Using the previous example, a line which reads GOTO 130

will create a branch to line 130, where execution will continue to the end of the program. There is no RETURN statement.

**HEX$**   This function returns a string representing the hexadecimal value of a numeric expression input in decimal form. This expression must range in value from −32,768 to 65,535. For example, HEX$(32) will return the number 20, which is the hexadecimal equivalent of 32 decimal.

IF   As is the case in other dialects, the IF statement decides the route of programming flow based upon the results of an expression. This statement is often preceded by an INPUT statement. The IF statement may be followed by a THEN and an ELSE statement, or by GOTO and ELSE. For example, take the line IF A$ = "YES" THEN 250 ELSE 300. This means that if A$, which has been input earlier, is equal to the expression "YES", then the program flow is routed to line 250. If A$ does not equal "YES", the program flow is routed to line 300. The THEN statement could be replaced in this example by a GOTO. The ELSE statement may or may not be used. IF must always be followed by a THEN or GOTO statement,

**INKEY$**   This variable is common to most BASIC dialects and is used to read a character from the keyboard. For example, the line X$ = INKEY$:IF A$ = "" THEN 40 causes the program to stop at this line and then branch to line 40 when any key on the keyboard is depressed.

INPUT   The INPUT statement is used within a program and stops execution until information is received from the keyboard. INPUT is followed by a phrase in quotes in many cases. This phrase serves as the screen prompt. For example, INPUT "YES OR NO",B$ asks the operator to input a yes or no answer. This line will most likely be followed by one containing an IF . . . THEN statement, which would act upon the input from the keyboard. INPUT may be used without an IF . . . THEN statement as well, such as INPUT "PRESS ENTER TO CONTINUE",B$. The program stops at this line but then continues when the Enter key is depressed. B$ is used here only as an example, and any unused string variable will suffice.

INPUT# This statement reads data items from a file or sequential device and assigns them to program variables. The expression is followed by the number used when the file was initially opened for input and by a variable that has an item in the file assigned to it.

INPUT$ This function returns a string of a specified number of characters read from the keyboard or from a file number.

KEY The KEY statement controls the ten soft keys, which are located on the left-hand side of the IBM Personal Computer's keyboard. It also turns the screen printout of the key designations on and off. KEY ON causes a printout at the bottom of the screen listing keys F1 through F10, along with their string expressions. The latter is an abbreviated listing of what each key does. KEY OFF removes this display. KEY LIST causes a separate printout of key functions to be displayed. KEYn,X$ is used to change key functions. For example, KEY 1, LIST would cause KEY 1 to print the word LIST on the screen. When this latter expression is followed by appropriate ASCII coding, the soft keys take on command functions and will automatically input and run a short command.

KILL This command deletes a file from diskette. If a file is named PGM, the command KILL "PGM.BAS" will erase the file from diskette. The .BAS is the full name of the file (along with PGM), as stored in DOS.

**LEFT$** This function causes the screen to return (print) the leftmost characters of a string expression. Let's assume that A$ -

"MY NAME IS RON". If the next line reads B$ - LEFT$(A$,2):PRINT B$, then the screen display will print out MY. This is the leftmost portion of A$, composed of the first two characters. If we inserted the line B$ = LEFT$(A$,5), then the first five characters would be output to the screen.

LEN The LEN function returns the number of characters in a string. As an example, A$ = "FRONT ROYAL, VA":PRINT LEN(A$) would cause a printout on the screen of fifteen, which is the total number of characters within the screen. Notice that the spaces have also been counted, as they are part of the string expression.

LET The LET statement, as in most dialects of BASIC, assigns the value of an expression to a variable. For example, LET A = 10 means that the variable A will always be equal to the number 10. However, in IBM BASIC, the LET statement is optional. The previous example could be replaced simply by A = 10. Since the expression is optional, there is no real reason to use it, as this will slow programming slightly.

LINE INPUT The LINE INPUT statement reads an entire line up to 256 characters from the keyboard and places it into a string variable, ignoring all delimiters. This expression is sometimes followed by a prompt, which is the string constant displayed on the screen before input is accepted. The prompt is then followed by a string variable that is the array element to which the line will be assigned. In Disk BASIC, LINE INPUT may be immediately followed by a semicolon to allow the cursor to remain on the same line as the response.

LIST The LIST command, when used by itself, will display all lines of the program currently in memory. You may also follow the expression with a line number, such as LIST 200. Line 200 will then be displayed on the screen. If you input LIST 100-200, then lines 100 through 200 will be displayed. You may edit lines using the LIST command, just as you would do with the EDIT command.

LLIST   This command is identical to the previous one, except all lines specified are output to the printer.

LOAD   The LOAD command retrieves a program from a specified memory device and reads it into current memory. This command is followed by a quotation mark and the name of the file. For example, LOAD"PGM loads the file named PGM into current memory.

LOCATE   The LOCATE statement positions the cursor on the screen at the point specified. This statement is followed by the screen position. For example, LOCATE 10,30 positions the cursor at row 10 and column 30. This statement may then be followed by a PRINT statement to allow information to be printed starting at the 10,30 position on the screen. The LOCATE and PRINT statements must be separated by a colon if they are included in the same program line. When used jointly, the LOCATE and PRINT statements take the place of PRINT@statements which are common to other dialects of BASIC. There is no PRINT@statement in IBM BASIC.

LOG   The LOG function returns the natural logarithm of a numeric expression to the screen. For example, PRINT LOG(56) would cause the screen to print out the natural logarithm of 56. You may also use variables with the LOG function and perform arithmetic operations with the parentheses. PRINT LOG(36/6) would return the natural logarithm of 36 divided by 6, or 6.

LPRINT   LPRINT is identical to the PRINT statement but outputs to the line printer. (See PRINT.)

LPRINT USING   LPRINT USING is similar to LPRINT, but it causes the printer to display a string constant. (See PRINT USING.)

MERGE   The MERGE command merges the line from an ASCII program file into the program currently in memory. This allows one program to be stored on diskette or cassette, while another portion of the program is being worked out in RAM. When this latter portion is completed, the two may be merged.

**MID$**   The MID$ function returns the requested part of the given string to the display. This function is followed by the name of the string and the starting and ending character position. As an example, PRINT MID$(A$,4,7) would cause the display to print that portion of A$ starting with the fourth character and ending seven characters past this point.

MOTOR   The MOTOR statement is used to turn the cassette recorder on and off. MOTOR 1 turns the machine on, while MOTOR 0 turns it off. If the MOTOR statement is used by itself, whenever it's encountered in a program, the state of the motor (on or off) will automatically be reversed. If the motor is on, it will be turned off when a MOTOR statement is encountered, and vice versa.

NAME   The NAME command is used to change the name of a diskette file. Assume that a program has been stored on diskette under the name "RED". The command NAME "RED.BAS" AS "BROWN.BAS" renames the file "BROWN". In each case, the .BAS designation is necessary, as all programs stored on diskette from BASIC are automatically given this designation within the filename.

NEW   The NEW command is often used prior to beginning a program. It deletes the program currently in memory and clears all variables. If this command is not used before beginning a new program with another program already in current memory, the lines of the program you're working on will automatically take the place of the lines bearing the same numbers in the older program.

**OCT$** This function returns a string to the screen that is equal to the octal value of a decimal numeric expression. For example, PRINT OCT$(24) will result in the screen displaying the number 30, which is the octal equivalent of decimal 24.

ON The ON statement is used in conjunction with a GOSUB and RETURN or GOTO to branch to one or more line numbers, depending upon the value of the expression. The ON statement may also be used in conjunction with the KEY statement to branch to another line number when the soft keys are used.

PLAY The PLAY statement is used in Advanced BASIC only. When coupled with a string expression, it outputs tones to the internal speaker. The PLAY statement is used to program computer music and is followed by string expressions composed of the letters A through G, which specify musical notes. There are many other string expression elements which set the octave, note length, pauses, and music style.

PRINT The PRINT statement is used to display data on the screen. It may be followed by a phrase in quotation marks. Here, it will reprint all characters within the quotes. This statement may also be followed by a numeric or screen variable. For example, the program line A = 1000:PRINT A will print the number 1000 on the screen. The line A$ = "ONE THOUSAND":PRINT A$ will cause the expression ONE THOUSAND to be printed.

PRINT USING The PRINT USING statement is used to display strings or numbers using a specific format.

PSET PSET, along with PRESET, are statements that are used to draw a point at a specified position on the display screen. This is used in graphics mode only and requires the IBM Color/Graphics Monitor Adapter. PRESET is almost identical to PSET, but if no color parameter is specified, the background color (0) is automatically selected. If a color designator is used, the two statements are identical. PSET is followed by the X,Y screen coordinates. X specifies the row, while Y indicates the column. Using PSET or PRESET, these coordinates will be followed by the desired color number, which must be in the range of 0 to 3. These expressions replace the SET statements common to other dialects of BASIC. IBM BASIC contains no SET statement.

RANDOMIZE The RANDOMIZE statement causes the program to stop in order to allow an integer expression to be input via the keyboard. This reseeds the random number generator, allowing numbers that are to be randomized (see RND) to be altered each time. The integer expression must be between $-32,768$ and $+32,767$. Each time the program is run, the program will stop and a prompt will be displayed on the screen, telling you to input a random number seed. You may also input a fixed number with the RANDOMIZE statement. This number will be automatically input to the random number generator each time the program is run, and there will be no pause.

READ The READ statement is common to most dialects of BASIC and reads the value from a DATA statement, assigning it to a variable.

REM The REM statement is a portion of a program that is not executed. It is included to explain the functioning of that portion of the program. Remarks that follow the REM statement are not displayed or acted upon during the program run, but are there to indicate a program function and are seen during line listing.

RENUM The RENUM command is used to renumber all program lines. When used by itself, it automatically numbers the lines in a sequence of 10. For example, if your program were

```
10 A = 5
15 B = 10
18 PRINT A + B
```

If the command RENUM were entered, the new program listing would be renumbered sequentially from 10 to 30:

```
10 A = 5
20 B − 10
30 PRINT A + B
```

Proper programming must be handled with adequate number spacing to allow for the insertion of new program lines. Sometimes, however, reworking a program causes all line spaces to be filled. When this occurs, you simply enter the RENUM command and then list the newly numbered program lines. You now have renumbering in increments of 10 and thus, more spaces between lines to add new program lines. The RENUM command also changes all line number references following GOTO, GOSUB, THEN and ELSE statements, so it is not necessary to go back through and make these corrections within the program lines to obtain the desired branching. An executable program will be just as executable after the RENUM command has been input.

The RENUM command may also be followed by numeric expressions that set the value of the first line number, the line in the current program where renumbering is to begin, and the increment to be used in the new program line sequence. For producing easy to understand programs, this command is extremely valuable.

RESET In IBM BASIC, the RESET command closes all files contained in diskette storage and clears the system buffer. If all files are already contained on diskette, the RESET command is the same as CLOSE.

**RIGHT$** The RIGHT$ function returns the right-most characters of a string expression. This is the reciprocal of the LEFT$ function. (See LEFT$).

RND The RND function returns a random number between 0 and 1. The same sequence of random numbers is generated each time the program is run unless the random number generator is reseeded. (See RANDOMIZE).

RUN The RUN command begins program execution. It may also be followed by a line number to begin execution at some point within the program. This command is available by depressing KEY F2 on the IBM Personal Computer keyboard.

SAVE The SAVE command is used to save a program in a file on cassette of diskette. The command SAVE"PGM" will cause the program to be filed and listed under the name PGM. When Cassette BASIC is used, the program is automatically filed on cassette tape. When Disk BASIC is used, the program is automatically filed on the default diskette drive (drive A). When used as shown, PGM will be saved in a compressed binary format rather than in ASCII. This conserves storage space. You may also save the program in ASCII by using SAVE"PGM", A.

SIN The SIN function calculates the trigonometric sine of a number. For example, PRINT SIN(20) returns the sine of 20 in a single-precision number.

SOUND The SOUND statement causes a tone to be generated through the internal speaker. The SOUND statement is followed by a numeric expression in the range of 37 to 32,767, which corresponds to the frequency of the tone. This may be followed by another numeric expression that determines the duration of the tone.

SQR The SQR function returns the square root of a numeric expression. For example, PRINT SQR(9) will return the number 3, this being the square root of 9.

STOP The STOP statement ends program execution and returns the machine to the command level.

SWAP The SWAP statement exchanges the values of two variables or array elements. For example:

```
10 A$ = "TWO":B$ − "FOR"
20 PRINT A$,B$
```

The screen printout from this program will be TWO FOR. Using the SWAP statement brings about a different printout:

```
10 A$ = "TWO":B$ = "FOR"
20 SWAP A$,B$
```

The screen printout will now be FOR TWO. The two expressions have been exchanged.

SYSTEM The SYSTEM command exits BASIC and returns to DOS.

TAB The TAB function advances the cursor to the column designated. For example, PRINT "HELLO" TAB (30) "THERE" will cause the screen to display HELLO at the left-hand side of the screen and THERE at column 30 on the same line.

**TIME$** THE TIME$ statement (or variable) sets or retrieves the current time. This is very similar to the DATE$ statement.

WAIT The WAIT statement suspends the execution of a program while monitoring the status of a machine input port. The program execution is halted until the specified port develops a prearranged bit pattern.

WHILE The WHILE statement is used in conjunction with a WEND statement to execute statements within a loop as long as a certain condition is true. If a statement is true, the loop is executed until the WEND statement is encountered. This returns execution to the original WHILE statement. If the expression is still true, the process is repeated. WHILE and WEND statements are similar to GOSUB and RETURN, as long as a certain condition is true.

WIDTH The WIDTH statement is used to set the width of any line in number of characters. If no WIDTH statement is used, the default is automatically 80 characters. This is the high-resolution mode. WIDTH 40 sets the display to output lines with a maximum of 40 characters, which is the medium-resolution mode.

WRITE The WRITE statement is very similar to the PRINT statement, and both are used to output data onto the screen. However, the WRITE statement inserts commas between the items.

PROGRAMMING IN BASIC

Most people who purchase the IBM Personal Computer also get a diskette drive and IBM DOS (Disk Operating System), though some opt for the less expensive cassette tape sortage medium. IBM DOS is preferred because of the advanced capabilities offered by this system.

When you first load IBM DOS, it is necessary to switch to BASIC or BASICA. You simply type in the date and the time when prompted to do so. When you receive the flashing prompt "A>" type in BASIC or BASICA (Advanced BASIC), and you are ready to begin programming.

PROGRAMMING IN DISK BASIC

Assuming that DOS has been properly loaded, you are in Disk BASIC and are receiving the BASIC prompt, it's an easy matter to enter your own programs. First of all, type:
NEW

and hit the Enter key. This tells the machine that you are entering a new program. Once this has been registered in memory, you will again receive the BASIC prompt. We will write an extremely simple program as an example. This will be written in the indirect mode, which requires each line to be numbered and is the standard mode for new program insertion. Our lines could be numbered from 1 to 10, assuming that the program will require a total of 10 lines. However, standard practice calls for numbers to be entered in increments of 10 (such as 10,20,30,...), since this allows for the insertion of additional lines should they be necessary.

The following program prints information on the monitor screen which is a duplicate of what was typed on each program line. Figure 8-1 shows how the program is constructed.

Let's examine each line individually. Line 10 issues a print instruction which is followed by a sentence enclosed in quotation marks. This tells the computer to print, "THIS IS A SAMPLE PROGRAM" on the screen. Lines 20 and 30 also give print instructions but are not followed by a phrase. These instructions tell the computer to skip two lines after printing what is on line 10. Line 40 is really a repeat of the first line, except the phrase has been changed. Lines 50 and 60 are the same as 20 and 30. Finally, line 70 causes "THIS IS THE END OF THE SAMPLE PROGRAM" to show. Line 80 indicates to the computer that the program is finished.

It is now time to run our program. This is done by typing:

RUN

Figure 8-2 shows what this program does on the computer monitor. Our original phrase, "THIS IS A SAMPLE PROGRAM", appears at the top. Then the computer automatically inserts two blank lines before printing the second phrase. Two more lines are inserted before the monitor displays, "THIS IS THE END OF THE SAMPLE PROGRAM". Our program has been run properly.

We can make the program even simpler by deleting lines 20, 30, 50, and 60. This will effectively remove the spacing between the three phrase lines when the program is being run. The result is shown in Fig. 8-3.

Figure 8-4 shows a simple mathematical program which requires the operator to insert a value when asked to do so by the monitor screen. Line 10 instructs the computer to print, "THAT IS AN IQ TEST". Lines 20 and 30 add two line spaces to the printout on the monitor screen, while line 40 causes, "ANSWER THE QUESTION TO RATE YOUR IQ" to appear. After two more line spaces, line 70 causes "PRESS ENTER WHEN READY" to appear on the screen. Notice that this line does not contain a print instruction but an INPUT. Since the phrase line is in quotation marks, it will be printed just as if a print instruction has been used with it, but INPUT indicates to the machine that it needs a keyboard input from the operator. Following

```
10   PRINT"THIS IS A SAMPLE PROGRAM"
20   PRINT
30   PRINT
40   PRINT"THE COMPUTER MONITOR WILL PRINT WHAT IS ON EVERY PROGRAM LINE"
50   PRINT
60   PRINT
70   PRINT"THIS IS THE END OF THE SAMPLE PROGRAM"
80   END
```

Fig. 8-1. A very simple program.

107

```
THIS IS A SAMPLE PROGRAM


THE COMPUTER MONITOR WILL PRINT WHAT IS ON EVERY PROGRAM LINE


THIS IS THE END OF THE SAMPLE PROGRAM
```

Fig. 8-2. Running this simple program.

the phrase is a semicolon, which is always used at the end of a string, followed by a B$. These latter symbols allow the information to be input and the program restarted by depressing the ENTER key. When an INPUT is typed in this manner along with the phrase in quotation marks, the monitor screen will automatically flash a "?" to indicate that input is needed on that line.

Line 80 actually contains two instructions for the computer. The first one, CLS, causes the monitor screen to erase all previously displayed data and moves the cursor to the top left of the screen. Notice that CLS is immediately followed by a colon. A colon must be used to separate two instructions or commands when they are contained in the same line. Following the colon is the next instruction. This is the one which will require the input referenced above. It states PRINT"1+1= ": Notice that the equal sign is followed by a space and then a quotation mark. This allows room for the flashing question mark, which will indicate to the operator that an input is needed. Again, line 80 tells the computer to do two things. First of all, it clears the monitor screen (CLS). Then it

prints the arithmetic question. We could have used two lines to accomplish this. Line 80 would simply say CLS, while line 81 would give the print instruction. This, however, would require more memory space, as two bytes would be required to insert line 81, plus two more bytes for the spacing between the line numbers and the actual instruction.

Moving on to line 90, we see INPUT X. The letter X designates the keyboard input which the operator is supposed to have typed in as per instructions in line 80. It certainly is not necessary to use the letter X. Letters A, B, C, etc. would do just as well. It is necessary, however, to establish some designator for the correct input value.

Things get interesting on line 110. It tells the computer what to print when input X equals various amounts. Line 110 contains the IF-THEN statement. Whenever IF is used in a statement, it must be followed by a THEN or an ELSE or a GOTO. What line 110 is saying is if X equals 2, then the computer must print the indicated phrase. Put simply, we are saying if such and such happens, then do so and so. Notice that no colons are used because only

```
THIS IS A SAMPLE PROGRAM
THE COMPUTER MONITOR WILL PRINT WHAT IS ON EVERY PROGRAM LINE
THIS IS THE END OF THE SAMPLE PROGRAM
```

Fig. 8-3. The program can be made simpler by deleting some lines.

```
10   PRINT"THIS IS AN IQ TEST"
20   PRINT
30   PRINT
40   PRINT"ANSWER THE QUESTION TO RATE YOUR IQ"
50   PRINT
60   PRINT
70   INPUT "PRESS ENTER WHEN READY";B$
80   CLS:PRINT"1+1 =  ";
90   INPUT X
110  IF X=2 THEN PRINT "YOU ARE SO INTELLIGENT"
120  IF X<>2 THEN PRINT "BOY, ARE YOU DUMB"
130  END
```

Fig. 8-4. A simple IQ test program.

one statement is given on line 110. IF and THEN are used as a single statement in this program.

Line 120 takes into account the possibility of a wrong answer being input to the machine. This is another IF-THEN statement and uses symbols to express if X does not equal 2, then print the indicated phrase. The symbols used between X and 2 indicate mathematical occurrences. The symbol immediately to the right of the X means less than, while the next symbol means more than. When combined in this manner, the machine is actually receiving the instruction if X is less than or more than 2, then print "BOY, ARE YOU DUMB". The computer has two options contained in line 110 and 120. If the X input value is 2, then the program actually stops at 110. If, however, you input any other value, the processor automatically goes to program line 120 and prints the correct output. Figure 8-5 shows how this program will appear when run. In this example, the correct answer (2) was input by the keyboard operator. If any number other than 2 had been entered, the monitor would have displayed, "BOY, ARE YOU DUMB".

Figure 8-6 shows another program which requires keyboard input by the operator. This one is used to figure power consumption given the correct values of voltage and current. This program runs Ohm's Law formula of P=IE, where P is power, I is current and E is voltage.

Program lines 10 and 20 are REM statements. A REM statement is a remark which is inserted into the program. It tells what the program is designed to do but is not actually printed on the screen. The output instructions to the display monitor begin in line 30, where the computer is instructed to print the indicated phrase. Line 40 calls for an input of the current value (I) in amperes. Line 50 instructs the computer to accept the keyboard input and line 60 calls for an input of the value in volts. Line 70 causes the computer to accept this value. Line 80 then redisplays the two input values, allowing the operator to make certain the correct values have been inserted. Line 90 is a LET statement, which assigns a value to P. The LET statement is not necessary in IBM BASIC, but it will work and is shown here for discussion purposes. In IBM BASIC, line 90 may be simplified by inputting: P=E*I. Again, the LET statement may be used, but it is superfluous in IBM BASIC. This is identical to the Ohm's Law formula. The computer will then take the given input values, multiply them and output the answer to the monitor, according to the instructions in line 100. Line 110 provides operator instructions (on the screen) to continue the program. In Disk BASIC, the F2 key is the equivalent of typing RUN into the machine. When it is depressed, the program will repeat, and new values of I and E may be inserted. Figure 8-7 shows two examples of

```
THIS IS AN IQ TEST

ANSWER THE QUESTION TO RATE YOUR IQ

PRESS ENTER WHEN READY?

1+1 =  ? 2

1+1 =  ? 2
YOU ARE SO INTELLIGENT
Ok
```

Fig. 8-5. When run, the IQ program will look like this.

```
10    REM THIS PROGRAM CONVERTS GIVEN VOLTAGE AND CURRENT
20    REM INTO POWER
30    PRINT"POWER PROGRAM FOR FIGURING P, GIVEN I AND E"
40    PRINT"CURRENT(I) IN AMPERES = ";
50    INPUT I
60    PRINT"VOLTAGE(E) IN VOLTS = ";
70    INPUT E
80    PRINT"I =";I,"E=";E
90    LET P = E*I
100   PRINT"POWER IN WATTS IS EQUAL TO ":PRINT P
110   PRINT"DEPRESS F2 TO CONTINUE"
```

Fig. 8-6. A power consumption program based on Ohm's Law.

this program using different input values. Figure 8-8 shows another power formula which is really the previous program that has been simplified a bit with a new mathematical equation inserted. This program is to be used when figuring power consumption based upon knowing the values of current (I) and resistance (R). The Ohm's law formula for this is $P=I^2R$. Note in this program that line 20 inputs the values of I and R. Note also that I and R are separated by a comma. This means that the input values typed in via the keyboard must be separated by a comma. Line 30 establishes the value of P, which uses the Ohm's Law formula direct. The asterisk key indicates multiplication. The way the formula is expressed in line 30 encompasses the I*I in parentheses. This is a typical mathematical function, which means that the value of I times I is then multiplied by the value of R, as indicated by another asterisk. The parentheses must be included or the formula will not work. Line 40 allows the monitor to display "POWER IN WATTS = (value)". Line 50 causes the program to automatically

```
POWER PROGRAM FOR FIGURING P, GIVEN I AND E
CURRENT(I) IN AMPERES = ? 2
VOLTAGE(E) IN VOLTS = ? 4
I = 2          E= 4
POWER IN WATTS IS EQUAL TO
 8
DEPRESS F2 TO CONTINUE

POWER PROGRAM FOR FIGURING P, GIVEN I AND E
CURRENT(I) IN AMPERES = ? 2.8888
VOLTAGE(E) IN VOLTS = ? 1606.42
I = 2.8888    E= 1606.42
POWER IN WATTS IS EQUAL TO
 4640.626
DEPRESS F2 TO CONTINUE
```

Fig. 8-7. Two examples of the power consumption program using different values.

```
10   PRINT"POWER PROGRAM"

20   INPUT"ENTER I,R ";I,R

30   LET P = (I*I)*R

40   PRINT"POWER IN WATTS = ":PRINT P

50   GOTO 10
```

Fig. 8-8. Another power consumption formula program.

repeat for the insertion of new values. The instruction simply tells the computer to go to line 10, which is the start of the program. Figure 8-9 shows an example of the actual running of the program.

Figure 8-10 shows another mathematical program which converts temperatures in Celsius to their Fahrenheit equivalent. This program is not really that much more complicated than the previous one, although more lines (and thus, more memory space) are used. We have visually cleaned this program up by inserting line spaces between the various printouts. The purpose of the ten lines has already been discussed. The only difference in this program is the LET statement in line 110, which establishes a value for Fahrenheit (F). Notice that in line 80, the Centigrade temperature (C) has already been input, so the computer will automatically process this value in the formula displayed in line 110. Note that C was chosen for clarification purposes. We could have used any other letter of the alphabet as long as it was properly substituted for C in line 110 and 140. This latter line causes the computer monitor screen to print "C IS THE EQUIVALENT OF (FAHRENHEIT)". Line 170 allows the operator to restart the program by pressing Enter. When this is done, the CLS statement clears the screen, and the GOTO statement returns the program to line 20. Note that line 170 has three separate statements, all separated by parentheses. The first statement

is the INPUT, the second is CLS, and GOTO is the third. This saves memory space. Figure 8-11 shows how the program will look when run.

While we are primarily talking here about writing our own programs in IBM Personal Computer BASIC, I mentioned earlier that some programs are already contained on DOS. To break things up a bit, I'll present a few here.

The Music Program displays a keyboard similar to the one shown in Fig. 8-12. This is actually a negative image of what is seen on the monitor screen, with black and white being reversed on the sample keyboard. The operator can choose from one of eleven musical selections by depressing letters A through K. It is not necessary to depress Enter to run the program. Should you press B, Sousa's Stars and Stripes Forever will be played over the internal speaker, one note at a time. A music symbol darts around the keyboard, indicating which piano keys are pressed to perform the piece.

Figure 8-13 shows a printout of the data run by the DOS Mortgage Program. The program initially prompts the operator to input a mortgage loan value (50,000), and interest rate (14.5) and a payback time (30 years). The program then uses these values (50,000 and 14.5) in a comparison display with other mortgage loan amounts and interest rates. Note that the program uses the input value as the low figure and proceeds upward from there. We can see

```
POWER PROGRAM
ENTER I,R ? 5.65,32
POWER IN WATTS =
  1021.52
POWER PROGRAM
ENTER I,R ?
```

Fig. 8-9. Running the power formula program.

111

```
10    REM CELSIUS TO FAHRENHEIT CONVERSION PROGRAM
20    PRINT"THIS PROGRAM CONVERTS TEMPERATURES FROM CELSIUS TO FAHRENHEIT"
30    PRINT
40    PRINT
50    PRINT"INSERT CELSIUS TEMPERATURE, THEN PRESS ENTER"
60    PRINT
70    PRINT
80    INPUT C
90    PRINT
100   PRINT
110   LET F=1.8*C+32
120   PRINT
130   PRINT
140   PRINT C; "C IS THE EQUIVALENT OF ":PRINT F; "F"
150   PRINT
160   PRINT
170   INPUT "PRESS ENTER TO RE-START";B$:CLS:GOTO 20
```

Fig. 8-10. This program converts temperatures from Celsius to Fahrenheit.

that a 50,000, 30-year mortgage at 14.5 percent results in a monthly payment of $612.28. We can also see the monthly payments for values from $52,000 to $66,000 and for interest rates up to 18 percent.

Figure 8-14 shows another part of the mortgage program in DOS. This is an amortization program using the same mortgage amount, rate and time figures as with the previous example. Note that the monthly payments are $612.28. The next portion of the printout shows the principal, interest, and balance for the first twelve payments. Payments for the second year can be displayed by inputting 2 in the line which reads, "OF 12 MONTH PERIOD ======>". To do this, you must obey the machine's instructions and press the space bar to continue.

```
THIS PROGRAM CONVERTS TEMPERATURES FROM CELSIUS TO FAHRENHEIT


INSERT CELSIUS TEMPERATURE, THEN PRESS ENTER



? 54



 54 C IS THE EQUIVALENT OF
 129.2 F


PRESS ENTER TO RE-START?
```

Fig. 8-11. When run, the temperature conversion program will look like this.

```
–––––––– selections ––––––––
A–MARCH    E–HUMOR   I–SAKURA
B–STARS    F–BUG     J–BLUE
C–FORTY    G–POP     K–SCALES
D–HAT      H–DANDY   ESC KEY–EXIT

ENTER SELECTION ==>
```

Fig. 8-12. The music program will display a keyboard.

Now for some more programming. Figure 8-21 shows a fairly simple program which can be added to and expanded over and over again to form one with several hundred program lines, depending upon how many questions you want to ask. I call this my intelligence test. Line 10 causes the screen to display "HOW SMART ARE YOU? THIS TEST WILL TELL IT ALL!". After a few spaces are skipped, line 40 displays "ANSWER THE FOLLOWING QUESTION". Line 60 gives the operator time to prepare for the quiz and when Enter is depressed, the actual test begins. Note in line 70 that two statements are used on the same line. CLS causes the screen to clear, and the first question, "WHO IS THE PRESIDENT OF THE USA?" is displayed, along with three choices (stated on lines 100-120). This pro-

MONTHLY MORTGAGE PAYMENT COMPARISONS								
30–YEAR MORTGAGE LOAN AMOUNTS								
50000	52000	54000	56000	58000	60000	62000	64000	66000
RATES								
14.50	612.28	636.77	661.26	685.75	710.24	734.73	759.22	783.72	808.21
14.75	622.24	647.13	672.02	696.91	721.80	746.69	771.57	796.46	821.35
15.00	632.22	657.51	682.80	708.09	733.38	758.67	783.96	809.24	834.53
15.25	642.23	667.92	693.61	719.30	744.99	770.68	796.36	822.05	847.74
15.50	652.26	678.35	704.44	730.53	756.62	782.71	808.80	834.89	860.98
15.75	662.31	688.80	715.29	741.79	768.28	794.77	821.26	847.76	874.25
16.00	672.38	699.27	726.17	753.06	779.96	806.85	833.75	860.64	887.54
16.25	682.47	709.77	737.06	764.36	791.66	818.96	846.26	873.56	900.86
16.50	692.57	720.28	747.98	775.68	803.39	831.09	858.79	886.49	914.20
16.75	702.70	730.81	758.91	787.02	815.13	843.24	871.35	899.45	927.56
17.00	712.84	741.35	769.86	798.38	826.89	855.41	883.92	912.43	940.95
17.25	722.99	751.91	780.83	809.75	838.67	867.59	896.51	925.43	954.35
17.50	733.16	762.49	791.82	821.14	850.47	879.80	909.12	938.45	967.77
17.75	743.35	773.08	802.81	832.55	862.28	892.02	921.75	951.48	981.22
18.00	753.54	783.68	813.83	843.97	874.11	904.25	934.39	964.53	994.68

Fig. 8-13. A printout of the data produced by the DOS mortgage program.

```
    MORTGAGE AMORTIZATION PROGRAM

ENTER MORTGAGE AMOUNT ===> 50000
ENTER INTEREST RATE =====> 14.5
ENTER NUMBER OF YEARS ===> 30
MONTHLY PAYMENTS ARE ====> 612.28

OF 12 MONTH PERIOD =======> 1
PYMNT PRINCIPAL     INTEREST     BALANCE
  1        8.11       604.17    49991.89
  2        8.21       604.07    49983.68
  3        8.31       603.97    49975.37
  4        8.41       603.87    49966.96
  5        8.51       603.77    49958.45
  6        8.62       603.66    49949.83
  7        8.72       603.56    49941.11
  8        8.82       603.46    49932.29
  9        8.93       603.35    49923.36
 10        9.04       603.24    49914.32
 11        9.15       603.13    49905.17
 12        9.26       603.02    49895.91

INTEREST FOR 12 PERIODS =    7243.27

PRESS SPACE BAR TO CONTINUE
```

Fig. 8-14. The amortization portion of the mortgage program.

gram differs from a previous IQ test program discussed in this chapter (the one where the operator must give the correct answer to $1 + 1 = $). This former program printed one statement when the correct answer was input and another statement when any but the correct answer was input.

This new program provides separate responses to any of the three answers selected. These instructions are provided in lines 210 through 230. Note that line 180 inputs "A," which is the alphabetic designation given to the first set of answers. Because of this, A may equal 1, 2, or 3. As expressed in line 210 by an IF-THEN statement, should input A equal 1 (Jimmy Carter), then the computer will display "DUMMY, HE WAS A FORMER PRESIDENT". If input A equals answer 2 (line 110), then another statement is printed. If A equals 3 (the correct answer), the computer will print, "YOU ARE VERY SMART".

This program can be expanded upon by

inserting additional program lines, as shown in Fig. 8-15. Here, two more spaces are added between the previous line and the operator is instructed to "PRESS ENTER TO CONTINUE". The next line (261) clears the screen (CLS) and the second statement prints, 'WHO DISCOVERED AMERICA?" From this point on, the same programming is repeated as before with different answers provided for the new question. Figure 8-16 shows the printout of an expanded version which is nearly identical to the portion shown in Fig. 8-17. Other than the different questions and answer options, the only major difference is discovered in lines 340, 500 and 670. The input alphabetic designations change with each question. Note that question 1 used input A, question 2 used input B, etc. The IF-THEN statements which follow each input reflect the alphabetic designator used for that question, but you can see that the program is really repeating the same statements over and over again.

I wanted to end this program with a way of rating the operator's score. This portion begins on line 730 with the input statement, "PRESS ENTER TO RATE YOUR SCORE". When Enter is depressed, line 740 clears the monitor screen and asks, "HOW MANY ANSWERS DID YOU GET CORRECT?" Type in the number of questions answered correctly. This becomes input E in line 770. More IF-THEN statements follow and print appropriate comments based upon the number of correct answers. While this latter portion of the program is slightly different from previous portions, it still follows the overall format

```
240 PRINT
250 PRINT
260 INPUT"PRESS ENTER TO CONTINUE" ;B$
261 CLS:PRINT"WHO DISCOVERED AMERICA"
```

Fig. 8-15. The intelligence test can be expanded by inserting additional program lines.

```
10      PRINT"HOW SMART ARE YOU? THIS TEST WILL TELL IT ALL!"
20      PRINT
30      PRINT
40      PRINT"ANSWER THE FOLLOWING QUESTIONS"
50      PRINT
60      INPUT"PRESS ENTER WHEN READY TO BEGIN";B$
70      CLS:PRINT"WHO IS THE PRESIDENT OF THE USA?"
80      PRINT
100     PRINT"1.JIMMY CARTER"
110     PRINT"2.LAWRENCE QUARK"
120     PRINT"3.RONALD REAGAN"
130     PRINT
140     PRINT
150     PRINT"SELECT 1,2, OR 3 AND PRESS ENTER"
160     PRINT
170     PRINT
180     INPUT A
190     PRINT
200     PRINT
210     IF A=1 THEN PRINT"***DUMMY, HE WAS A FORMER PRESIDENT***"
220     IF A=2 THEN PRINT"***LARD HEAD, HE'S AN OBSTETRICIAN***"
230     IF A=3 THEN PRINT"***YOU ARE VERY SMART***"
240     PRINT
250     PRINT
260     INPUT"PRESS ENTER TO CONTINUE" ;B$
261     CLS:PRINT"WHO DISCOVERED AMERICA"
262     PRINT
270     PRINT
280     PRINT"1.CHRISTOPHER COLUMBUS"
290     PRINT"2.FELIX THE CAT"
300     PRINT"3.JOAN OF ARC"
310     PRINT"MAKE YOUR SELECTION AS BEFORE--BE SURE TO PRESS ENTER"
320     PRINT
330     PRINT
340     INPUT B
350     IF B=1 THEN PRINT"***YOU MUST BE A GENIUS***"
360     IF B=2 THEN PRINT"***YOU'VE GOT TO BE KIDDING***"
370     IF B=3 THEN PRINT"***WRONG! THAT ANSWER BURNS ME UP"
380     PRINT
390     PRINT
400     INPUT"PRESS ENTER TO CONTINUE" ;B$
410     CLS:PRINT"WHY DO YOU HEAR THUNDER BEFORE SEEING THE LIGHNING FLASH?"
420     PRINT
430     PRINT
440     PRINT"1.BECAUSE YOU DIDN'T LOOK QUICKLY ENOUGH"
450     PRINT"2.BECAUSE LIGHT TRAVELS FASTER THAN SOUND"
460     PRINT"3. ARE YOU KIDDING? YOU SEE THE FLASH THEN HEAR THE THUNDER"
470     PRINT"MAKE YOUR SELECTION--PRESS ENTER"
480     PRINT
490     PRINT
500     INPUT C
510     IF C=1 THEN PRINT"***THAT'S A WRONG ANSWER, THUNDERHEAD***"
520     IF C=2 THEN PRINT"***THE STATEMENT IS CORRECT--YOUR ANSWER IS WRONG"
530     IF C=3 THEN PRINT"***GEE, THAT'S RIGHT! DID YOU EVER THINK OF BECOMING A
        COMPUTER***"
540     PRINT
550     PRINT
560     INPUT"IF YOU DARE TO CONTINUE, PRESS ENTER AGAIN";B$
570     CLS:PRINT"WHAT IS 5 TIMES 6?"
```

Fig. 8-16. Printout of the expanded version of the intelligence test.

```
580    PRINT
590    PRINT
600    PRINT"1.30"
610    PRINT"2.56"
620    PRINT"3.88"
630    PRINT
640    PRINT"SELECT ONLY ONE ANSWER, THEN PRESS ENTER"
650    PRINT
660    PRINT
670    INPUT D
680    IF D=1 THEN PRINT"***THAT IS A CORRECT ANSWER***"
690    IF D=2 THEN PRINT"***WRONG! GO BACK TO SCHOOL***"
700    IF D=3 THEN PRINT"***WRONG! WAS THE QUESTION TOO HARD FOR YOU?***"
710    PRINT
720    PRINT
730    INPUT"PRESS ENTER TO RATE YOUR SCORE";B$
740    CLS:PRINT"HOW MANY ANSWERS DID YOU GET CORRECT?"
750    PRINT
760    PRINT"TYPE IN THE NUMBER, THEN PRESS ENTER";B$
770    INPUT E
780    IF E=4 THEN PRINT"YOU ARE TRULY GENIUS MATERIAL--PERFECT SCORE!!!"
790    IF E=3 THEN PRINT"NOT BAD! THE NEXT TIME YOU'LL GET IT PERFECT"
800    IF E=2 THEN PRINT"YOU SHOULD HAVE TRIED HARDER"
810    IF E=1 THEN PRINT"OH WELL, MAYBE YOU WERE ASLEEP"
820    IF E=0 THEN PRINT"YOU'RE IN A HEAP OF TROUBLE"
830    END
```

Fig. 8-16. Continued from page 115.

```
10     PRINT"HOW SMART ARE YOU? THIS TEST WILL TELL IT ALL!"
20     PRINT
30     PRINT
40     PRINT"ANSWER THE FOLLOWING QUESTIONS"
50     PRINT
60     INPUT"PRESS ENTER WHEN READY TO BEGIN";B$
70     CLS:PRINT"WHO IS THE PRESIDENT OF THE USA?"
80     PRINT
100    PRINT"1.JIMMY CARTER"
110    PRINT"2.LAWRENCE QUARK"
120    PRINT"3.RONALD REAGAN"
130    PRINT
140    PRINT
150    PRINT"SELECT 1,2, OR 3 AND PRESS ENTER"
160    PRINT
170    PRINT
180    INPUT A
190    PRINT
200    PRINT
210    IF A=1 THEN PRINT"***DUMMY, HE WAS A FORMER PRESIDENT***"
220    IF A=2 THEN PRINT"***LARD HEAD, HE'S AN OBSTETRICIAN***"
230    IF A=3 THEN PRINT"***YOU ARE VERY SMART***"
```

Fig. 8-17. A simple intelligence test program.

quite closely. This program is basically made up of print statements, input statements and IF-THEN statements. While I ended my program after four questions, you could easily expand it to 400, although a great deal of typing time would be required to enter lines 10 through 5000 or so.

While this program was written with fun in mind, most readers will probably be able to realize the educational benefits which such a program might offer. History questions, math problems, even computer logic problems may all be inserted into this simple program and run with education in mind. With the excellent editing functions of the IBM Personal Computer and the DOS program, an original program could be updated with new questions and answers in a fairly short period of time while still leaving in the IF-THEN responses. You would want to make certain, however, that any new answer options were inserted so that the correct answer falls under the same number (1, 2, 3) as the previous correct answer did. Subprograms could be written into this one which would provide tutoring information in regard to a specific question and maybe even ask a similar backup question. A GOTO command at the end of the subprograms could bring the program back to where it was exited.

Biorhythm programs have excellent application to the IBM Personal Computer. While writing this book I did not have one on hand written specifically for the IBM Personal Computer, so I garnered one from *55 Advanced Computer Programs in BASIC*, by Wm. Scott Watson, (PUBLISHED BY TAB Books Inc.). I was also testing the IBM Personal Computer BASIC language to see if it was directly compatible with TRS-80 Level II BASIC. Mr. Watson's programs were run on the Radio Shack machine. I found all programs written in Level II BASIC that I tested on the IBM Personal Computer to be wholly compatible. To check

on this, I contacted IBM and posed the question to a technician. The answer I got was, "One could assume that the two languages would be compatible in most instances." As of this writing, I have found little problems in writing Level II BASIC programs directly into the IBM Personal Computer, as long as the programs are to be run in text mode. However, this does not mean that a TRS-80 program can be directly input. A fair amount of modification will often be necessary, and in graphics mode, complete revamping is often required.

The biorhythm program is shown in Fig. 8-18. I did make a few minor changes to suit me, but the program printed in Mr. Watson's book should work just as well. This is the most complex program presented thus far, and whether or not you believe in biorhythms, I am sure you will find the results to be very interesting and certainly pleasing.

When the program is initially run, it asks for three keyboard inputs. These include the current date, the birthdate and the number of days to be displayed on the graph. An equivalent of the monitor display and the input answers is shown in Fig. 8-19. Enter must be depressed with each keyboard insertion. Upon the last insertion, the monitor screen displays what is shown in Fig. 8-20. This gives you the option of plotting your physical cycle only, the cognitive cycle only, the sensitivity cycle only or all cycles. In most practical applications, the user will select A and then press Enter. Figure 8-21 provides an example of the monitor display at this point, which explains the meaning of the characters which will appear on the graph about to be plotted. Note that P is the physical cycle, S indicates sensitivity, while C is the cognitive or mental cycle. Upon pressing Enter, another display is output to the monitor, telling the person's birthdate, the day on which they were born, the number of days they have been alive and their age to two decimal places.

```
10    CLS:CLEAR 64:DIM A(150)
20    PRINT CHR$(23):PRINT TAB(12) "BIORYTHM":PRINT STRING$(32,"+"):PRINT
30    FOR I=1 TO 12:READ A(I):NEXT I
40    FOR I=101 TO 112:READ A(I):NEXT I
50    DATA 0,31,59,90,120,151,181,212,243,273,304,334
60    DATA 31,28,31,30,31,30,31,31,30,31,30,31
70    A(55)=6.28318
80    GOTO 150
90    X=(V/X-INT(V/X))*A(55)
100   Y=SIN(X)
110   X=X*57.295755#
120   Y=(Y*18)+44
130   Y=INT(Y)
140   RETURN
150   INPUT "ENTER TODAY'S DATE EXAMPLE: 6,2,1980 ";M,D,Y
160   A=M:B=D:C=Y
170   GOSUB 260
180   Z=T
190   INPUT "ENTER BIRTHDATE EXAMPLE: 9,9,1959 ";M,D,Y
200   E=M:F=D:G=Y
210   GOSUB 260
220   V=T-Z
230   V=ABS(V)
240   REM
250   GOTO 440
260   H=Y-1800
270   I=INT(H/4)
280   J=INT(I/25)
290   L=INT((H+200)/400)
300   K=0
310   IF I*4<>H GOTO 350
320   IF J*100<>H GOTO 350
330   IF L*400-200<>H GOTO 350
340   K=1
350   T=365*H+1-J+L-K
360   T=T+A(M)+D-1
370   IF M<3 GOTO 390
380   T=T+K
390   IF INT(H/4)<>H/4 GOTO 420
400   IF M>2 GOTO 420
410   T=T-1
420   N=T-7*INT(T/7)
430   RETURN
440   PRINT:PRINT
450   INPUT "HOW MANY DAYS ON GRAPH ";O
460   CLS
470   GOTO 1460
480   PRINT "THE POTENTIAL FOR ACCIDENTS TO OCCUR IS GREATEST WHEN"
490   PRINT "ONE OR MORE OF YOUR CYCLES CROSSES THE CENTER LINE."
500   PRINT "GRAPH SYMBOLS:"
510   PRINT "X  --CENTER LINE"
520   PRINT "P  --PHYSICAL CYCLE (23-DAY)"
```

Fig. 8-18. One of many biorhythm programs available on the market.

```
530     PRINT "S  --SENSITIVITY CYCLE (28-DAY)"
540     PRINT "C  --COGNITIVE CYCLE (33-DAY)"
550     PRINT
560     INPUT "PRESS ENTER TO CONTINUE";B$:CLS
570     PRINT "YOUR BIRTHDAY IS ";:P=E:GOSUB 1070:PRINT F;G
580     PRINT "YOU WERE BORN ON A ";:Q=N+1:GOSUB 1190
590     PRINT ", ";V;" DAYS (";INT((V/365)*100)/100;"YEARS) AGO!"
600     PRINT
610     PRINT "HERE ARE YOUR BIORYTHM CYCLES"
620     PRINT "STARTING AT ";:P=A:GOSUB 1070:PRINT B;C
630     PRINT "AND ENDING AT ";
640     S=A:R=B+O-1:T=C
650     IF S<12 GOTO 670
660     S=1:T=T+1:GOTO 700
670     IF S<>2 GOTO 700
680     IF INT(T/4)<>T/4 THEN 700
690     K=1
700     IF R<=A(S+100)+K GOTO 730
710     R=R-(A(S+100)+K):IF S<>1 THEN S=S+1:K=0
720     GOTO 650
730     P=S:GOSUB 1070:PRINT R;T
740     INPUT "PRESS ENTER TO CONTINUE";B$:CLS
750     PRINT TAB(7);"DATE";TAB(25)"(-)";TAB(43)"(X)";TAB(61)"(+)"
760     PRINT
770     U=V+N:U=U-7*INT(U/7):B=B-1:U=U-1:V=V-1:K=0
780     FOR I=1 TO O:V=V+1:B=B+1:U=U+1: IF A<>2 THEN 810
790     IF INT(C/4)<>C/4 THEN 810
800     K=1
810     IF B<=A(A+100)+K THEN 830
820     A=A+1:B=1
830     IF U<7 THEN 850
840     U=0
850     IF A<=12 THEN 870
860     A=1:C=C+1
870     IF (A<>E)+(B<>F) THEN 890
880     PRINT TAB(33);"** HAPPY ";ABS(C-G);" BIRTHDAY **"
890     W=U+1:GOSUB 1380
900     PRINT "    ";:A(25)=A:GOSUB 1260:PRINT B;C;
910     IF L$="P" OR L$="A" GOTO 920 ELSE GOTO 930
920     X=23:GOSUB 90:A(30)=Y
930     IF L$="S" OR L$="A" GOTO 940 ELSE GOTO 950
940     X=28:GOSUB 90:A(35)=Y
950     IF L$="C" OR L$="A" GOTO 960 ELSE GOTO 970
960     X=33:GOSUB 90:A(40)=Y
970     M=0:FOR L=19 TO 66:PRINT TAB(L);
980     IF A(30)=L THEN PRINT "P";:GOTO 1030
990     IF A(35)=L THEN PRINT "S";:GOTO 1030
1000    IF A(40)=L THEN PRINT "C";:GOTO 1030
1010    IF 44=L THEN PRINT "X";
1020    IF 66=L THEN PRINT
1030    M=M+1:IF M<>4 THEN 1040:L=100
1040    NEXT L
```

```
1050    NEXT I
1060    END
1070    IF P=1 THEN PRINT "JANUARY";:RETURN
1080    IF P=2 THEN PRINT "FEBRUARY";:RETURN
1090    IF P=3 THEN PRINT "MARCH";:RETURN
1100    IF P=4 THEN PRINT "APRIL";:RETURN
1110    IF P=5 THEN PRINT "MAY";:RETURN
1120    IF P=6 THEN PRINT "JUNE";:RETURN
1130    IF P=7 THEN PRINT "JULY";: RETURN
1140    IF P=8 THEN PRINT "AUGUST";:RETURN
1150    IF P=9 THEN PRINT "SEPTEMBER";:RETURN
1160    IF P=10 THEN PRINT "OCTOBER";:RETURN
1170    IF P=11 THEN PRINT "NOVEMBER";:RETURN
1180    PRINT "DECEMBER";:RETURN
1190    IF Q=1 THEN PRINT "FRIDAY";:RETURN
1200    IF Q=2 THEN PRINT "SATURDAY";:RETURN
1210    IF Q=3 THEN PRINT "SUNDAY";:RETURN
1220    IF Q=4 THEN PRINT "MONDAY";:RETURN
1230    IF Q=5 THEN PRINT "TUESDAY";:RETURN
1240    IF Q=6 THEN PRINT "WEDNESDAY";:RETURN
1250    PRINT "THURSDAY";:RETURN
1260    IF A(25)=1 THEN PRINT "JAN";:RETURN
1270    IF A(25)=2 THEN PRINT "FEB";:RETURN
1280    IF A(25)=3 THEN PRINT "MAR";:RETURN
1290    IF A(25)=4 THEN PRINT "APR";:RETURN
1300    IF A(25)=5 THEN PRINT "MAY";:RETURN
1310    IF A(25)=6 THEN PRINT "JUN";:RETURN
1320    IF A(25)=7 THEN PRINT "JUL";:RETURN
1330    IF A(25)=8 THEN PRINT "AUG";:RETURN
1340    IF A(25)=9 THEN PRINT "SEP";:RETURN
1350    IF A(25)=10 THEN PRINT "OCT";:RETURN
1360    IF A(25)=11 THEN PRINT "NOV";:RETURN
1370    PRINT "DEC";:RETURN
1380    IF W=1 THEN PRINT "FRI";:RETURN
1390    IF W=2 THEN PRINT "SAT";:RETURN
1400    IF W=3 THEN PRINT "SUN";:RETURN
1410    IF W=4 THEN PRINT "MON";:RETURN
1420    IF W=5 THEN PRINT "TUE";:RETURN
1430    IF W=6 THEN PRINT "WED";:RETURN
1440    PRINT "THU";:RETURN
1450    END
1460    PRINT "ENTER YOUR GRAPH CHOICE:"
1470    PRINT "P ----- PLOT PHYSICAL CYCLE ONLY"
1480    PRINT "C ----- PLOT COGNITIVE CYCLE ONLY"
1490    PRINT "S ----- PLOT SENSITIVITY CYCLE ONLY"
1500    PRINT "A ----- PLOT ALL CYCLES"
1510    PRINT
1520    INPUT "ENTER YOUR CHOICE (P, C, S, OR A) ";L$
1530    IF L$<>"P" AND L$<>"S" AND L$<>"C" AND L$<>"A" GOTO 1520
1540    CLS:GOTO 480
```

Fig. 8-18. Continued.

```
                    BIORHYTHM
+++++++++++++++++++++++++++++++++++++++++++++

ENTER TODAY'S DATE EXAMPLE: 6,2,1980 ? 2,14,1983
ENTER BIRTHDATE EXAMPLE: 9,9,1959 ? 8,16,1948


HOW MANY DAYS ON GRAPH ? 10
```

Fig. 8-19. When the program is run, it requests three inputs, as shown here.

Additionally, the biorhythm which is about to be displayed will begin on a certain date and end on another, so this information is provided here, although it will also be referenced on the graph itself. This display is shown in Fig. 8-22.

At this point, the program tells the computer to display the biorhythm for the period of 2-14-83 to 2-23-83. Depressing Enter causes the display to be printed on the monitor. The result is shown in Fig. 8-23. The birthdate used for this example is my own, and if you believe in biorhythms (I don't), you will most likely be very concerned about me for this period of time. According to the chart, all of my cycles (with the exception of 2-14 and 2-23) fall into the negative side of the graph. According to biorhythm experts (?), this means my physical state, mental condition and sensitivity are all in bad shape. My sensitivity is coming back up, however, and you can even notice that my cognitive and physical cycles are beginning to swing back toward the positive.

In order to find out where my destiny goes from here, the program is rerun using the same basic information, but when it asks for the number of days on the graph, I would insert 10 to see what the next ten days (after 2-23-83) will bring. The resulting printout for the following ten days is shown in Fig. 8-24. Eureka! It would appear that my biorhythm cycle is back in the positive again after 2-28.

IBM advertises the Personal Computer as being an all-around device which may be used for everything from children's video games (with the optional Color/Graphics Adapter, a color monitor or color television/video modulator) to business applications. In thinking about the latter, I contacted my friend and fellow author, Howard Parmington, at Microlearn Computer Products in Winchester, Virginia. He has developed a program called "THE FIDO SCALE - FACTORS INFLUENCING DOG ORIENTATION". The scale is loosely based on behavioral principles and focuses on those factors influencing a dog's orientation to its home, master and surroundings.

The Fido Scale consists of three areas which are rated by the dog owner: (1) Thinking about dogs; (2) Dog behavior; and (3) Owner/ dog compatibility. Howard points out that while the Fido Scale can give insight into a dog's behavior, it is solely intended for the amusement of dog owners. It is not intended for nor is it useful in the identification of

```
ENTER YOUR GRAPH CHOICE:
P ----- PLOT PHYSICAL CYCLE ONLY
C ----- PLOT COGNITIVE CYCLE ONLY
S ----- PLOT SENSITIVITY CYCLE ONLY
A ----- PLOT ALL CYCLES
ENTER YOUR CHOICE (P, C, S, OR A) ?
```

Fig. 8-20. The program then asks which cycles you wish to see plotted.

121

```
THE POTENTIAL FOR ACCIDENTS TO OCCUR IS GREATEST WHEN
ONE OR MORE OF YOUR CYCLES CROSSES THE CENTER LINE.
GRAPH SYMBOLS:
X    --CENTER LINE
P    ---PHYSICAL CYCLE (23-DAY)
S    --SENSITIVITY CYCLE (28-DAY)
C    --COGNITIVE CYCLE (33-DAY)


PRESS ENTER TO CONTINUE?
```

Fig. 8-21. At this point, the program will explain the meaning of the different cycles.

psychological stresses that the dog or the dog owner may encounter.

The program is not presented here because it is tremendously long and copyrighted by Microlearn Computer Products, which sells the rating service. I just wanted to see if the program could be applied to the IBM Personal Computer. It took a bit of debugging, because it was originlly written in another version of BASIC, but after a few hours, Howard and I worked out all of the problems and indeed, it ran beautifully on my machine with 128K memory.

To input information using the Fido Scale, it is necessary for the dog owner to fill out four questionnaires, portions of whch are shown in Fig. 8-25 through 8-28. Once the questionnaires are completed, there is a fairly lengthy process involved in inputting it to the computer. The resulting printout is extremely lengthy, involving nearly fifty printer forms.

Figure 8-29 shows one of these sheets which rates the need for support, tells the owner how he/she scored and even makes comments about the score in this area alone. Finally, a summary is provided to tell the dog owners just how well their dogs are matched with them as far as compatibility is concerned. This is shown in Fig. 8-30. The Fido Scale is an idea that was dreamed up some years ago, and since the program is unique, it has been quite carefully guarded for the sole use of its author and chief marketing agent.

Still with the idea of a home computer business in mind, we tried another idea from *Making Money With Your Microcomputer* (TAB Book No. 1506). This book contains mostly ideas about the types of businesses a computer owner might wish to get into and does not really delve into programs or programming. Some home computer operators have been successful in marketing word definition guide

```
YOUR BIRTHDAY IS AUGUST 16 1948
YOU WERE BORN ON A TUESDAY, 12592  DAYS ( 34.49 YEARS) AGO!

HERE ARE YOUR BIORYTHM CYCLES
STARTING AT FEBRUARY 14  1983
AND ENDING AT FEBRUARY 23  1983
PRESS ENTER TO CONTINUE?
```

Fig. 8-22. The program then provides further information on the biorhythm to be displayed.

```
        DATE                (-)                     (X)              (+)

MON    FEB 14  1983
                            S              C              X P
TUE    FEB 15  1983
                            S        C            P    X
WED    FEB 16  1983
                            S    C        P        X
THU    FEB 17  1983
                             SC     P              X
FRI    FEB 18  1983
                            C  P               X
SAT    FEB 19  1983
                            CF       S         X
SUN    FEB 20  1983
                            P            S       X
MON    FEB 21  1983
                            P              S   X
TUE    FEB.22  1983
                             CF              S
WED    FEB 23  1983
                              CF            X   S
Ok
```

Fig. 8-23. A sample biorhythm chart.

```
        DATE             (-)                  (X)                (+)

THU    FEB 24  1983
                         C  P            X           S
FRI    FEB 25  1983
                           C    P    X              S
SAT    FEB 26  1983
                               C      P              S
SUN    FEB 27  1983
                               C   X    P              S
MON    FEB 28  1983
                               C              P       S
TUE    MAR 1   1983            X  C              P    S
WED    MAR 2   1983            X       C           P S
THU    MAR 3   1983            X          C        SP
FRI    MAR 4   1983            X            C S   P
SAT    MAR 5   1983            X             S  C P
Ok
```

Fig. 8-24. Entering different dates produces a chart for the next ten days.

```
                    THE  FIDO  SCALE  -
    FACTORS  INFLUENCING  DOG  ORIENTATION


/-----------------------------------------------------------------------------------/
/ DOG'S NAME                                    / AGE AND SEX                        /
/-----------------------------------------------------------------------------------/
/ HEALTH                    / WEIGHT            / YEARS UNDER YOUR OWNERSHIP         /
/-----------------------------------------------------------------------------------/
/ BREED                                         / PEDIGREED?                         /
/-----------------------------------------------------------------------------------/
/ % TIME SPENT INDOORS      / % TIME AWAY FROM HOME   / SIZE OF LITTER              /
/-----------------------------------------------------------------------------------/
```

Fig. 8-25. Portion of the Fido Scale questionnaire (courtesy Microlearn Computer Products).

sheets to bookstores. Each sheet contains the more difficult words from a particular book and serves as a minidictionary to be used while reading the book. Naturally, a different computer printout is used for each individual book title. This is quite a useful tool and has proven satisfactory for the home computer enthusiast to make a little spending money, but I wanted to tailor a program which would allow those persons owning home computers to use available storage to contain the minidictionary.

The program shown in Fig. 8-31 is the first thing I came up with. All of the difficult words from one book have been loaded into the IBM Personal Computer (via this program),

along with simplistic definitions of each. Figure 8-32 shows a word list, which is used to reference the proper input commands to key the definition. When you wish to know the definition of any of the 45 words, you type in the number and press Enter. The display shown in Fig. 8-33 is the result.

While this program includes definitions for only 45 words, there really is no limit (except in memory space) to the expansion of this program. It would then be fair to say that this program could be used to insert a massive dictionary of definitions, although its use would still require an equally massive and numbered word guide.

```
22.  MY DOG IS TRULY 'MAN'S BEST FRIEND'.                                SA       A      UN       D       SD
23.  ABOVE ALL, A DOG SHOULD PLEASE ITS OWNER.                           SA       A      UN       D       SD
24.  AN OWNER SHOULD LIE DOWN WITH HIS/HER DOG WHEN IT CANNOT SLEEP.      SA       A      UN       D       SD

25.  I THINK EVERYONE COULD BENEFIT FROM OWNING A DOG.                    SA       A      UN       D       SD
26.  DOGS SHOULD BE SEEN AND NOT HEARD.                                   SA       A      UN       D       SD
27.  DOGS SHOULD NOT BE SCOLDED FOR SHOWING THEIR AFFECTION TO STRANGERS. SA       A      UN       D       SD

28.  AN OWNER SHOULD DEFEND HIS/HER DOG AGAINST CRITICISM.                SA       A      UN       D       SD
29.  MY DOG IS MORE PLEASANT THAN MOST CHILDREN I KNOW.                   SA       A      UN       D       SD
30.  I AM SYMPATHETIC TO MY DOG'S FEELINGS.                              SA       A      UN       D       SD
```

Fig. 8-26. Sample questions from the Fido Scale (courtesy Microlearn Computer Products).

```
        PART II: DOG BEHAVIOR


                                    NUMBER 1. BEHAVIOR HAS NOT BEEN OBSERVED
                                    NUMBER 2. BEHAVIOR OCCURS A LITTLE
                                    NUMBER 3. BEHAVIOR OCCURS FAIRLY OFTEN
  PLEASE CIRCLE YOUR RESPONSE       NUMBER 4. BEHAVIOR OCCURS QUITE OFTEN
                                    NUMBER 5. BEHAVIOR OCCURS A GREAT DEAL



  1.  IS NOT WELL COORDINATED          1       2       3       4       5
  2.  SEEMS DEPRESSED                   1       2       3       4       5
  3.  IS TOO CONCERNED ABOUT HAVING OTHERS LIKE HIM/HER  1   2   3   4   5

  4.  SEEMS TO BE TENSE                   1       2       3       4       5
  5.  GETS MAD EASILY                     1       2       3       4       5
  6.  IS A MESSY EATER                    1       2       3       4       5
```

Fig. 8-27. Portion of the Fido Scale questionnaire relating to dog behavior (courtesy Microlearn Computer Products).

From a business standpoint, this program would be marketed only to home computer users who were reading the book or books whose words were included. It certainly doesn't have the potential of the original idea, which was to print out a hard copy list for sale to bookstores that would sell it to those persons buying certain books. However, from a programming standpoint, this minidictionary is quite interesting, if not highly practical.

```
     PART III:  OWNER-DOG COMPATABILITY

  PART IIIA: COMMON INTERESTS
  PLEASE CIRCLE THE APPROPRIATE LETTER


  I WOULD RATHER:                          MY DOG WOULD RATHER:


          *** A ***      *** B ***                 *** A ***       *** B ***

  A B  1.  TAKE A WALK    OR WATCH TELEVISION   A B  1.  LIE IN THE SUN   OR FROLIC IN THE SNOW
  A B  2.  GO TO A PARTY  OR STAY HOME          A B  2.  BE GROOMED      OR BE 'NATURAL'
  A B  3.  TELL SOMEONE OFF OR KEEP IT TO MYSELF A B  3.  PROTECT ME     OR RUN AND HIDE
  A B  4.  BE HUGGED      OR NOT TOUCHED        A B  4.  GO EXPLORING    OR STAY AT HOME
  A B  5.  BE INDOORS     OR BE OUTDOORS        A B  5.  WAG HIS TAIL    OR MOPE AROUND

  A B  6.  LAUGH          OR CRY                A B  6.  BE INDOORS      OR BE OUTDOORS
  A B  7.  DO SOMETHING NEW OR STAY WITH A ROUTINE A B 7. BE PETTED      OR NOT BE PETTED
  A B  8.  CONTRIBUTE TO CHARITY OR BUY NEW CLOTHES A B 8. GROWL AT A STRANGER OR IGNORE A STRANGER
  A B  9.  TAKE A BATH    OR GO WITHOUT SHAVING A B  9.  BE WITH OTHER DOGS OR BE BY HIM/HERSELF
  A B 10.  GO SWIMMING    OR HAVE A SNOWBALL FIGHT A B 10. CHASE A BALL   OR TAKE A NAP
```

Fig. 8-28. Another portion of the Fido Scale relating to owner/dog compatibility (courtesy Microlearn Computer Products).

```
┌─────────────────────────────────────────────────────────────────────┐
│               NEED  FOR  SUPPORT                                      │
│                                                                       │
│               ADJUSTED FACTOR SCORE = 60                              │
│ NEED FOR SUPPORT REFERS TO THE DEMONSTRATED DESIRE OF YOUR DOG TO DEPEND ON │
│ OTHERS IN VIRTUALLY ALL AREAS OF LIVING.  TYPICALLY, SUCH OVERDEPENDENCY RESULTS │
│ FROM OVERPROTECTION ON THE PART OF THE DOG OWNER.                      │
│                                                                       │
│ YOUR RATINGS FOR THIS FACTOR ARE AS FOLLOWS (1=LOW OCCURENCE;5=HIGH OCCURENCE): │
│                                                                       │
│           3    3.   IS TOO EAGER TO PLEASE                            │
│                                                                       │
│           3    9.   SEEKS CONSTANT PRAISE                             │
│                                                                       │
│           3   15.   WANTS OTHERS TO DO THINGS FOR HIM/HER             │
│                                                                       │
│           3   26.   DEPENDS ON OTHERS TO INITIATE ACTIVITY            │
│                                                                       │
│ AS COMPARED TO RATINGS FOR OTHER DOGS, THE SCORE FOR YOUR DOG ON THIS FACTOR IS │
│ AVERAGE AND SUGGESTS THAT YOUR DOG IS SOMEWHAT DEPENDANT ON YOU OR OTHER HUMANS │
│ FOR THE FULFILLMENT OF HIS/HER NEEDS, BUT THIS PROBABLY DOES NOT INTERFERE WITH │
│ YOUR DOG'S EXPRESSION OF INDIVIDUALITY.  IN FACT, YOUR DOG MAY APPEAR A BIT LAZY │
│ BUT IS QUITE CAPABLE OF TAKING CARE OF HIM/HERSELF IF NEED BE. THESE CHARACTER- │
│ ISTICS ARE PERHAPS REFLECTIVE OF A EASY GIVE-AND-TAKE MANAGEMENT STYLE ON THE │
│ PART OF THE DOG OWNER.                                                │
└─────────────────────────────────────────────────────────────────────┘
```

Fig. 8-29. After running the Fido Scale program, a length report is printed out, One page of which is shown here (courtesy Microlearn Computer Products).

```
┌─────────────────────────────────────────────────────────────────────┐
│            SUMMARY  OF  PARTS  A  &  B:                               │
│                                                                       │
│               OVERALL  COMPATABILITY                                  │
│                                                                       │
│                                                                       │
│ PART  A                                                               │
│                                                                       │
│ IN PART A, YOU AND YOUR DOG SHARED COMMON INTERESTS IN 0 OF 10 AREAS.  YOU │
│ MIGHT REVIEW PART A FOR THOSE SPECIFIC AREAS IN WHICH YOU AND YOUR DOG AGREED │
│ AND THOSE IN WHICH YOU DISAGREED.  ON A SCALE OF 1-100, THE COMPATABILITY SCORE │
│ FOR COMMON INTERESTS WAS 0.                                           │
│                                                                       │
│                                                                       │
│ PART  B                                                               │
│                                                                       │
│ IN PART B, YOU INDICATED THAT YOUR DOG BEHAVED CONSISTANT WITH YOUR EXPECTATIONS │
│ ON 0 OF 20 AREAS.  AGAIN, REVIEW PART B FOR SPECIFICS.  ON A SCALE OF 1-100, │
│ THE COMPATABILITY SCORE FOR THE CONGRUENCE BETWEEN EXPECTATIONS AND ACTUAL │
│ BEHAVIOR WAS 0.                                                       │
│                                                                       │
│                                                                       │
│ PARTS  A  &  B                                                        │
│                                                                       │
│ BY SUMMING THE COMPATABILITY SCORES FOR PARTS A & B, YOU MAY OBTAIN YOUR OVER- │
│ ALL COMPATABILITY SCORE.  ON A SCALE OF 1-100, THE OVERALL COMPATABILITY SCORE │
│ WAS 0.  SINCE NO ABSOLUTE CUT-OFF SCORE WOULD ACCURATELY DICHOTOMIZE   │
│ COMPATABILITY VS INCOMPATABILITY, SUFFICE IT TO SAY THAT THE HIGHER THIS SCORE, │
│ THE MORE LIKELY YOU AND YOUR DOG ARE TO ENJOY YOUR RELATIONSHIP.       │
└─────────────────────────────────────────────────────────────────────┘
```

Fig. 8-30. The summary page of the Fido Scale program rates both the dog and owner (courtesy Microlearn Computer Products).

```
10   PRINT"INSERT WORD NUMBER FROM LIST"
20   PRINT
30   PRINT
40   INPUT A
50   PRINT
60   PRINT
70   PRINT
80   PRINT"THE DEFINITION IS:"
90   PRINT
100  IF A=1 THEN PRINT"*****ABLE TO CONTAIN A GREAT DEAL*****"
110  IF A=2 THEN PRINT"*****ABOLISH; CANCEL*****"
120  IF A=3 THEN PRINT"*****ABSOLUTE RULER*****"
130  IF A=4 THEN PRINT"*****ABUNDANT; PLENTIFUL*****"
140  IF A=5 THEN PRINT"*****BEYOND WORDS; INEXPRESSIBLE*****"
150  IF A=6 THEN PRINT"*****BUXON; FULL BOSOMED*****"
160  IF A=7 THEN PRINT"*****CAPABLE OF PRODUCING DEEP RICH RESONANT SOUND*****"
170  IF A=8 THEN PRINT"*****CAREFUL OR CAUTIOUS*****"
180  IF A=9 THEN PRINT"*****TALKATIVE; GARRULOUS*****"
190  IF A=10 THEN PRINT"*****CHARACTERIZED BY DELUSIONS OF GRANDEUR*****"
200  IF A=11 THEN PRINT"*****COMIC; LUDICROUS*****"
210  IF A=12 THEN PRINT"*****COARSE; OFFENSIVE*****"
220  IF A=13 THEN PRINT"*****EXTRAVAGANTLY CHIVALROUS OR ROMANTIC*****"
230  IF A=14 THEN PRINT"*****GOOD; SATISFACTORY*****"
240  IF A=15 THEN PRINT"*****GOVERNMENT BY A FEW*****"
250  IF A=16 THEN PRINT"*****GOVERNMENT BY ONE SUPREME RULER*****"
260  IF A=17 THEN PRINT"*****GOVERNMENT BY WEALTHY*****"
270  IF A=18 THEN PRINT"*****HEINOUS; SCANDALOUS*****"
280  IF A=19 THEN PRINT"*****INCLINED TO CHANGE WITHOUT REASON;UNPREDICTABLE****
*"
290  IF A=20 THEN PRINT"*****LACK OF SPIRIT OR INTEREST*****"
300  IF A=21 THEN PRINT"*****LACKING CONFIDENCE IN ONE'S SELF*****"
310  IF A=22 THEN PRINT"*****LEADERSHIP OR DOMINANCE*****"
320  IF A=23 THEN PRINT"*****LETHARGIC; LACKING IN ENERGY*****"
330 IF A=24 THEN PRINT"*****MAKING BLISSFUL; JOYFUL*****"
340  IF A=25 THEN PRINT"*****MEANINGLESS FLATTERY OR SILLY TALK*****"
350  IF A=26 THEN PRINT"*****NO LONGER CAPABLE OF PRODUCING; EXHAUSTED*****"
360  IF A=27 THEN PRINT"*****NOT LIKING TO TALK; UNCOMMUNICATIVE*****"
370  IF A=28 THEN PRINT"*****OF ANTIQUES*****"
380  IF A=29 THEN PRINT"*****ORIGINATING IN THE INTELLECT; INTANGIBLE*****"
390  IF A=30 THEN PRINT"*****PURE; MOST PERFECT*****"
400  IF A=31 THEN PRINT"*****ROTATING; REVOLVING*****"
410  IF A=32 THEN PRINT"*****RUDDY; RED (AS RELATED TO SKIN)*****"
420  IF A=33 THEN PRINT"*****SELF-ASSURANCE; POISE*****"
430  IF A=34 THEN PRINT"*****SLOW TO UNDERSTAND OR PERCEIVE; INSENSITIVE*****"
440  IF A=35 THEN PRINT"*****SMALL GROUP OF PERSONS JOINED IN SECRET DESIGN OR S
CHEME*****"
450  IF A=36 THEN PRINT"*****SUDDEN ATTACK OF SYMPTOMS OF A DISEASE*****"
460  IF A=37 THEN PRINT"*****TALKING MUCH; PARTICULARLY ABOUT UNIMPORTANT THINGS
*****"
470  IF A=38 THEN PRINT"*****THREE DOTS (. . .) USED TO INDICATE THE OMISSION OF
 WORDS*****"
480  IF A=39 THEN PRINT"*****TO ENTICE*****"
490  IF A=40 THEN PRINT"*****TO THROW OF SCUM*****"
500  IF A=41 THEN PRINT"*****TREMBLING; FEARFUL; TIMID*****"
510  IF A=42 THEN PRINT"*****UNEXCITABLE; SHOWING NO EMOTION*****"
520  IF A=43 THEN PRINT"*****UNSPOKEN; IMPLIED*****"
530  IF A=44 THEN PRINT"*****VERY SAD; MOURNFUL*****"
540  IF A=45 THEN PRINT"*****WITHOUT SHAPE OR DEFINITE FORM*****"
550  PRINT
560  PRINT
570  PRINT
580  INPUT"PRESS ENTER TO CONTINUE";B$
590  CLS:GOTO 10
```

Fig. 8-31. A minidictionary program.

1.	CAPACIOUS
2.	ABROGATED
3.	DESPOT
4.	COPIOUS
5.	INEFFABLE
6.	SONSY
7.	SONOROUS
8.	CHARY
9.	VOLUBLE
10.	MEGALOMANIA
11.	HARLEQUIN
12.	RIBALD
13.	QUIXOTICISM
14.	COPASETIC
15.	OLIGARCHY
16.	AUTOCRACY
17.	PLUTOCRACY
18.	FLAGITIOUS
19.	CAPRICIOUS
20.	LANGUOR
21.	DIFFIDENT
22.	HEGEMONY
23.	LANGUID
24.	BEATIFIC
25.	FLUMMARY
26.	EFFETTE
27.	TACITURN
28.	ANTIQUARIAN
29.	NOETIC
30.	QUINTESSENTIAL
31.	VERTIGINOUS
32.	SATURNINE
33.	APLOMB
34.	OBTUSE
35.	CABAL
36.	PAROXISM
37.	GARRULOUS
38.	ELLIPSIS
39.	INVEIGLE
40.	DESPUMATE
41.	TREMULOUS
42.	STOLID
43.	TACIT
44.	LUGUBRIOUS
45.	AMORPHOUS

Fig. 8-32. This word list is used as input to receive the definitions.

```
INSERT WORD NUMBER FROM LIST


? 24



THE DEFINITION IS:

*****MAKING BLISSFUL; JOYFUL*****



PRESS ENTER TO CONTINUE?
```

Fig. 8-33. The computer will print out a definition after a word is input.

You've probably already noticed that all of the programs discussed thus far required numeric variables for keyboard input to the computer. We have used the standard input command, which requires numeric variables and will not allow whole words to access definitions (in the latter case).

We can make the minidictionary program far more useful to the computer operator by allowing the entire word to be input and then displaying the definition on the monitor screen. In this case, the words themselves, or more specifically, the individual letters (characters) which make up the words become the variables. The Personal Computer is quite easy to program in this latter mode, as shown in Fig. 8-34. This is a duplicate of the previous program, in that it provides the same definitions for the 45 words that with the previous program, had to be printed on a separate list, and is numbered sequentially. This new program allows you to input the 45 words directly. When a word is entered, the computer will search for the variable.

Looking at the program, line 10 is an input command which causes the monitor screen to display the phrase, "ENTER WORD:". This is followed by a comma and the A$. These latter

```
10   INPUT "ENTER WORD: ",A$
20   PRINT
30   PRINT
40   PRINT
50   IF A$="CAPACIOUS" THEN PRINT"ABLE TO CONTAIN A GREAT DEAL"
60   IF A$="ABROGATED" THEN PRINT"ABOLISH"
70   IF A$="DESPOT" THEN PRINT"ABSOLUTE RULER;TYRANT"
80   IF A$="COPIOUS" THEN PRINT"ABUNDANT; PLENTIFUL"
90   IF A$="INEFFABLE" THEN PRINT"BEYOND WORDS; INEXPRESSIBLE"
100  IF A$="SONSY" THEN PRINT"BUXOM; FULL BOSOMED"
110  IF A$="SONOROUS" THEN PRINT"CAPABLE OF PRODUCING DEEP, RICH RESONANT SOUND"
120  IF A$="CHARY" THEN PRINT"CAREFUL OR CAUTIOUS"
130  IF A$="VOLUBLE" THEN PRINT"TALKATIVE; GARRULOUS"
140  IF A$="MEGALOMANIA" THEN PRINT"CHARACTERIZED BY DELUSIONS OF GRANDUER"
150  IF A$="HARLEQUIN" THEN PRINT"COMIC; LUDICROUS"
160  IF A$="RIBALD" THEN PRINT"COARSE; OFFENSIVE"
170  IF A$="QUIXOTICISM" THEN PRINT"EXTRAVAGENTLY CHIVALROUS OR ROMANTIC"
180  IF A$="COPASETIC" THEN PRINT"GOOD; SATISFACTORY"
190  IF A$="OLIGARCHY" THEN PRINT"GOVERNMENT BY A FEW"
200  IF A$="AUTOCRACY" THEN PRINT"GOVERNMENT BY ONE SUPREME RULER"
210  IF A$="PLUTOCRACY" THEN PRINT"GOVERNMENT BY THE WEALTHY"
220  IF A$="FLAGITIOUS" THEN PRINT"HEINOUS; SCANDALOUS"
230  IF A$="CAPRICIOUS" THEN PRINT"INCLINED TO CHANGE WITHOUT REASON; UNPREDICTAB
LE"
240  IF A$="LANGUOR" THEN PRINT"LACK OF SPIRIT OR INTEREST"
250  IF A$="DIFFIDENT" THEN PRINT"LACKING CONFIDENCE IN ONE'S SELF"
260  IF A$="HEGEMONY" THEN PRINT"LEADERSHIP OR DOMINANCE"
270  IF A$="LANGUID" THEN PRINT"LETHARGIC; LACKING IN ENERGY"
280  IF A$="BEATIFIC" THEN PRINT"MAKING BLISSFUL; JOYFUL"
290  IF A$="FLUMMARY" THEN PRINT"MAENINGLESS FLATTERY OR SILLY TALK"
300  IF A$="EFFETTE" THEN PRINT"NO LONGER CAPABLE OF PRODUCING; STERILE"
310  IF A$="TACITURN" THEN PRINT"NOT LIKING TO TALK; UNCOMMUNICATIVE"
320  IF A$="ANTIQUARIAN" THEN PRINT"OF ANTIQUES"
330  IF A$="NOETIC" THEN PRINT"ORIGINATING IN THE INTELLECT; INTANGIBLE"
340  IF A$="QUINTESSENTIAL" THEN PRINT"PURE; MOST PERFECT"
350  IF A$="VERTIGINOUS" THEN PRINT"ROTATING; REVOLVING"
360  IF A$="SATURNINE" THEN PRINT"RUDDY; RED (AS RELATING TO THE SKIN)"
370  IF A$="APLOMB" THEN PRINT"SELF-ASSURANCE; POISE"
380  IF A$="OBTUSE" THEN PRINT"SLOW TO UNDERSTAND OR PERCEIVE; INSENSITIVE"
390  IF A$="CABAL" THEN PRINT"SMALL GROUP OF PERSONS JOINED IN SECRET DESIGN OR S
CHEME"
400  IF A$="PAROXISM" THEN PRINT"SUDDEN ATTACK OF SYMPTOMS OF A DISEASE"
410  IF A$="GARRULOUS" THEN PRINT"TALKING MUCH; PARTICULARLY ABOUT UNIMPORTANT TH
INGS"
420  IF A$="ELLIPSIS" THEN PRINT"(...) THREE DOTS USED TO INDICATE THE OMMISSION
OF WORDS"
430  IF A$="INVEIGLE" THEN PRINT"TO ENTICE"
440  IF A$="DESPUMATE" THEN PRINT"TO THROW OFF SCUM"
450  IF A$="TREMULOUS" THEN PRINT"TREMBLING; FEARFUL; TIMID"
460  IF A$="STOLID" THEN PRINT"UNEXCITABLE; SHOWING NO EMOTION"
470  IF A$="TACIT" THEN PRINT"UNSPOKEN; IMPLIED"
480  IF A$="LUGUBRIOUS" THEN PRINT"VERY SAD; MOURNFUL"
490  IF A$="AMORPHOUS" THEN PRINT"WITHOUT SHAPE OR DEFINITE FORM"
500  PRINT
510  PRINT
520  PRINT
530  INPUT"PRESS ENTER TO CONTINUE";B$
540  CLS:GOTO 10
```

Fig. 8-34. Here, the words can be input directly.

two characters serve as a string designator. Lines 20 through 40 simply cause the monitor screen to skip three lines. The remainder of the program is made up of 45 IF-THEN statements. Starting at line 50, the computer is told, "IF (the string variable) is equal to (word) THEN PRINT (definition)". The A$ symbol is used for all 45 words. In previous programs, this would be equivalent to, "IF A=1 THEN PRINT (definition)". Notice that the input words, as typed into lines 50-490, are surrounded by quotation marks. This ties the entire string together. The dollar sign following the A variable indicates to the machine that a character string will follow. This program is more efficient and useful than the previous minidictionary and contains less lines. On the Personal Computer, it's just as easy to program for direct word input as it is to program for a numeric designator. This latter program does away completely with the separate list, as all words and definitions are contained within memory. Figure 8-35 shows how this program appears on the monitor screen when the word "CAPACIOUS" has been input. I omitted the fancy asterisks which surrounded each definition in the previous program, but you could certainly include them in yours, along with a number of other features to make the display more pleasing to the eye.

```
ENTER WORD: CAPACIOUS



ABLE TO CONTAIN A GREAT DEAL



PRESS ENTER TO CONTINUE?
```

Fig. 8-35. Screen printout when the word capacious has been input.

This has been a brief overview of IBM BASIC, especially as it relates to Disk BASIC. If I were to list all of the capabilities of this language and machine combination, it would fill several large volumes. While IBM Disk BASIC and TRS-80 Level II BASIC are very similar, there are differences in the two, especially relating to graphics operations. For example, the Level II PRINT X,Y statement is an unknown in IBM BASIC, but can be directly replaced with LOCATE X,Y:PRINT "(word or phrase)". If you use Level II to aid you in writing your own programs into IBM BASIC, it will be necessary to make the needed changes. Again, this applies mostly to the graphics mode. I experienced very little difficulty in entering other programs in Level II BASIC.

Be assured that every program presented throughout these pages has actually been loaded into the IBM Personal Computer, debugged and tested for proper operation. The pages of program lines included here are reproductions (direct) from the computer printouts output by my machine. You should be able to load them directly into your Personal Computer and have them work as described here.

With fairly complex programs, it is quite easy to make more than one input error at the keyboard, so you will depend quite a bit on the editing and debugging capabilities of this machine and the DOS. The BASIC error messages which will be output to the monitor should a program error occur will aid you in the debugging procedure.

ERROR MESSAGES

Following is a list of error messages which may be output when operating under Disk BASIC. Each indicates a program error or a keyboard function error, and many will print the program line in which the error has taken place. They can save you hours of frustrating "trial and error" debugging, and you will find that they help shorten the time needed to load, debug and run your programs.

NEXT without FOR. This means that a variable in a NEXT statement doesn't correspond to any previously executed FOR statement variable. This error message is displayed when a NEXT statement is encountered *before* its corresponding FOR statement has been executed.

SYNTAX ERROR. This is the error message you will probably experience most often. This indicates that a line has been encountered somewhere in the program which contains an incorrect sequence of characters. This message will always be followed by the line number in which the error has occurred. Your first step will be to access the individual line by typing EDIT (line number) and then pressing Enter. What you will be looking for are such things as misspelled statements or commands, incorrect punctuation, unmatched quotation marks, parens, etc. A syntax error may not be as apparent as you would think. Go over each character displayed on the program line in which the error occurred. Sometimes, a semicolon will look like a colon, and vice versa. Since both are triggered by the same key (one in lowercase and one in uppercase), it is quite easy for this type of error to occur.

RETURN without GOSUB. This error message indicates that a RETURN statement has been encountered for which there is no previous GOSUB statement. RETURN must always follow GOSUB in order to return from a subroutine to a main program.

Out of Data. This simply means that you are asking the computer to read a program or program section for which there are no data statements. This occurs when a READ statement is executed somewhere within the program when there are no DATA statements with unread information remaining.

Illegal Function Call. This error message

may be generated for many reasons. It can mean that a parameter that is out of range is passed to a system function. It may also be displayed by the monitor due to a negative or extremely large subscript, an improper argument to a function or statement, or an attempt to list or edit a BASIC program which is protected.

Overflow. This error message indicates that a number is too large to be represented in BASIC's number format. This overflow will cause execution to stop.

Out of Memory. This often means that the program you're trying to input is just too large for available memory. In some cases, this can be overcome by using CLEAR at the beginning of your program to set aside more memory area.

Undefined line number. This occurs when you attempt to reference or call up a line in a BASIC program that doesn't exist. For example, if your program contains lines 10 through 1000 and you enter a LIST command for line 1010, the Undefined line number message will be displayed because line 1010 is nonexistent in the program. The same will occur should you enter the EDIT command followed by this nonexistent line number. This error message can be used to advantage in editing. For example, if you edit out a complete program line and wish to make certain it has been done, you would key in the line number. If your deletion had taken place, this message would appear on the screen. Most often, however, this error message simply means that you have made a keyboard error, either when writing the program or when trying to access a particular line number. (For example, typing in "list 1000" when you really mean "list 100".)

Subscript Out of Range. This message indicates that an array element is referenced with the wrong number of subscripts or that a subscript lies outside the dimensions of the array. This can be caused by putting a subscript on a variable that is not an array or by incorrectly coding a built-in function.

Duplicate Definition. Indicates that you have tried to define the size of the same array twice. This may happen in one of several ways, such as if two DIM statements are given for the same array, or if a DIM statement is given for an array after the default dimension of 10 has been established for that array. It may also happen if an OPTION BASE statement has been encountered after an array has been dimensioned, either by a DIM statement or by default.

Division by Zero. This message indicates that in an expression, you tried to divide by zero, or you tried to raise zero to a negative power. Machine infinity with the sign of the numerator is supplied as the result of the division, or positive machine infinity is supplied as the result of the exponentiation, and execution continues.

Illegal Direct. This means that a statement that is invalid in direct mode is entered as a direct mode command; i.e., DEF SEG.

Type mismatch. This message occurs when you give a string value where a numeric value was expected, or vice versa. It may also be caused by trying to SWAP single and double precision values, etc.

Out of String Space. BASIC will allocate string space dynamically until it runs out of memory. This message means that string variables have caused BASIC to exceed the amount of free memory remaining after doing housecleaning.

String too long. This message will appear when you try to create a string which is more than the maximum of 255 characters long.

String Formula Too Complex. This is caused when a string expression is too long or too complex. To correct this error, break the expression into smaller expressions.

Can't Continue. This message indicates that you tried to use CONT to continue a program that has halted due to an error, has been modified during a break in execution, or does not exist.

Undefined User Function. This error is caused when you attempt to call function before defining it.

No RESUME. This message means that the program branched to an active error trapping routine as a result of an error condition or an ERROR statement. The routine does not have a RESUME statement. (An END, STOP, or RETURN was found before a RESUME statement.)

RESUME Without Error. This is caused when a RESUME statement is encountered before an error trapping routine is entered.

Unprintable Error. This message indicates that an error message is not available for the error condition which presently exists. It is usually caused by an ERROR statement with an undefined error code.

Missing Operand. This means that an expression contains an operator, such as * or OR, with no operand following it.

Line Buffer Overflow. Indicates that you tried to enter a line that has too many characters.

Device Timeout. This message will appear if BASIC did not receive information from an input/output device within a predetermined amount of time. In Cassette BASIC, this would only occur while trying to read from the cassette or write to the printer.

Device Fault. This is caused by a hardware error indication returned by an interface adapter. In Cassette BASIC, this will only occur when a fault status is returned from the printer interface adapter.

FOR without NEXT. This will occur when a FOR is encountered without a matching NEXT. That is, a FOR was active when an

END, STOP, or RETURN was encountered.

Out of Paper. This message occurs when the printer is out of paper or when the printer is not turned on. You should insert paper (if necessary), verify that the printer is properly connected, and that the power is on. The program can then be continued.

WHILE without WEND. This indicates that a WHILE statement does not have a matching WEND. That is, a WHILE was still active when an END, STOP or RETURN statement was found.

WEND without WHILE. This message occurs when a WEND is encountered before a matching WHILE is executed.

FIELD Overflow. This means that a FIELD statement is attempting to allocate more bytes than were specified for the record length of a random file in the OPEN statement. It may also mean that the end of the FIELD buffer was encountered while doing sequential I/O (PRINT#, WRITE#, INPUT#, etc.) to a random file.

Internal Error. Indicates that an internal malfunction has occurred in BASIC, so report to the dealer where your computer was purchased the conditions under which message appeared.

Bad File Number. This message indicates that a statement references a file with a file number that is not OPEN or is out of range of possible file numbers which was specified at initialization. It may also mean that the device name in the file specification is too long or invalid, or the filename was too long or invalid.

File Not Found. This is caused by a LOAD, KILL, NAME, FILES, or OPEN which references a file that does not exist on the disk in the drive specified.

Bad File Mode. This message means that you tried to use PUT or GET with a sequential file or a closed file to MERGE a non-ASCII file or to execute an OPEN with a file mode other than input, output, append, or random.

File Already Open. You tried to OPEN a file for sequential output or append when the file is already OPEN.

Device I/O Error. An error occurred on a device I/O operation. DOS cannot recover from the error.

File Already Exists. When this message is indicated, it means that the filename specified in a NAME statement is identical to a filename already in use on the disk.

Disk Full. This message means that all disk storage space is in use.

Input Past End. This is an end-of-file error. An input statement was executed for a null (empty) file, or after all the data in a sequential file was already input. To avoid this error, use the EOF function to detect the end of a file. This error also occurs if you try to read from a file that was opened for output or append.

Bad Record Number. This message indicates that in a PUT or GET statement, the record number is either greater than the maximum allowed (32767) or equal to zero.

Bad File Name. This is an indication that an invalid form is used for the filename with BLOAD, BSAVE, KILL, OPEN, NAME, or FILES (e.g., a filename starting with a period).

Direct Statement in File. This message indicates that a direct statement was encountered while LOADing or CHAINing to an ASCII format file. The LOAD or CHAIN is terminated. The ASCII file should consist only of statements preceded by line numbers. This may occur because of a line feed character in the input stream.

Too Many Files. This is caused when an attempt is made to create a new file (using SAVE or OPEN) when all directory entries on the disk are full, or the file specification is invalid.

Device Unavailable. This message will

occur when you try to OPEN a file to a device which doesn't exist. Either you do not have the hardware to support the device (such as printer adapters for a second or third printer), or you have disabled the device. For example, you may have used /C:0 on the BASIC command to start Disk BASIC. That would disable communications devices.

Communication Buffer Overflow. This is caused when a communication input statement is executed but the input buffer is already full. You should use an ON ERROR statement to retry the input when this condition occurs. Subsequent inputs will attempt to clear this fault unless characters continue to be received faster than the program can process them. If this is the case, there are a number of things you might do. First, you could increase the size of the communications buffer using the /C: option when you start BASIC. Secondly, you could implement a "hand-shaking" protocol with the other computer to tell it to stop sending long enough so you can catch up. Or you may use a lower data rate to transmit and receive.

Disk Write Protect. This message will occur when you try to write to a disk that is write-protected.

Disk not Ready. The disk drive door is open or a disk is not in the drive. Place the correct disk in the drive and continue the program.

Disk Media Error. This error occurs when the controller attachment card has detected a hardware or media fault. Most often, this means that the disk has gone bad. Copy any existing files to a new disk and reformat the bad disk. If formatting fails, the disk should be discarded.

Advanced Feature. This is an indication that your program used an Advanced BASIC feature while you were using Disk BASIC. Start Advanced BASIC (BASICA) and rerun your program.

In conclusion, I think you will find the IBM Personal Computer, coupled with DOS, to be a rewarding combination. If you are just starting in the microcomputer field, the support information provided by IBM in their BASIC manual, DOS manual, and Guide to Operations manual will help you along in a mode of learning which is more pleasing than frustrating. Beginners, however, should first read through the BASIC manual to get an understanding of how the language is used in general. Then go to the Guide to Operations, especially the section on DOS and BASIC. These pages take you through some simple programming techniques, showing you how to use both BASIC and the features offered by DOS. From this point on, the DOS manual will allow you to expand your capabilities and take advantage of the features which are exclusive to this mode of operation.

If you already have experience, carefully read through IBM's BASIC manual to be alert to discrete changes in IBM's BASIC. If computers are very new to you, you will find the help of a more experienced person useful. IBM's material is very thorough and stated in simple-to-understand language, but some additional input will help you over the trouble spots. The IBM materials are not designed to provide a complete education in microcomputers, but rather to inform of the direct operation of their machine, programming techniques, etc. It helps to have the advice of someone who is a little past the beginner stage.

Chapter 9

Problem Determination

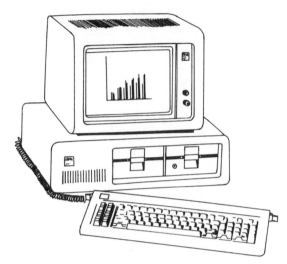

The IBM Guide to Operations provides an excellent section entitled Problem Determination Procedures (PDP) that will help you resolve operational and system failures. It poses a series of observations for you to answer yes or no when checking the results. By following these steps, you can probably tell if service is needed or what actions must be taken to make the system work.

The Problem Determination Procedures involve the use of the Diagnostic Aids disk or cassette. This program contains a series of tests to help in locating a specific problem or problems with any of the four components in the system. These four units are known as CRUs or customer-replaceable units and include the System Unit, Keyboard, Display and Printer. Apparently, there were a few bugs in the first Diagnostics disk offered by IBM. The problems only showed up when certain options were used. IBM informed me that their new Debug Diagnostics program is labeled as Version 3.00. You might check your program if a problem seems to be indicated when none is encountered in the actual operation.

First of all, make certain that the units which comprise your Personal Computer system are connected in strict accordance with the instructions in the Guide to Operations manual. It is quite easy to accidentally connect the keyboard output plug into the cassette jack at the rear of the System Unit and vice versa. Also, it is quite possible to connect the IBM Monochrome Display to the jack which provides output to the color graphics display or to connect a color graphics monitor to the monochrome output. The jacks and plugs for these two outputs and devices are interchangeable.

Before loading the Diagnostics disk or cassette, activate the switch on the right rear of the System Unit. If you are using the IBM Monochrome Display, turn both front panel controls to full clockwise. Upon switch activation, a flashing cursor should appear in the upper left-hand corner of the display screen in about four seconds. Afterwards, a short beep will be heard from the speaker. The beep indicates that all of memory has been tested and takes approximately fifteen to twenty seconds to occur if you have 128K or up to 45 seconds with 264K. Following the beep, "IBM Personal Computer" will appear on the screen above the flashing cursor. This is the mini-test and indicates that all is functioning well to this point. This test is internally generated and doesn't use the IBM Diagnostic disk or cassette.

If all goes well, then your basic system is functioning properly. If, however, you get no screen display or any response from the System Unit other than one short beep, there's a good chance that a problem exists within the System Unit. You may receive error messages on the screen, such as:

XXX 201
601
131
Parity check X

You may also receive one short beep from the System Unit and random characters or no response at all from the monitor. These conditions indicate a possible problem in the System Unit. Any error messages that appear may not remain on the screen for more than a second or so, so look quickly and make note of them. If you should get the one short beep from the System Unit and the screen displays XXXX followed by the number 301, this indicates a problem within the keyboard. A short beep followed by a funny screen display such as rolling, shadows, flickering, etc. indicates a display problem. Any of these problems will probably mean that your System Unit, keyboard and/or monitor will have to be serviced.

A call to IBM's Boca Raton headquarters will get you the information needed, along with the location of your nearest service facility. Before making this call, however, switch off your System Unit and reexamine your connections. If the test indicated that you have a keyboard problem, check your connections between the receptacle at the rear of the System Unit and the keyboard. Is the plug connected to the proper jack? Is it inserted all the way? If the test indicated a defective display monitor, then check the connections here. Is the power plug properly inserted in its receptacle at the rear of the System Unit? Is the "D" plug properly inserted in the IBM Monochrome Adapter receptacle (or color monitor receptacle for a color graphics display)? Now, run the test one more time by activating the System Unit. If you get the same results, then contact IBM. Before placing the call, make a note of exactly what happened when you ran the test. Did you get a beep from the System Unit? If so, how long did it take to receive it? What did your screen display (if anything)? Were there any error messages generated?

Of course, if you got absolutely nothing (no beep, no display, etc.), possibly your computer is not receiving power. Check the wall receptacle by plugging in an electric lamp or other device which is known to be working and see if it is operating properly. If not, try a different outlet and rerun the tests.

If you do not get a beep and you know your System Unit is receiving power, this is an indication that the power supply is not operating or has shut down due to a malfunction within the System Unit. This is an intelligent power supply and will shut off part of its output if circuit conditions are not correct. The beep is called a Power Good signal and indicates the presence of +/− 5 volts and +/− 12 volts output. Even though you're sure that you have power at the wall outlet, there could be a break in the System Unit cord. At the right rear of the System Unit there is a screened vent which is used to channel air out of the power supply compartment for efficient cooling. When you activate the System Unit switch, the fan should begin to operate. If it doesn't, insert voltmeter probes in the end of the System Unit cord that attaches to the rear panel. You should receive a reading of approximately 115 volts ac. If voltage is low or nonexistent, then the problem lies within this cord, which can probably be replaced by a standard extension cord with a bit of jury rigging. If voltage checks out all right here, this may indicate a wiring break between the power receptacle at the rear of the unit and the power supply transformer. Such a condition should be noted when you talk to your IBM service representative.

The IBM System Unit is not exactly owner-serviceable, but there are a few checks you can perform that may be of some help and which are not included in the IBM Guide to Operations. If you're not getting a Power Good signal (beep), then there is a possibility that the disk drive(s) may not be operating correctly, causing an overload. Also, any of the options inserted in the system expansion slots may be causing the overload. Since these options can be owner-installed, it is fair to assume that you can perform your own personal minicheck by removing them one at a time. First take the power plug out of the wall receptacle. Remove the cover of the System Unit. Remove the two screws at the far left and right of the back section and slide the cover forward. When the rear of the cover reaches the front panel of the System Unit, pull the front upward and it should slide off easily.

Examine the option boards. Are the edge connectors firmly mated with their receptacles on the system board? Is there any apparent damage, such as broken components, obvious cracks in circuit boards, etc.? If so, make note of the damaged areas. Facing the front of the System Unit, the power supply is contained in a black box located in the right rear section. On the left side of this box, two power plugs and their associated wiring exit. The plugs are attached to mating receptacles on the system board. Make certain these plugs are firmly in place. Examine the ribbon cable used to connect the disk drive(s) to the drive adapter. If all seems well, check the power connectors from the power supply box to the back left-hand edge of the circuit board(s) mounted on the top of the disk drive(s). There are several more plugs in this area, all of which should be firmly mated to their proper receptacles. If you find any of the plugs loose, carefully tighten them by pushing them into their mating receptacles. Now, reinsert the plug in the wall and run the minitest again. If your machine checks out all right, the cover may be replaced. If not, remove the plug from the wall outlet and proceed.

Starting at the left-hand side of the system expansion slots, remove the first card. Removal is accomplished by loosening the set screw at the rear of each option board, removing it completely and then carefully prying the board out of its slot. When the first board is removed, reconnect the power plug to the wall outlet and test your unit again, waiting for the beep. If you still get nothing, remove another board after turning the power off and unplugging the cord. Do not replace the one which has already been removed. Run the minitest again. Continue removing boards from the system expansion slots until the beep is heard. Remember to unplug the unit each time a board is removed. If you still get nothing, then the problem lies elsewhere (probably on the system board or in the power supply).

On the other hand, if you finally remove a board and the minitest produces a beep, then set aside the last board removed. Now, reinsert the first board you took out (again, with the power plug removed from the wall). Once the reinstallation procedure is complete, run the minitest again. If you get a beep, leave the board in place and install another one. If you do not get a beep, remove the board again and install the second one which was originally removed. Continue this process until you determine which boards cause the system to fail the minitest. Make note of your findings before talking to IBM service personnel.

If removal of the option boards does nothing, there is one last condition you might look for. This would be a loose IC or two on the system board. Sometimes, ICs are not properly mated in their sockets. Some of the ICs on the system board are wired in directly, while others use sockets. If an IC is obviously not seated firmly in its appropriate socket, then carefully remove it and note whether or not the pins are properly aligned. If not, correct the situation by bending the misaligned pins inward or outward. Now, reinsert the IC in its socket. Look closely at the memory modules which lie on the left front of the system board. These should have white dots painted at one end. All of the ICs must be inserted with the dots pointing toward the rear of the System Unit. Since they will fit either way, there is a slight possibility that one or two may have been installed in reverse order. If this is the case, gently pull them from their sockets, reverse them and then reinstall. Also, note the positions of each individual switching element in the system board DIP switches (2). Check their positions with your Guide to Operations manual to make certain that they are properly aligned. This is about all you can do on your own, so if you cannot get proper test results, contact IBM.

The same minitest applies when using a standard television set or color graphics monitor in place of the IBM Monochrome Dis-play. Make certain, however, that this external monitor is operational before it is connected to the System Unit.

The IBM 80 CPS Matrix Printer has a built-in test function which may be run without any connection to the IBM System Unit. Make certain your printer is working properly before any connections are made to the rest of the system. The printer must be plugged into a wall outlet since it does not receive power from the System Unit.

IBM DIAGNOSTIC AIDS DISK

Assuming that your Power-On test has checked out all right (flashing cursor, power good beep, and proper display), then it is time to use the Diagnostic Aids disk or cassette to run further tests. These additional tests provide a more thorough going-over of the entire system and can detect malfunctions which the Power-On test can't.

To load the disk version, insert the Diagnostics disk into drive A and turn the System Unit switch to the on position. Figure 9-1 shows what the screen will display. Note in the second line that Version 1.00 is displayed. Your Diagnostics routine will most likely be Version 2.00 or 3.00. If you do not get this display, then there is most likely a problem with your System Unit. If, however, the Power-On test discussed previously checked out all right, you should see a fascimile of Fig. 9-1 on your screen.

To effectively run the Diagnostics test, it will be necessary to format a data disk. If you have only one drive, remove the Diagnostics disk and insert the data disk. You are now ready to format, so you will select Option 1, as indicated by the display prompt ("Format Disk"). Depress the 1 key and then press Enter. In addition to the information which previously appeared on the display, this action will add the question, "Which drive contains

```
The IBM Personal Computer DIAGNOSTICS
Version 1.00 (C) Copyright IBM Corp 1981

SELECT AN OPTION

0 - RUN DIAGNOSTIC ROUTINES
1 - FORMAT DISKETTE
2 - COPY DISKETTE
9 - EXIT TO SYSTEM DISKETTE



INSERT  DIAGNOSTIC DISKETTE  IN DRIVE A AND ENTER
THE ACTION DESIRED
```

Fig. 9-1. When the diagnostic aids disk has been inserted, the screen will appear as shown here (courtesy IBM).

disk to be formatted?" If you have a two-drive system, insert a scratch disk into drive B and type in "B." If not, remove the Diagnostics disk from the single drive and insert the scratch disk. Then type "A" and press Enter. Whichever drive you specified (A or B) will not be activated and after about thirty seconds, the disk drive will stop and the screen will reprint what it formerly displayed, asking you to enter the option desired. This signifies that formatting is complete and you are ready to move on to the Diagnostics routines. If this entire action did not come off as described, recheck to make certain the disk to be formatted was properly inserted. The write-protect tab must be removed. If you find no problem here, try another disk and repeat the steps.

Assuming that the formatting routine was carried out properly, you are now ready to run the Diagnostics routines (Option 0). Depress the 0 key and hit Enter. Make sure your Diagnostic Aids disk has been reinserted into drive A. The screen will display the devices installed in and connected to the System Unit. This is shown in Fig. 9-2. You should already be aware of what options and peripherals your system is composed of. Check these against the list displayed on the screen. Notice that you are

prompted to answer if this list checks with what you know you have. If it does not, this indicates a problem within the System Unit. This could mean that one of your option boards is not properly installed. You can check this by removing the cover and checking the unit which was not recorded on the list. If no problem is found here, your System Unit probably needs service. If the list was correct, save for the omission of the printer, check to make certain that your printer was actually turned on and that the printer-to-system unit cable is properly installed. If not, make the needed corrections and run the test again.

Assuming that the results received on your display screen are in line with the correct results described here, continue on to the next portion of the test by answering the prompt by typing Y (for yes) and then hitting Enter. This indicates that the tests have gone well to this point.

Upon depressing the Enter key, your screen should provide a System Checkout menu like the one shown in Fig. 9-3. At this time, select Option 0 (run tests one time) and again press Enter. Almost immediately, the monitor will display "System Unit 100". This indicates that the program is now checking

```
THE INSTALLED DEVICES ARE


SYSTEM BOARD
192KB MEMORY
KEYBOARD
MONOCHROME & PRINTER ADAPTER
COLOR/GRAPHICS ADAPTER
2 DISKETTE DRIVE(S) & ADAPTER
MATRIX PRINTER


IS THE LIST CORRECT (Y/N) ?
```

Fig. 9-2. A listing of the installed devices in the system is displayed.

area 100 of the System Unit memory. After fifteen seconds or so, the screen will display five rows of blocks and prompt you to press each key on the keyboard. Each time you depress a key, one of the blocks will be filled in by the character it is designed to input. When all of the keys have been pressed once, all of the blocks should contain an appropriate character. The prompt then asks you if the screen is correct. Typing Y and then pressing Enter will cause the system to go on to the next check. If all blocks are not filled in, you would type an N

```
SYSTEM CHECKOUT

0 - RUN TESTS ONE TIME
1 - RUN TESTS MULTIPLE TIMES
2 - LOG UTILITIES
9 - EXIT DIAGNOSTIC ROUTINES

ENTER THE ACTION DESIRED
?
```

Fig. 9-3. A system checkout menu.

for no, press Enter and receive a display that tells you to have the System Unit serviced.

If this portion of the test went all right, upon typing Y and pressing Enter, you will see a display which is similar to the one shown in Fig. 9-4. This is a hard copy printout of what is displayed on the screen, but does not accurately reflect some of the graphics involved. For example, the second line in this figure will be much brighter than the first on the monitor. The third line from the bottom is not seen at all on the screen, while the next line blinks and the last line is underlined. A monitor can display a lot more than our printout. When used with a color monitor, an additional screen printout will show the colors blue, green, cyan, red, magenta, yellow and white. If there are problems here, this again points to the System Unit; but if everything is okay, press Y and Enter again to continue. You will now see a display of every character your Personal Computer can print. If this is correct, the normal Y/Enter sequence takes you to the next stage, which is identical to the individual test per-

```
DISPLAY ATTRIBUTES


THIS LINE IS AT NORMAL INTENSITY.
THIS LINE IS INTENSIFIED.
THIS LINE IS IN REVERSE VIDEO.
THIS LINE IS NOT VISIBLE.
THIS LINE IS BLINKING.
THIS LINE IS UNDERLINED.




IS THE SCREEN CORRECT? (Y/N)
```

Fig. 9-4. A hard copy printout of a diagnostics test to check graphics.

formed on the printer, but is in graphics form. This is shown in Fig. 9-5, which again is the printout. On the screen, these figures are displayed in black on a bright green background. This display should match the printer self-test display. The IBM Guide to Operations provides pictorial descriptions of what you should see during each of these tests.

Those persons who have color graphics monitors will be required to perform four or five additional tests to check out the performance of the Personal Computer with these non-IBM supplied devices. Those with IBM Monochrome Displays will skip these steps, and the equivalent of what is shown in Fig. 9-6 will be seen on the monitor. I performed these tests using a system unit with two disk drives. This required two formatted disks containing no useful information to be placed in drives A and B. You must remember to remove the original Diagnostic Aids disk from drive A before going further. If your System Unit contains a single disk drive, then the message will be altered to read, "Insert scratch disk in drive A. Press Enter when ready." Make certain the scratch disk(s) are installed as the prompt indicates. When this has been done depressing the Enter key will cause the disk drive to be activated. If you have two drives, the second one will be activated after the first one stops cycling. If the test has gone properly, you will get a display identical to the one seen in Fig. 9-7. This is a printer test, and your results should accurately display what is seen here. If this printout is correct and all other steps went according to this description, your entire system has been put through the mill and has come out with flying colors. If the printout is not correct, it may be necessary to have your printer and cable serviced.

Throughout these tests, make note of any error messages. These will be displayed on the IBM Monochrome Monitor with a solid green background. Figure 9-8 shows examples of two error messages. One indicates that one of the disks was equipped with a write-protect feature and must be replaced. The other indicates a problem within the System Unit, Section 601.

```
80X25 DISPLAY
 !"#$%&'()*+,-./0123456789:;<=>?@ABCDEFGHIJKLMNOPQRSTUVWXYZ[\]^_`abcdefghijklmn
 !"#$%&'()*+,-./0123456789:;<=>?@ABCDEFGHIJKLMNOPQRSTUVWXYZ[\]^_`abcdefghijklmno
 "#$%&'()*+,-./0123456789:;<=>?@ABCDEFGHIJKLMNOPQRSTUVWXYZ[\]^_`abcdefghijklmnop
 #$%&'()*+,-./0123456789:;<=>?@ABCDEFGHIJKLMNOPQRSTUVWXYZ[\]^_`abcdefghijklmnopq
 $%&'()*+,-./0123456789:;<=>?@ABCDEFGHIJKLMNOPQRSTUVWXYZ[\]^_`abcdefghijklmnopqr
 %&'()*+,-./0123456789:;<=>?@ABCDEFGHIJKLMNOPQRSTUVWXYZ[\]^_`abcdefghijklmnopqrs
 &'()*+,-./0123456789:;<=>?@ABCDEFGHIJKLMNOPQRSTUVWXYZ[\]^_`abcdefghijklmnopqrst
 '()*+,-./0123456789:;<=>?@ABCDEFGHIJKLMNOPQRSTUVWXYZ[\]^_`abcdefghijklmnopqrstu
 ()*+,-./0123456789:;<=>?@ABCDEFGHIJKLMNOPQRSTUVWXYZ[\]^_`abcdefghijklmnopqrstuv
 )*+,-./0123456789:;<=>?@ABCDEFGHIJKLMNOPQRSTUVWXYZ[\]^_`abcdefghijklmnopqrstuvw
 *+,-./0123456789:;<=>?@ABCDEFGHIJKLMNOPQRSTUVWXYZ[\]^_`abcdefghijklmnopqrstuvwx
 +,-./0123456789:;<=>?@ABCDEFGHIJKLMNOPQRSTUVWXYZ[\]^_`abcdefghijklmnopqrstuvwxy
 ,-./0123456789:;<=>?@ABCDEFGHIJKLMNOPQRSTUVWXYZ[\]^_`abcdefghijklmnopqrstuvwxyz
 -./0123456789:;<=>?@ABCDEFGHIJKLMNOPQRSTUVWXYZ[\]^_`abcdefghijklmnopqrstuvwxyz{
 ./0123456789:;<=>?@ABCDEFGHIJKLMNOPQRSTUVWXYZ[\]^_`abcdefghijklmnopqrstuvwxyz{|
 /0123456789:;<=>?@ABCDEFGHIJKLMNOPQRSTUVWXYZ[\]^_`abcdefghijklmnopqrstuvwxyz{|}
 0123456789:;<=>?@ABCDEFGHIJKLMNOPQRSTUVWXYZ[\]^_`abcdefghijklmnopqrstuvwxyz{|}~
 123456789:;<=>?@ABCDEFGHIJKLMNOPQRSTUVWXYZ[\]^_`abcdefghijklmnopqrstuvwxyz{|}~

IS THE SCREEN CORRECT? (Y/N)
```

Fig. 9-5. Another printout of a portion of the diagnostics test.

```
 ****  WARNING  ****
DATA WILL BE DESTROYED

INSERT SCRATCH DISKETTE IN ALL DRIVES
PRESS ENTER WHEN READY
?
```

Fig. 9-6. A check of the performance of the IBM Monochrome Display.

The IBM Diagnostic Aids diskette or cassette greatly assists even the novice microcomputer operator in system checkout procedures. When I ran my first test, I encountered a problem. The procedure halted at the midway point and would not continue. A check with IBM indicated that I had been erroneously sent the old Diagnostic Aids version. The new version ran perfectly.

I have provided some service information of my own regarding the checking of option board installations, loose wiring connectors, etc. If you are not familiar with general test procedures, do not even attempt to remove the cover of the System Unit. If you would normally install your own options, then you can get through this procedure with little difficulty,

```
 !"#$%&'()*+,-.
0123456789:;<=>
@ABCDEFGHIJKLMN
PQRSTUVWXYZ[\]^
`abcdefghijklmn
pqrstuvwxyz{|}~
 !"#$%&'()*+,-.
0123456789:;<=>
@ABCDEFGHIJKLMN
PQRSTUVWXYZ[\]^
`abcdefghijklmn
pqrstuvwxyz{|}~
 !"#$%&'()*+,-.
```

Fig. 9-7. A display of the printer test.

```
SYSTEM UNIT      500
ERROR - 07 WRITE PROTECT
 0:05:43
ERROR - SYSTEM UNIT     601
```

Fig. 9-8. Examples of two error messages that may occur.

as all of my "miniinternal check" involves the same basic procedures that IBM recommends. Do not be tempted to tinker with some of the adjustable controls. It will probably not work and you will probably void your warranty as well.

If you do go inside the cabinet of the System Unit, make certain the power plug is removed from the wall. Don't depend upon the on/off switch to remove all power from the unit. You're not likely to encounter potentials greater than about 15 volts dc, which is certainly below the lethal level, but you must remember that these are the levels present when the system is functioning properly. You wouldn't be inside the cabinet if this were the case, so suspect anything. While not likely, it is possible that 115 volts ac could be present anywhere and could cause a serious electrical shock. In almost every case, when the diagnostics routine indicates that a portion of your system must be serviced by IBM, this is the way it's got to be. Of course, a call to your IBM Service Center or the main headquarters in Boca Raton, Florida, may put you in touch with a technician who may offer service information over the telephone if the problem seems to be user-correctable and if you demonstrate to him in a few words your ability to perform a few minor tests.

PREVENTIVE MAINTENANCE

While not directly specified in the IBM Guide to Operations, a few preventive maintenance tips are in order. These are mostly common sense procedures, but are mentioned here for the beginner. Make certain all diskettes are safely stashed away in their protective covers to keep out dust and prevent scratching of the tracks. These devices should not be subjected to extremely high or low temperatures and should be stored in a fairly dry environment which is free from high relative humidity. Do not allow them to be bent or misshapen. Special disk files are available which will keep them secure, but two pieces of stiff cardboard on either side of the disk will serve the same purpose.

When your disk drives are not in use, keep the doors closed to prevent dust, dirt and foreign objects from entering. Remove dust from the surface of the cabinet or drive doors with a slightly damp cloth, one which will leave a little lint behind. Keep the area surrounding your microcomputer clean. Be on the lookout for small pieces of wire, paper clips, etc. which can easily enter the disk drive openings. These objects can also foul your printer drive mechanism.

Treat all power cords and interconnecting cables with care. If these are severely bent, mashed or subjected to a great deal of weight, the internal conductors can break or short. In signal cables, this can cause malfunctions, which are difficult to isolate.

Do not operate your computer in environments which create a great deal of vibration. Areas which contain heavy motorized equipment, generators, etc. can create a constant vibration that can sometimes cause power plugs, connectors, etc. to work loose.

Try to operate your Personal Computer system on an electrical circuit which does not also provide power to motorized devices or any device which draws a great deal of current, especially when being initially turned on or off. When my computer was first installed, I had one large extension cord which was fitted with a splitter receptacle. Into this splitter I attached the power cable for the System Unit, the printer, and my IBM typewriter. Whenever I had a problem in the computer and would simultaneously switch the typewriter on or off, all data was lost.

The circuitry and packaging which makes up the hardware portion of the IBM Personal Computer system are quite efficient and rugged as well. The IBM Personal Computer is as strong as any other microcomputer but still must be treated with kid gloves. If your System Unit falls off a wobbly legged table, however, it would be quite easy to break a circuit board or two. Of course, if the same thing happened to the monitor containing a depressurized cathode-ray tube, the results could be disastrous. Note that the System Unit is encased in a metal-covered chasis, and the same applies to the keyboard. The latter portion of the IBM Personal Computer is probably the unit which could be subjected to the most abuse since it is portable. For this reason, the keyboard unit is extremely rugged. It does contain plastic keys, however, which could be broken if subjected to a high impact shock.

The power supply fitted in the System Unit is rated at 63.5 watts of continuous operation. This allows the system to remain on 24 hours a day if necessary. It's a good idea, though, to shut the machine down if it is not to be operated for any great length of time. The power supply has fused primary protection and will automatically shut down should a failure occur within the System Unit.

After several months of usage, it would probably be a good idea to remove the System Unit case and go over the circuit boards and chassis with a low-pressure airgun to clean out dust and debris. At most electronics stores, you can buy a can of pressurized air that will allow you to direct a gust of air at various points in the chassis. This type of cleaning should be done in a relatively dust-free environment or you're liable to bring in more dust than you blow out.

The surface of the keyboard is the area most likely to receive a buildup of dirt, oil and grime. For goodness sakes, wash your hands before using the keyboard. A daily or weekly cleaning with a slightly damp cloth will keep your keyboard in like-new condition. I found the pressure needed to activate the keys to be quite minimal, so it's not necessary to slap the keys like you would a manual typewriter. The electronic conditions that are set up by pressing each key involve the mechanical movement of the key itself. This means that each key has so many cycles of operation before it will fail . . . but fail it will eventually. I am certain that IBM has tested the keyboard to make certain that total keying operations number in the hundreds of thousands or even millions. This is far and above the number of depressions that will be made during many, many years of operation. However, if you stab at the keys using excessive pressure, this will certainly shorten the anticipated life. Again, easy does it.

Connect the signal cables to the System Unit gently. If a plug has some difficulty in mating with its appropriate receptacle, ease it into place and then tighten the locking bolts securely. If you try and force a plug into its receptacle, you are likely to bend pins which may necessitate replacing the receptacle or plug entirely. The plugs will only mate with the receptacles one way, so make certain you have the pins properly aligned before attempting insertion. Since multicontact plugs and receptacles often appear identical (at first glance) to other plugs and receptacles, make certain you are attempting to mate the correct plug with its appropriate receptacle. Anyone who has attempted to insert a 16-pin plug into a 15-pin receptacle will know what I'm talking about. It just won't work.

Preventive maintenance procedures may occasionally require you to remove the cover from the System Unit in order to clean the interior and make certain all plugs are properly mated with their appropriate connectors. Also, when installing new options such as an additional disk drive, color graphics adapter, etc., it will be necessary to remove, exchange and insert new circuit boards. A printed circuit board is a very sturdy device, but only when properly mounted. When removed from their mounts, these boards can easily be broken. Be careful when removing or installing any circuit board, because these are the times when they're more prone to damage. A hairline fracture in a printed circuit board may be created by placing undue and uneven stresses across one portion. These types of breaks may not even be noticed through visual inspection and often require a magnifying glass to be seen. Such fractures, however, will cause the circuit board to operate erratically or not at all. The system option boards contain edge connectors which mate with multi-contact receptacles on the system board. This is often a tight fit, so it is necessary to gingerly "wiggle" the board into place. The color graphics adapter and the monochrome display/printer adapter boards run the length of the System Unit's chassis. Two guide slots have been installed on the inside front panel, into which one edge of the card is inserted. This is not true for the other option boards. When installing these two options, you must make certain that the edge connectors are properly aligned with their receptacles and that the front panel slot is aligned with the board edge. The rear panel slots mate with the other edge of the board where the screw-in mount is attached. If you should install one of these long boards and miss the front panel slot, uneven pressure will be applied from the leading edge to the center. This could eventually cause a hairline fracture.

When installing any circuit card with an edge connector, carefully align the connector with its receptacle and then gently rock the board into place. Make sure that the connector and receptacle are tightly mated. Otherwise the board won't work or it may work for a period of time and then become intermittent or fail.

The circuit boards mounted atop the disk drive unit contain receptacles for power plugs which exit the power supply box. These are tight friction fits, so it is necessary to apply a bit of pressure to get a proper mating. Here, it is very easy to break the edge of a circuit board, so apply equal pressure on top of the board near the edge while mating the plug. When removing the plug, you must pull up slightly on the board edge while pulling downward on the power plug.

Whenever the cover is removed from the System Unit, make sure the surrounding environment is clear of any debris, especially metal shavings, paper clips and small hardware in general. Before replacing the cover and activating the unit, closely examine the entire interior to make certain that no metallic objects remain. Small screws, metal shavings, etc. can create instantaneous short circuits. One of its main purposes of the System Unit cover is to prevent falling objects from coming in contact with the circuit components. When the cover is removed, if you should drop even a fairly lightweight object into the interior, you could easily break a circuit board, an integrated circuit or any number of other components. For this reason, never operate the System Unit for any length of time (or any other unit) with the cover removed. If you must work on the interior of the System Unit over a period of several days, replace the cover each time your operation is to be halted for any long period. It is not necessary to replace the cabinet mounting screws until your repair or installation procedure is complete, but make certain that the cover is temporarily put back in place until you are ready to resume service operations.

It has been previously mentioned that a *slightly* damp cloth may be used to clean the *exterior* of the System Unit, printer, keyboard and display. However, do not use this cleaning technique on the interior of any piece of electronic equipment. Moisture can cause short circuits if power is applied before it has time to evaporate. If you should accidentally spill water into the circuit components, carefully wipe away as much as possible and then allow the circuit to sit for several hours (or more, if necessary) to make certain all remaining moisture has evaporated. I have seen pieces of electronic equipment operate perfectly after being totally submerged in water . . . but only after a drying out period which lasted for several days and was aided by a heat lamp. By the same token, I have seen similar pieces of equipment fail completely when power was applied too soon. Power transformers are especially subject to water infiltration. Of course, there is no reason for water to get into your Personal Computer unless you are very careless. But accidents can happen, so if you do have some water infiltration, make certain it is completely removed before power is applied.

As far as cabinets are concerned, the Personal Computer system uses metal for those found on the System Unit and keyboard. The IBM monitor and printer, however, are closed in plastic cases, so these two units will be more subject to enclosure breakage. If you should accidentally crack an enclosure, this must be repaired or replaced immediately. A damaged enclosure can allow dust to enter the interior of the circuitry. This may cause no real problems in the monitor, but may cause the printer to operate erratically or not at all after a period of time. A minor case breakage can often be repaired with a piece of tape, bonding compound, etc. However, a major crack will weaken the integrity of the entire enclosure and a replacement should be ordered. Be extremely careful when handling monitors. The cathode-ray tube can literally explore if cracked, creating a real health hazard.

In summary, preventive maintenance of the IBM Personal Computer system is quite easily accomplished. System checkout and problem determination have been lowered to the simplest of procedures with the aid of the IBM Diagnostic Aids disk or cassette and the Guide to Operations manual. With these aids, anyone should be quite capable of checking out the entire system within fifteen minutes or so. If you should have a problem, the Diagnostic Aids will probably locate the trouble area and allow for a quick repair.

Chapter 10

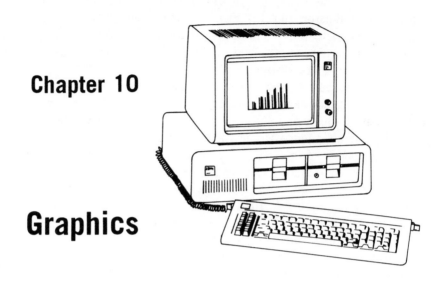

Graphics

The Personal Computer's monochrome monitor is not really capable of displaying graphics. Although it offers the highest resolution of any personal computer monochrome display (it can produce up to 25 80-column lines, rather than the 24 80-column lines offered by its closest competitor), the adapter board just wasn't designed for graphics purposes. This was done as a tradeoff to allow the system to provide extremely versatile operation in areas which lay outside the graphics field.

In order to obtain high-resolution graphics with this system, you must purchase IBM's Color/Graphics Monitor Adapter, available for about $300. In addition you must purchase a monochrome or color monitor, which IBM does not supply. Any of the standard units available for microcomputer purposes can be easily interfaced with the Color/Graphics Adapter. You can also use your black-and-

white or color television receiver if you also purchase an rf modulator and connect its output to your television antenna terminals. If you intend to work in a high-resolution graphics mode, you will most likely need the IBM monochrome display, along with the display and printer adapter card.

There are three methods of accessing the Color/Graphics Monitor Adapter output. For direct drive monitors, there is a 9-pin "D" shell connector. This provides individual output for the colors red, green, and blue (found on pins 3, 4, and 5, respectively). Pins 6, 8, and 9 form the output terminals for intensity, horizontal drive, and vertical drive, respectively.

For standard video monitors there is a phono jack located on the monitor adapter output panel which outputs a composite video signal of approximately 1.5 volts peak-to-peak amplitude.

If you wish to use your own television

receiver, there is a special output section located on the circuit board. This must be accessed by removing the System Unit's cover, a 4-pin Berg strip, of which only pins 1, 3, and 4 are used. Pin 1 outputs a positive 12 volt dc to power the modulator; pin 3 is the composite video output; and pin 4 connects to logic ground. Once a plug is attached to this Berg strip, the cable must be routed out of the System Unit between the enclosure and chassis. There is also an additional 6-pin Berg strip for connection of a light pen.

The Color/Graphics Monitor Adapter has two basic modes of operation: alphanumeric and graphics. Each mode provides further options in color and black-and-white. In the alphanumeric mode, every display character position is defined by two bytes in the regen buffer (part of the display adapter, not system memory). Both the color and black-and-white display adapters use the two-byte character/attribute format shown in Fig. 10-1.

```
DISPLAY CHAR CODE BYTE   ATTRIBUTE BYTE
7  6  5  4  3  2  1       7  6  5  4  3  2  1
```

Fig. 10-1. The two-byte character/attribute format.

Using a color television, the adapter will allow for display of up to 25 rows of 40 characters each, with a maximum of 256 characters. The adapter board contains 2,000 bytes of Read/Write Memory (RAM), an 8 by 8 character box, outputting 7 by 7 double-dotted characters.

Using a color monitor with direct drive input capability, you can display up to 25 rows of 80 characters each, as established by 4,000 bytes of Read/Write Memory on the adapter board. There are three color graphics modes of operation. Low resolution provides 160 horizontal points and 100 vertical points and up to sixteen colors, including black and white.

Medium resolution outputs at 320 points horizontally, 200 vertical and four colors. High resolution contains 640 horizontal points, 200 vertical points, and outputs black and white only. Low resolution color graphics requires an 8000-byte Read/Write Memory, medium resolution color graphics, and black-and-white high-resolution graphics require 16,000 bytes, contained on the adapter card. It should be pointed out that low-resolution color graphics are not supported in read-only memory.

Using the IBM monochrome display with its appropriate adapter, you can draw pictures with the line and block characters. Blinking, reverse image, invisible, highlighted, and underscored characters are also supported. Using the Color/Graphics Monitor Adapter, you can also operate in the text mode, but this option allows you to display the text in sixteen different colors. You can also display in just black and white by setting parameters on the Screen or Color statements. You also get complete graphics capability to draw complex pictures. This graphics capability makes all points addressable in medium and high resolution. This is more versatile than drawing with the special line and block characters which you have in text mode. Graphics refers to the special capability of the Color/Graphics Monitor Adapter. The use of the extended character set with special line and block characters is not considered to be graphics.

An example of the monitor screen and its various print coordinates is seen in Fig. 10-2. Characters are presented in 25 horizontal lines across the screen; each line is composed of a maximum of 80 characters. The horizontal lines are numbered from 1 to 25; the character positions on each line are numbered 1 through 80 in high-resolution mode, and 1 through 40 in medium resolution. In IBM BASIC, the LOCATE statement is used to print a character at a particular point on the screen. For example,

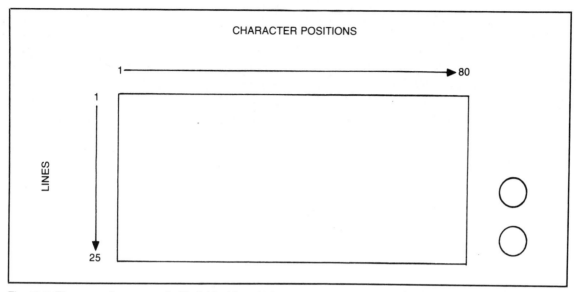

CHARACTER POSITIONS

1 ——————————————→ 80

1

LINES

25

Fig. 10-2. The screen is composed of individual lines (25) and character positions, (80 in high-resolution mode).

the upper left-hand corner of the screen is identified by:

LOCATE 1,1

The position at the top center of the screen, in high-resolution mode, would be identified by:

LOCATE 1,40

The first number indicates the horizontal line; the second number indicates the character position on that line.

With IBM DOS, line 25 is usually reserved for the Soft Key display, which simply indicates the functions of the ten soft keys. However, you may write over this area by simply typing in "KEY OFF" and then pressing Enter. This will remove the soft key display and make this area available for input display use.

In graphics programming using color, you will constantly hear the terms foreground and background. Foreground and background colors are set up by following the color graphic

statements with numerical designations. Some people have difficulty understanding what these terms mean, so to put it simply, the foreground is the character and the background is the space around the character. Foreground and background colors are established using the COLOR statement.

Using IBM Advanced BASIC (BASICA), you can select from a total of sixteen colors (Fig. 10-3). To experience these colors, it is necessary to have the optional Color/Graphics Monitor Adapter and a suitable color monitor or color television receiver and modulator.

BLACK(0)	GRAY(8)
BLUE(1)	LIGHT BLUE(9)
GREEN(2)	LIGHT GREEN(10)
CYAN(3)	LIGHT CYAN(11)
RED(4)	LIGHT RED(12)
MAGENTA(5)	LIGHT MAGENTA(13)
BROWN(6)	YELLOW(14)
WHITE(7)	HIGH INTENSITY WHITE(15)

Fig. 10-3. In medium resolution, sixteen colors are available in Advanced BASIC with the use of the Color/Graphics Monitor Adapter.

149

To do serious color graphics work, it is necessary to purchase IBM DOS. This gives you the Advanced BASIC capability, which is primarily aimed at advanced graphics work. In standard BASIC, the only graphics function is POINT, which prints the color of a point at specified coordinates on the screen. In Advanced BASIC, however, you have the additional statements CIRCLE, DRAW, GET, PAINT, and PUT, explained in Chapter 8 (Fig. 10-4).

CIRCLE	PAINT
COLOR	PRESET
DRAW	PSET
GET	PUT
LINE	SCREEN

Fig. 10-4. Statements in BASIC which are used for the graphics mode of operation.

When operating in the graphics mode, you handle coordinates completely different from text mode. In text mode there are only 25 horizontal lines and 40 character positions in medium-resolution mode. In graphics mode, there are 320 points horizontally and vertically in medium resolution. As before, these points are numbered from left to right and from the top of the screen to the bottom. This count starts at zero. In text mode, the upper left-hand corner is identified by 1.1. In graphics mode, this same portion of the screen is identified as 0,0, while the lower right corner is 319,199.

In high-resolution mode (black and white only), there are 640 horizontal points and the same 200 vertical points. The lower right-hand corner, then, would be at coordinate 639,199. It should be pointed out that text characters can still be displayed while you are in the graphics mode, and they will be the same size as in text mode. In medium resolution, the on-screen characters may be displayed in four colors, which are identified by numerals 0, 1, 2,

and 3. These numbers act in conjunction with the COLOR statement, which sets a palette of three colors identified by the numerals 1, 2, and 3. The four character colors can be any of sixteen different colors, which are referenced by the COLOR statement. The numerical color designation, that specifies the color pink with one COLOR statement may specify the color green with another. When the palette is changed with a new COLOR statement, all colors on the screen change to match this new palette. This allows for the complete set of colors to be changed by substituting a new numeral in the COLOR statement instead of going through the other color graphic statements and making repeated changes.

SETTING UP THE COLOR GRAPHICS

Assuming that the color graphics board has already been installed in the Personal Computer System Unit, then you have three choices as to how you may proceed. Before going on to the various monitoring arrangements, be sure that you have set the system board DIP switch 1 to reflect your monitor option. If you're using a high-resolution graphics monitor (80 by 25), then switch 5 should be on and 6 off. If you're using a medium-resolution television or monitor (40 by 25), switch 5 should be off and 6 on. When using both the Monochrome Display and a separate color/graphics monitor, switches 5 and 6 should be off. Be certain of your switch settings, particularly when the Monochrome Display is to be used in conjunction with a separate color monitor. If switches 5 and 6 are not in the off position, you can blow a fuse inside the Display.

If you have a direct drive color monitor, all you need is a mating "D" plug to attach to the connector on the rear of the System Unit. If you have a standard video monitor which accepts composite video signals, then use the phono jack directly above the 9-pin "D" shell connector. This may also be used for video input to a self-powered rf modulator. Most modulators designed for use with computers, however, are not self-powered and will depend upon the computer itself to supply an operating potential of 12 volts dc. Here, the 4-pin Berg connector located on the Color/Graphics Monitor Adapter board must be accessed.

In setting my computer up for color graphics, I decided the best route to take would be to use an rf modulator. I purchased the Sup'R'Mod V manufactured by M & R Enterprises in Santa Clara, California. It cost about $65 and is directly compatible with the IBM Personal Computer. I suspect the compatibility here is attributed to the fact that the input cable is terminated in a 4-pin Berg plug, which is actually a part of an adapter that fits a 5-pin DIN connector for which the input plug was originally designed. In other words, you go from a 5-pin male DIN connector to a 5-pin female receptacle and then into the 4-pin Berg plug which mates with the connector on the Color/Graphics Adapter board. A few inches from the Berg plug, there is a toroid core, around which the four wires are wrapped about seven times. This forms an interference trap which prevents many of the electronic functionings of the computer from interfering with television reception, both at your monitor screen and at nearby sets. A check with IBM in Boca Raton, Florida, assured me that this particular modulator was indeed compatible with their computer, as are many other types. All rf modulators are pretty much alike, although the inexpensive units often do not provide a stable signal output. I popped the lid on my modulator, which is shown in Fig. 10-5, and discovered it to be a very neat arrangement. Its performance with various television receivers was excellent. However, you should always use a receiver which has automatic fine tuning.

I experienced a distortion problem when using an inexpensive black-and-white television that did not offer the AFT feature. The poor performance may have been attributable to the television's inability to handle the computer output.

If you are experienced in television repair, you might be able to do away completely with the modulator by simply tapping into the first video amplifier stage in any receiver after bypassing the IF amplifiers and tuner. The Personal Computer produces an output from its Color/Graphics Monitor Adapter board of approximately 1.5 volts peak-to-peak. This is more than adequate to drive the first video amplifier stage in most television receivers and more than adequate for most rf modulators.

Fig. 10-5. The Sup'R'Mod V rf modulator.

(Mine would automatically cut off if the video output exceeded 1.5 volts. This never happened, so it can be assumed that the output level in the computer is slightly less. I measured 1.2 volts from mine.)

I did not elect to access the internal video amplifier in my monitor because for research purposes, it was necessary to test different types of television receivers. The labor required to obtain input from the video amplifier in each would certainly have not been worth the effort, especially when a video modulator can be obtained so easily. Since most people will use a video modulator, this makes a more appropriate discussion for this book.

My video modulator had a selectable VHF output, preset to channel 3 or 4. Some will allow selection of other VHF channels, while others have outputs in the UHF frequency band. Connection was fairly simple. It was necessary to loosen the two rear enclosure screws on the System Unit, slide the cover forward and then locate the 4-pin Berg connector on the adapter board. If you have other boards installed around the graphics board, it will be a fairly tight fitting procedure in making the plug connection. Note: The 4-pin Berg connector on the adapter board has the second pin clipped away. Only three pins are used for modulator connection. Pin 1 supplies the +12 volts dc, pin 2 is not used, pin 3 is the composite video connector, and pin 4 serves as video and dc ground. Before connecting any modulator, you must establish which leads on the modulator plug are designed to accept the various outputs. Don't go by the pin numbers on the modulator itself. For example, the plug on my modulator is labeled pin 1 for ground connection, whereas pin 1 on the Berg connector on the adapter board is +12 volts dc. This modulator plug is compatible with the computer by simply reversing it (the plug will fit either way). By connecting pin 1 on the plug to

pin 4 on the adapter board, the ground requirement is met. This brings the other plug connections in line. Pin 4 on the modulator plug accepts 12 volts dc, while pin 2 is the composite video terminal. If you modify other modulators to fit this board, you must determine what inputs are needed and then make suitable connections.

I had a bit of a problem fitting the toroidal adapter inside the System Unit case so it did not bar the enclosure from being fitted back in place. The Color/Graphics Monitor Adapter board is a long one and should be fitted in either the third or fourth system expansion slot from the right. The board will fit in the remaining three slots, but slots 3 and 4 contain special card guides on the inside of the front panel to better secure the card.

With the adapter board in the third slot from the right, I ran the short length of cable around the rear of the boards in slots 4 and 5 and allowed the toroid to hang down near the keyboard input plug inside the System Unit. This brought the adapter plug which is designed to mate with the DIN connector very close to the circular knockout in the System Unit rear panel. Removing the knockout allowed me to insert the adapter plug through the rear of the unit, where the modulator may be connected or disconnected as desired.

My modulator contained a 4-inch length of 300-ohm cable fitted with connectors for direct attachment to the VHF terminals of the receiver. The modulator unit then hangs in place but is fitted with two adhesive foam pads to allow it to be attached to the back of the receiver. My modulator contained a panel-mounted slide switch which allows selection of drive from the computer or from a separately connected television antenna cable which is accessed by a terminal strip on the side of the unit.

With everything in place, I tuned my color

television receiver to channel 4, making sure the modulator channel select switch was also in this position. I activated the computer while I watched the television screen. It became immediately apparent that the modulator was getting power, as the television screen was completely blanked (picture goes completely black or gray, no static lines). After the power-on test was completed by the computer, the flashing cursor appeared and screen printout was seen. It was necessary to adjust the fine tuning a bit, along with the contrast and brightness controls on the television receiver for best reproduction. To this day, I have not experienced any interference on my television monitor, nor received complaints from surrounding television owners.

When using a television receiver for monitoring purposes, you may select either medium resolution or high resolution screen printout. By the time I got around to the graphics portion of my research, I had become used to viewing the high resolution display of the IBM Monochrome monitor. The results obtained in *text mode* using a television receiver as the monitor was disappointing by comparison. The low resolution mode is easiest to read on the screen, but you effectively have half the space you do when using the Monochrome Display. You can switch to an equivalent high-resolution display by entering WIDTH 80 at the keyboard or with the Screen 2 command. Now, you have a full high-resolution display equivalent to the Monochrome Monitor . . . but only as far as screen space is concerned. When operating in the text mode, I found the high-resolution display print

to be extremely hard to read. In graphics mode, it was excellent, but I would not want to work for any length of time in the text mode while in high resolution. For this reason, most text mode operations using a separate monitor were done in medium resolution. If you don't use the IBM Monochrome Display and want to do some serious text mode operations using another type of monitor, I recommend you work with a high resolution direct drive type. Of course, after a period of time, you might become accustomed to reading the extremely narrow, close-fitting characters which are displayed on a television screen in high resolution, but this can be a real strain on the eyes. I know because I tried it with over ten different television receivers, none of which performed as well as the IBM Monochrome Display.

USING GRAPHICS

As a first test, I loaded DOS into my machine and then entered Advanced BASIC and ran some of the sample programs. On the DOS disk you may select about seven color graphics programs, which include a race car game, pie chart, an example of art and several others which produce highly colorful displays.

When going from the graphics mode to text mode when using the Monochrome Display Adapter and the Color/Graphics Adapter, it is necessary to run a short program to get the System Unit to output to one or the other. This information was not originally included with the programs and literature supplied to me by IBM. A call to their Technical Department was most productive, and I was given the programs orally over the telephone. When using the IBM

```
10 KEY OFF:CLS
20 WIDTH 80:DEF SEG=0:A=PEEK(&H410): POKE &H410, (A AND &HCF) OR &H20
30 WIDTH 40: SCREEN 1: SCREEN 0: LOCATE ,,1,6,7
40 KEY ON
```

Fig. 10-6. To switch to the color/graphics monitor, this program is used.

```
10 KEY OFF: CLS
20 WIDTH 40: DEF SEG=0: A=PEEK(&H410): POKE &H410,A OR &H30
30 WIDTH 80: LOCATE ,,1,12,13
40 KEY ON
```

Fig. 10-7. In order to return to the monochrome display, this program is run.

DOS and both adapters and monitors, the System Unit will automatically default to the IBM Monochrome Display. To switch to the Color/Graphics Monitor, use the program shown in Fig. 10-6. When this is run, the IBM Monochrome Display will be deactivated and output is automatically fed to the television modulator.

To go back to the monochrome display again, another program is required, shown in Fig. 10-7. Both monitors will not work simultaneously, so it will be necessary to load both in the DOS directory. This is done by getting into DOS and then going to BASIC. Enter *NEW* and then type in the first program. When you are finished, type SAVE" (name of program). This will automatically load it in the DOS file directory. Do the same for the next program, giving it a different name, of course. I called my program which switches to the graphics monitor "CGA" for color graphics adapter. The other program was named "MONO" for monochrome.

Once you have entered your programs and committed them to the directory, to switch back and forth, enter Disk BASIC, type LOAD" (name of program), and then press Enter. The program you selected will be read from the DOS disk. Then enter RUN and press the Enter key again. The monitor which is controlled by the program you have selected will automatically be activated. To switch to the other monitor, run the other program using the same input technique. You can eliminate the separate Load/Run functions by typing LOAD" (program name)", R. When you hit Enter, the program will automatically be loaded and run without further keyboard input.

Using these programs, I found the switch from one adapter to the other to be quite convenient and accomplished in a a few seconds. I prefer to use the monochrome display for all entries in text mode and the color graphics display for graphics work only, although the latter monitor may be used for text mode as well. Unfortunately, there is not enough space available on the System Unit top to properly mount both the IBM Monochrome Display and a television receiver. The top of the Monochrome Display is slightly slanted and since this unit contains a plastic enclosure, I do not recommend setting anything in this location. It may be necessary for you to provide space on your operating table for the television monitor or to install a small wall-mounted shelf close to the System Unit and Monochrome Display. During some of my operations, I used a large screen console color television receiver. The screen was so large that the set could be seen easily from across the room.

Chapter 11

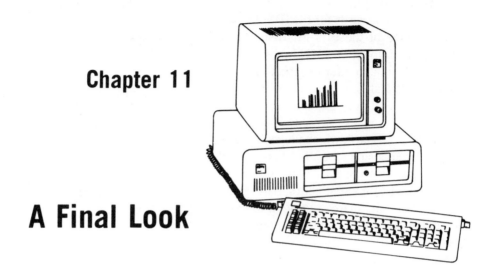

A Final Look

When I first began writing this book, there was a very evident lack of software and accessories available for the IBM Personal Computer, both from IBM and other companies who market products for microcomputers. However, more and more companies are now writing programs specifically for the IBM Personal Computer. Many of the programs are not new, but they have been rewritten in IBM BASIC. Additionally, many companies now offer accessories and replacement adapter cards for the IBM Personal Computer.

IBM-COMPATIBLE
SOFTWARE AND PERIPHERALS

Each month, something new is on the market. For example, Phase One Systems in Oakland, California, recently announced a multi-user operating system for the IBM Personal Computer. It will handle up to 32 users and provides for optional passwords and shared, private, and public files. In talking with Dick Wrenn, Director of Sales for Phase One Systems, I found that he was quite excited about the potential this operation system offers to business users. It seems that if the operator was not aware that he or she was using a microcomputer, they would tend to think there was a mainframe system processing the data.

At the present time, this operating system costs approximately $1,500 and requires 128K RAM, a monochrome display adapter, and a 5¼-inch floppy disk adapter with two drives, in addition to a 5M Winchester hard disk drive. More information can be obtained by contacting Phase One Systems, 7700 Edgewater Drive, Suite 830, Oakland, California, 94621; (415) 562-8085.

In the area of hardware, Corona Data Systems, Inc. of Westlake Village, California, offers a Winchester disk system for the IBM Personal Computer that actually fits inside the

System Unit in one of the slots originally allocated for a disk drive. The 5MB system retails for about $2,000, and 10MB version costs approximately $2,500.

Several companies now manufacture memory expansion cards for the IBM Personal Computer. One of these is Microsoft, which offers boards from 64 to 256K bytes. Another company, which also offers system expansion boards, is Apparat, Inc. in Denver, Colorado. They offer several different boards, some containing memory and some not. The Apparat Clock/Calendar Board, which plugs into one of the system expansion slots, is a hardware device that provides the CPU with the current time in seconds, minutes, hours, date, month, and year. This eliminates the need to set the time and date every time the computer is turned on. The date and time are automatically maintained whenever the computer is turned off by a battery-operated circuit. A rechargeable ni-cad battery will supply power for the clock whenever the computer is off for up to three months. The battery is automatically recharged while the computer is on. Software is provided on a diskette that allows operation through an autoexec file when the computer is powered on. Figure 11-1 provides complete specifications for the Apparat Clock/Calendar Board.

Another popular board from this same company is the Combo Card, a multipurpose plug-in adapter board. It combines the functions of a parallel printer adapter and asynchronous communications adapter. The connections from the card to the printer are shown in Fig. 11-2; Fig. 11-3 shows the cable connections between the card and the RS-232-C modem.

Pin No.	Signal	Pin No.
1	−Strobe	1
2	+Data Bit 0	2
3	+Data Bit 1	3
4	+Data Bit 2	4
5	+Data Bit 3	5
6	+Data Bit 4	6
7	+Data Bit 5	7
8	+Data Bit 6	8
9	+Data Bit 7	9
10	−Acknowledge	10
11	+Busy	11
12	+P. End	12
13	+Select	13
14	−Auto Feed	14
32	−Error	15
31	−Initialize Printer	16
36	−Select Input	17
*	Ground	18 - 25

Printer ... Combo Card

* 19, 21, 23, 25, 27, 29, 30, 33

Fig. 11-2. Connections for the Combo Card to a printer (courtesy Apparat, Inc.).

The IBM Personal Computer has five slots available. If you install a color graphics adapter, a disk drive controller, a memory card, a parallel printer adapter, and an asynchronous communications adapter, there is no room left for any other hardware adapters such as a Clock/Calendar. Apparat, Inc. has developed a multi-purpose card that has the capabilities of a printer adapter, an asynchronous communications adapter, and an Apparat Clock/Calendar on one board. It fits into one slot inside the computer. All of the functions of the Combo Card operate identically to the single board versions, so there is no need for special software drivers. All IBM Personal Computer software should operate without any modifications. The printer connector is pin

Size:	5.5 inches × 4 inches
	32 Contacts each side, 100″ centers,
Card Edge Connector:	Gold plated, .062″ thick
OSC. Frequency:	32.768 kHz, XTAL controlled
Board Type:	Double side, Plated through holes,
	.062 material, Solder mask, Silk screen
Warranty:	90 Days, Parts and labor
Software:	Supplied

Fig. 11-1. Specifications for the Apparat Clock/Calendar Board (courtesy Apparat, Inc.).

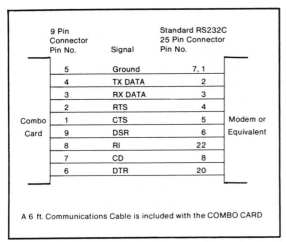

Combo Card	9 Pin Connector Pin No.	Signal	Standard RS232C 25 Pin Connector Pin No.	Modem or Equivalent
	5	Ground	7, 1	
	4	TX DATA	2	
	3	RX DATA	3	
	2	RTS	4	
	1	CTS	5	
	9	DSR	6	
	8	RI	22	
	7	CD	8	
	6	DTR	20	

A 6 ft. Communications Cable is included with the COMBO CARD

Fig. 11-3. Cable connections between the Combo Card and the RS-232-C modem (courtesy Apparat, Inc.).

compatible with IBM's printer cable. The parallel printer and asynchronous communication adapter are software compatible, thus requiring no modification to the IBM software. A diskette is provided for the Clock/Calendar that lets you patch the Personal Computer Disk Operating System to load the IBM software clock. In addition, a program is provided on the diskette to set the date and time. Figure 11-4 lists the features of the Combo Card; complete specifications are given in Fig. 11-5.

Apparat also sells add-on memory cards, monitors, RGB color monitors, and disk drives, all of which are IBM compatible. Apparat software includes game programs, finance programs, among others. One interesting hardware item is an IBM expansion prototype card, a blank card that will fit in one of the system expansion slots. It contains a 3.5-by-8-inch wirewrap area that will hold up to 85 14-pin ICs. Such a card may be used to build specialized capabilities into an IBM Personal Computer.

Corvus Systems of San Jose, California, now offers an externally located Winchester disk system for the IBM Personal Computer.

Their integrated family of 6-, 11-, and 20-megabyte disk systems lets you operate the IBM Personal Computer with the speed, convenience, and flexibility of more sophisticated systems. In effect, Corvus mass-storage peripherals transform the IBM machine into a powerful business, professional, and educational tool. You can have all records on line in a centralized file for immediate access. With the Corvus Mirror, you can also support your mass storage system with economical videotape backup. More than 6,000 of these systems are in daily use in a broad variety of applications worldwide.

Corvus mass storage systems offer the IBM Personal Computer user the established reliability of Winchester technology. The disk drive is enclosed in a sealed environment with a recirculating air system to keep dust, smoke,

Parallel Printer Adapter
Standard Centronics Parallel Printer Interface
Completely Software Compatible
Supports Two Addresses
8 Bit Bidirectional I/O Option
Uses Standard IBM Printer Cable

Asynchronous Adapter
EIA RS-232C
Programmable Baud Rate
50-9600 Baud
Even, Odd, or No Parity
Supports Both Port Addresses
Completely Software Compatible
Communications Cable Included

Clock/Calendar
Hours, Minutes, Seconds
Date, Month, Year
Rechargeable 3 Month Battery Back-up
Quartz Crystal Time Base
Uses OKI MSM5832 Clock Chip
Includes Software Diskette
Automatically Sets the IBM PC's Software Clock

Fig. 11-4. Combo Card features (courtesy Apparat, Inc.).

Size:	14 Inches × 4 Inches
Card Edge Connector:	32 Contacts Each side, .100 center., Gold Plated, .062 Thick.
Clock/Calendar Osc. Freq.:	32.768 kHz. Xtal Controlled
Baud Rate Osc. Freq.:	1.8432 MHz. Xtal Controlled
Board Type:	Double side, plated through connectors .062 material, solder mask, silk screen
Warranty:	90 days, Parts and Labor
Optional Accessories:	Printer Cable, and a variety of Modems.

Fig. 11-5. Combo Card specifications (courtesy Apparat, Inc.).

and other foreign particles from reaching the disk surface. Low-mass read/write heads dramatically improve system dependability. Because of the inherent reliability of the Corvus design, these units require no preventive maintenance.

All Corvus Disk Systems require only minimum support from the IBM Personal Computer. The microcomputer-based Corvus intelligent controller translates high-level command sequences into a form intelligible to the disk drive, manages bidirectional data transfer between disk drive and CPU interface, and performs a number of essential functions to guarantee data integrity. These functions include read-after-write verify, automatic error retries, sector buffering, transparent formatting with CRC (cylic redundancy check) error detection, and high-speed transfer using DMA (direct memory access).

Corvus provides all the software needed to use the mass-storage system with the IBM Personal Computer. You receive drivers for the IBM Disk Operating System provided by IBM, as well as a unique linkage program that attaches itself to the diskette-based IBM DOS. The driver and linkage program itself requires only 1K of memory. Total compatibility with the IBM DOS commands and utilities lets you take advantage of the fast 6 to 20 megabytes of on-line storage.

The 6 megabyte disk system configures at two drives (A and B), with 2.648 megabytes of formatted memory each. The 11 megabyte disk system also configures as two drives (A and B), with 5.096 megabytes of formatted memory each. The 20 megabyte drive configures as three drives (A,B, and E), with 6.296 megabytes of formatted memory each. The experienced user can create up to 10 separate volumes on one disk system, the largest of which can be up to 8 megabytes. In the standard configuration, all Corvus Disk Systems will appear as drives A and B, thereby allowing the purchaser to use existing programs with little or no modification.

Corvus provides several utilities for disk system diagnostics, controller code update, and operation of their Mirror storage backup system. Presently, all Corvus disk systems for the IBM Personal Computer are supplied with software and utility programs on 5¼-inch diskettes. These programs will also be made available on 8-inch diskettes, should a need develop for them in the future.

All Corvus Disk Systems come with a six month parts and labor warranty. Warranty extensions of up to 24 additional months are available at additional cost. Figure 11-6 provides complete specifications for the Corvus systems.

Tecmar, Inc. in Cleveland, Ohio, has jumped into the IBM Personal Computer scene with the Tecmar Expansion Series, advertised as the first and only complete line of expansion options for the IBM Personal Computer. Tecmar also offers a range of system expansion boards, but remember that the IBM System Unit can only hold a maximum of five. You pretty much have to assume that two of these will already be occupied by the Monochrome/Printer Card and the Disk Drive Adapter Card, so this leaves only three. If you wish to have color/graphics capability, another slot is taken by this card, and memory expansion will take a fourth. This leaves only one

Data Organization	6 MB	11 MB	20 MB
Capacity (megabytes)			
Unformatted	6.7	11.3	20.5
Formatted	5.7	10.8	19.7
Disks			
Number	2	2	3
Data Surfaces	4	3	5
Diameter	4	3	5
(inces/centimeters)	5.25/13.3	8/20.32	8/20.32

Performance	6 MB	11/20 MB
Access Times (milliseconds)		
Minimum	43	6
Maximum	240	65
Average	125	35
Latency Time		
Average (milliseconds)	6.25	8.33
Disk Rotational Speed (RPM)	4,800	3,600
Peak Transfer Rate		
(kilobytes/second)	960	648

Physical Dimensions	6 MB	11/20 MB
Height (inches/centimeters)	5.3/13.5	6.375/16.19
Width (inches/centimeters)	14.5/36.8	14.50/36.83
Depth (inches/centimeters)	15.0/38.1	23.00/58.42

Environmental Specifications

Temperature	
Operating (F/C)	50° to 120°/10° to 50°
Non-operating	−40 to 140°/−40° to 60°
Variation	18°F per hour
Humidity (non-condensing)	
Operating	10 to 80%
Non-operating	10 to 90%
Altitude, Operating	
(feet/meters)	−1,000 to 10,000/−305 to 3,050

Power Requirements

Voltage	110/120 or 220/240 volts	
	(selectable), 50/60 Hz, single	
	phase alternating current	
Consumption	6MB:	125 volt amperes
	11/20 MB:	250 volt amperes

Fig. 11-6. Corvus Winchester Disk System specifications (courtesy Corvus Systems).

remaining, and that will probably be quickly filled by Asynchronous Communications Adapter, Game Control Adapter, etc. The fact of the matter is, there are just not enough expansion slots to handle all of the many expansion cards now available.

Tecmar has solved this problem by offering a complete system expansion. This is a separate chassis. The chassis is the same size as the System Unit and contains its own power supply, plus six additional system expansion slots. The extra power supply is necessary, because the one contained within the IBM System Unit is not capable of providing power for more than five cards. Since one expansion slot will be taken up by connecting the new chassis, you will have a total of ten expansion slots with the combination. Tecmar offers memory expansion cards, disk expansion, and several different interfaces. They continue to look for new needs to meet and are inviting input from customers and owners of the IBM Personal Computer regarding their needs in hopes of being able to offer new expansion products.

One drawback to the IBM Personal Computer system lies in the fact that no high-resolution graphics can be handled by the Monochrome Display. It is necessary to purchase a color/graphics adapter card, which will supply a composite video output or a direct-drive RGB output for direct-drive monitors. The first output is designed to be connected to a video modulator to drive a standard television receiver. The latter, however, feeds a direct-drive monitor; and at present, IBM does not offer such a product. Amdek in Arlington Heights, Illinois, offers several IBM compatible monitors. Several other companies offer direct-drive monitors as well and supply the appropriate cables for interfacing their units with IBM Personal Computers.

It may seem as though everyone has suddenly jumped into the IBM accessory market. This is true in a way, but it's not as startling as it might seem. IBM has released their Personal Computer at a time when the interest in microcomputers has never been greater. We are fast approaching the time when microcomputer ownership will be the rule rather than the exception. Many of the companies offering IBM-compatible accessories have previously offered accessories for other types of popular microcomputers. In many instances, gearing up to handle a new computer, such as the IBM machine, is simply a matter of building the proper interface cables. True, several companies seem to be concentrating solely on IBM, but many others have simply expanded the products they already sell to include the IBM line. The new products offered every month are often overwhelming in numbers, so only a sampling has been discussed here. By the time this book is released, undoubtedly, the selection in the IBM accessory market will at least have doubled.

It has been rumored that sales of the IBM Personal Computer in 1981 and 1982 were far and above even the most optimistic imaginings of the IBM sales force, and that IBM is gearing up to sell one million Personal Computers in 1983. To check out the true popularity of the IBM Personal Computer, I talked with Art Sherman of Frederick Computer Products in Frederick, Maryland. His store carries a very large line of microcomputers and accessories, including the IBM machine. Mr. Sherman stated that the IBM Personal Computer was fast becoming the biggest seller and that the machine was being purchased by many people who had never owned a microcomputer before. In looking through his stock room, I noted a veritable mountain of IBM Personal Computers and accessories neatly boxed and stored from floor to ceiling.

The marketing of an IBM product by a company that is not owned or officially a part of IBM is quite unusual. While you will find IBM Personal Computers at ComputerLand and a few other national outlets, you will not find a great deal of single-location businesses that offer this machine. IBM standards are quite rigid, and many computer outlets simply cannot meet them. Frederick Computer Products offers in-store service of all machines they sell, and service personnel took part in a spe-

cial IBM service seminar for dealers.

The first IBM Personal Computer system I had in my possession was on loan from IBM in Boca Raton, Florida. When this one was returned, I purchased my own system from Frederick Computer Products. Before I was allowed to take delivery, the entire system was set up in my presence and thoroughly checked using an expanded Diagnostic Diskette, which does everything the standard Diagnostic Aids diskette does, plus it checks diskette drive motor speed and several other parameters. This is a service that is not provided by some computer outlets, which sell you a box of equipment and little else. This, of course, is unacceptable and not found in most IBM outlets.

One of the most popular accessories for my machine is a speech synthesizer which is manufactured by Votrax Division of Federal Screw Works in Troy, Michigan. Named the Votrax Type-'N-Talk, this diminutive "voice box" is relatively inexpensive and interfaces directly with the IBM Asynchronous Communications Adapter. Shown in Fig. 11-7, the Votrax synthesizer is a text-to-speech device. This means it will say just about anything you type into the computer . . . and it says it with surprising clarity. Long gone are the days

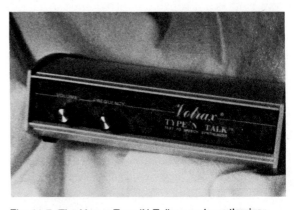

Fig. 11-7. The Votrax Type-'N-Talk speech synthesizer.

when each individual word was arrived at after long hours of programming. When you type in "hello," the synthesizer's speaker says "hello." True, you sometimes have to spell words phonetically, but one quickly picks up on this. For example, if you input the word "computer," the synthesizer will say "compooter." However, if you input "compeuter" or "comp uter," the synthesizer pronounces it just like you and I pronounce it. It is amazing to discover the number of long-time microcomputer users who have never operated their machines with the aid of a voice synthesizer. Most have seen or heard them on television, but few have experienced their use first-hand. Such a device is bound to attract attention from this group, as well as from another group made up of died-in-the-wool anti-computerists. Outputting data from its Asynchronous Communications Adapter at a rate of 9600 baud, the IBM Personal Computer interfaces very nicely with the Votrax Synthesizer, and Votrax supplies the interconnecting cable.

PERSONAL REFLECTIONS

Throughout this book, I have tried to insert any impressions I have experienced while becoming familiar with this new machine. Since IBM considers the first-time computer buyer to be a prime target for their new machine, I feel that it is necessary to include discussions especially for him or her.

Let's assume that you plan to purchase or have purchased an IBM Personal Computer and know little or nothing about computers, or for that matter, how to actually operate a computer. I think you will find the *IBM Guide to Operations* quite helpful, along with the *IBM BASIC* book. The latter is more useful as a reference tool than as a guide to learning BASIC. The book is an education in IBM BASIC, which differs from other dialects of this same language, but a person who knows nothing about BASIC would do well to enlist the aid of a more experienced computer hobbyist in order to attain a level of knowledge which will allow the complete usage of this very powerful BASIC dialect.

One of the best methods of learning BASIC, in my opinion, is to start out with an extremely simple program of ten or twenty lines or less. You can find these in many different computer books and magazines. Stay away from graphics during this stage of the training process, because IBM BASIC is quite different from all of the other dialects when operating in this mode.

Input the simple program via the keyboard and make sure it is operational. Then, use the IBM BASIC manual to try and understand what each line does, using the program run on the monitor screen as a guide. Some of the simple programs presented in an earlier chapter of this book may aid you here.

When your program is operational and you begin to understand just what has taken place, you can begin to modify and note the results. Let's take the following program as an example.

```
10 FOR X = 1 TO 10
20 PRINT X
30 NEXT
```

This program demonstrates a program loop that is established by FOR . . . NEXT statements. The first line sets the range of values for the variable X. The next line tells the computer to display the value of X on the screen. The final line simply returns the program to line 10, so the loop repeats itself. The screen printout from this program will be:

1
2
3
4

```
5
6
7
8
9
10
```

If you omit line 20, you would see no results on the screen or elsewhere, but the computer would still count from 1 to 10.

Now, refer to the IBM BASIC manual. You will find a complete explanation of the FOR and NEXT statements, although this program demonstrates their functions quite clearly. You might next move on to an explanation of the PRINT statement. In this discussion, you will find that if you follow the X in line 20 by a semicolon, as in:

```
20      PRINT X;
```

the screen will display:

```
1   2   3   4   5   6   7   8   9   10
```

In the first screen printout, the numbers were listed vertically, but the addition of the semicolon at the end of line 20 causes a horizontal printout. This single fact will aid you in many types of future programming. If you had simply used the manual alone, this point may not have made itself immediately known. However, when you read the manual to explain the operation of a working program, the knowledge comes much faster.

Learning to program a computer for the first time is overwhelming to many. After a day or so, one begins to expand on the knowledge that has already been garnered, and there is a rapid ascent to a moderate level of proficiency. The trick here is to avoid becoming discouraged, or from a more practical standpoint, to quit programming for a while when you be-

come discouraged. Discouragement generally leads to making the same mistake or acting upon an incorrect assumption again and again. For example, recently I was writing a fairly elaborate program on my IBM machine. I reached a point where I simply couldn't come up with the right combination to perform a certain function. I worked on the problem for five hours straight and got absolutely nowhere. In disgust, I shut the machine down and retreated to my den, vowing to give up computers forever. To say I was discouraged was a blatant understatement. I rested on my couch for no more than five minutes, and as soon as I had relaxed a little, the answer to my problem popped into my head. I immediately reactivated the computer and input four program lines, which solved the problem and allowed me to continue. Add to this the fact that the needed lines were extremely simple, and you can see just what discouragement does to anyone at any level of programming proficiency.

Undoubtedly, first-time computer owners will want to jump right in and try to do everything at once. This is one of the joys of owning a microcomputer, but this is seldom accomplished, especially by the rank beginner. At this stage, you are learning a new language, and this experience can be compared to learning French, Spanish, or some other foreign language. Fortunately, BASIC is English-oriented so you can pick up on it in a very short period of time, but you still have to learn it.

If you remember that the computer is a mathematical device and that mathematics in itself is a language, the learning process will not be as difficult. Anything in the physical universe can be described mathematically, although the language we call mathematics may have to be added to in order to describe newly found conditions. In most instances, the computer draws a picture, prints something on the screen, or performs other operations based upon a mathematical formula. This may be contained within the on-board memory or input via the keyboard. For example, let's assume that an automobile is traveling to a distant city 100 miles away. Assume also that the average speed of the automobile is 50 mph. How long will it take the automobile to reach its destination? You can do this one in your head, and the answer would be two hours. Ths answer was figured by means of a mathematical formula, but that formula has already been committed to the on-board memory in our brain, and we don't even think about the mathematics involved. Written on a computer line, the formula might read:

$$T = D/S$$

where, T is travel time, D is distance, and S is speed. If you inserted this formula into a program line, allowing the values of D and S to be input via the keyboard, the next line might read:

PRINT T

Upon receiving the values of D and S, the computer would automatically divide the former by the latter and print the value of T, which would be two hours, in this example.

You can figure out this simple problem in your head, but let's assume that the city is 122.5 miles away and that the average speed is 43.68 miles per hour. Most of us anyway cannot quickly insert these values and come up with an answer, even though we have retained the formula in our heads. We know we have to divide the distance by the speed, but the numbers are just too complicated. Once armed with the formula, the computer, however, does not make a distinction between numbers to seven decimal places and even whole numbers. To the computer, a number is a number, and all it

needs is a formula to figure out what to do with the input information. Using the same program as before, the screen would instantly display the answer, which is 2.8044871 hours. The computer doesn't have us beat in thinking power . . . only in speed.

Like most people who hold the name IBM in awe, I expected any computer manufactured by this company to be nothing short of excellent. I was certainly not disappointed. I found the system to be extremely easy to operate and the advanced features to be quite helpful in speeding up programming time. The Alternate key feature allows whole commands or statements to be input when two keys are simultaneously pressed. It takes a bit of practice to get away from typing in whole words, such as PRINT, for example, when the same word may be input by simply pressing ALT plus P. The editing function available with IBM DOS lets you to quickly make corrections to lines without having to retype them completely. This and other advanced features quickly become almost automatic. One tends to become almost oblivious to the convenience and speed these offer until one tries the same thing on another computer that does not offer these advantages.

One major problem at present is the lack of software and programming books written specifically for the IBM Personal Computer. As has been previously pointed out, many of the text-mode programs written for other computers can be input without modification to the IBM Personal Computer and will run very well. Others, however, will require complete revamping. Remember, however, that these other machines have been around for many years as compared with the IBM Personal Computer, which is still in its infancy. The same lack was experienced by early owners of other machines which have now reached a high level of popularity. As popularity increases, so does available software.

I do not believe the software scarcity is any reason to put off purchasing an IBM Personal Computer, if that is the machine you would most like to have. The IBM machine is probably the most talked about microcomputer on today's market, and its popularity is soaring. Companies that sell software and publishers who market programming books are jumping on the bandwagon. The present lack of software is simply due to the fact that this computer's popularity has soared more rapidly than these companies can produce the needed programs. This situation will be quickly corrected.

More than any other machine, I have had fun with my IBM Personal Computer. I have used it for serious business programming and have also written a large number of game and entertainment programs for personal and family use.

Appendix

Appendix

ASCII CHARACTER CODES*

ASCII Value	Character	ASCII Value	Character	ASCII Value	Character
0	(null)	32	(space)	64	@
1	☺	33	!	65	A
2	☻	34	''	66	B
3	♥	35	#	67	C
4	♦	36	$	68	D
5	♣	37	%	69	E
6	♠	38	&	70	F
7	(beep)	39	'	71	G
8	◘	40	(	72	H
9	(tab)	41	)	73	I
10	(line feed)	42	*	74	J
11	(home)	43	+	75	K
12	(form feed)	44	,	76	L
13	(carriage return)	45	-	77	M
14	♫	46	.	78	N
15	☼	47	/	79	O
16	►	48	0	80	P
17	◄	49	1	81	Q
18	↕	50	2	82	R
19	‼	51	3	83	S
20	¶	52	4	84	T
21	§	53	5	85	U
22	▬	54	6	86	V
23	↨	55	7	87	W
24	↑	56	8	88	X
25	↓	57	9	89	Y
26	→	58	:	90	Z
27	←	59	;	91	[
28	(cursor right)	60	<	92	\
29	(cursor left)	61	=	93	]
30	(cursor up)	62	>	94	∧
31	(cursor down)	63	?	95	—

*(Courtesy IBM Corp.)

ASCII Value	Character	ASCII Value	Character	ASCII Value	Character
96	`	134	å	171	½
97	a	135	ç	172	¼
98	b	136	ê	173	¡
99	c	137	ë	174	«
100	d	138	è	175	»
101	e	139	ï	176	▒
102	f	140	î	177	▒
103	g	141	ì	178	▓
104	h	142	Ä	179	│
105	i	143	Å	180	┤
106	j	144	É	181	╡
107	k	145	æ	182	╢
108	l	146	Æ	183	╖
109	m	147	ô	184	╕
110	n	148	ö	185	╣
111	o	149	ò	186	║
112	p	150	û	187	╗
113	q	151	ù	188	╝
114	r	152	ÿ	189	╜
115	s	153	Ö	190	╛
116	t	154	Ü	191	┐
117	u	155	¢	192	└
118	v	156	£	193	┴
119	w	157	¥	194	┬
120	x	158	Pt	195	├
121	y	159	ƒ	196	─
122	z	160	á	197	┼
123	{	161	í	198	╞
124	|	162	ó	199	╟
125	}	163	ú	200	╚
126	~	164	ñ	201	╔
128	Ç	165	Ñ	202	╩
129	ü	166	ª	203	╦
130	é	167	º	204	╠
131	â	168	¿	205	═
132	ä	169	⌐	206	╬
133	à	170	¬	207	╧

ASCII Value	Character	ASCII Value	Character	ASCII Value	Character
208	⊥	224	α	240	≡
209	∓	225	β	241	±
210	┬	226	Γ	242	≥
211	╙	227	π	243	≤
212	╘	228	Σ	244	⌠
213	╒	229	σ	245	⌡
214	╓	230	μ	246	÷
215	╫	231	τ	247	≈
216	╪	232	Φ	248	°
217	┘	233	Θ	249	•
218	┌	234	Ω	250	·
219	█	235	δ	251	√
220	▄	236	∞	252	ⁿ
221	▌	237	$\varnothing$	253	²
222	▐	238	ϵ	254	■
223	▀	239	∩	255	'blank

UNIT SPECIFICATIONS*

System Unit

Size: Width—20″, Depth—16″, Height—5.5″
Weight: Without diskette drive—21 lbs.
          With one drive—25 lbs.
          With two drives—28 lbs.
Electrical: 120 volts ac
Cycle Time: Main storage—410 nanoseconds
              Access—250 nanoseconds
Memory: 40K built-in read only memory (ROM)
          16K to 256K user memory
Standard:
    Keyboard for data and text entry
    Cassette player jack for cassette attachment
    Five expansion slots for additional memory and display, printer, communications and game adapters
    Built-in speaker for musical programming
    Power-on automatic self-test of system components
    BASIC language interpreter, 16K memory

Keyboard

    Size: Width—20″, Depth—8″, Height—2″
    Weight: 6 lbs.
    Keys: 83 full-function for data and text entry: includes 10 for numeric entry and cursor control and
            10 special function for scrolling, editing, etc.
            Easy access to 256 characters (ASCII and Special)
    Keyboard: Adjustable typing angle
                Detached from system unit and connected by six-foot cable for flexibility
                All keys automatically repeat

Matrix Printer

    Size: Width—16″, Depth—15″, Height—4″
    Weight: 12.5 lbs.
    Features:
        80 characters-per-second printing
        Continuous feed, multi-part paper
        Self-diagnostic checks to assure proper operation
        12 type styles to suit various printing needs
        Page spacing and column skip for word processing
        Bi-directional printing for increased speed
        40, 66, 80 or 132 characters-per-line formats
        Out-of-paper, alarm
        Replaceable ribbon cartridge and print head

Monochrome Display

    Size: Width—15″, Depth—14″, Height—11″
    Weight: 17 lbs.
    Display Functions:
        25 lines of 80 characters on 11½″ screen
        Underlining, high intensity blinking characters and reverse image for highlighting information
        Non-display for security data
        Upper and lower case display for word processing
        Brightness and contrast controls for reading comfort

*(Courtesy IBM Corp.)

IBM KEYWORDS

A keyword may be typed by pressing a single letter key simultaneously with the ALT key. Each letter (when in the alternate mode) will cause the keyboard to input an entire command, thus cutting down on input time.

AUTO	A		MOTOR	M
BSAVE	B		NEXT	N
COLOR	C		OPEN	O
DELETE	D		PRINT	P
ELSE	E		RUN	R
FOR	F		SCREEN	S
GOTO	G		THEN	T
HEX$	H		USING	U
INPUT	I		VAL	V
KEY	K		WIDTH	W
LOCATE	L		XOR	X

Note: The letters J, Q, Y, and Z have no function in the alternate mode.

NONINTRINSIC MATHEMATICAL FUNCTIONS

The IBM Personal Computer is a powerful mathematical tool. However, IBM BASIC may not offer certain functions in direct form. The following list explains the method of programming by which these nonintrinsic functions may be arrived at.

Function		
Cosecant	SEC(A)	= 1/COS(A)
Cotangent	CSC(A)	= 1/SIN(A)
Hyperbolic cosine	COSH(A)	= (EXP(A)+EXP(−A))/2
Hyperbolic Cosecant	CSCH(A)	= 2/(EXP(A)+EXP(−A))
Hyperbolic cotangent	COTH(A)	= (EXP(A)+EXP(−A)
Hyperbolic secant	SECH(A)	= 2/EXP(A)=EXP(−A))
Hyperbolic tangent	TANH(A)	= (EXP(A)−EXP(−A))
Inverse cosine	ARCCOS(A)	= 1.570796 − ATN(A/SQR(1−A*A))
Inverse cosecant	ARCCSC(A)	= ATN(1/SQR(A*A−1)) + (A<0)*3.141593
Inverse cotangent	ARCCOT(A)	= 1.57096−ATN(A)
Inverse hyperbolic cosecant	ARCCSCH(A)	= LOG((1+SGN(A)*SQR(1+A*A))/A)
Inverse hyperbolic cosine	ARCCOSH(A)	= LOG(A+SQR(A*A−1))
Inverse hyperbolic cotangent	ARCCOTH(A)	= LOG((A+1)/(A−1))/2
Inverse hyperbolic secant	ARCSECH(A)	= LOG((1+SQR(1−A*A))/A)
Inverse hyperbolic sine	ARCSINH(A)	= LOG(A+SQR(A*A+1))
Inverse hyperbolic tangent	ARCTANH(A)	= LOG((1+A)/(1−A))/2
Inverse secant	ARCSEC(A)	= ATN(SQR(A*A−1))+(A<0)*3.141593
Inverse sine	ARCSIN(A)	= ATN(A/SQR(1−1*A))
Secant	SEC(A)	= 1/COS(A)

NUMERIC BASE EQUIVALENTS

Decimal	Binary	Hexadecimal	Octal
0	00000000	00	000
1	00000001	01	001
2	00000010	02	002
3	00000011	03	003
4	00000100	04	004
5	00000101	05	005
6	00000110	06	006
7	00000111	07	007
8	00001000	08	010
9	00001001	09	011
10	00001010	0A	012
11	00001011	0B	013
12	00001100	0C	014
13	00001101	0D	015
14	00001110	0E	016
15	00001111	0F	017
16	00010000	10	020
17	00010001	11	021
18	00010010	12	022
19	00010011	13	023
20	00010100	14	024
21	00010101	15	025
22	00010110	16	026
23	00010111	17	027
24	00011000	18	030
25	00011001	19	031
26	00011010	1A	032
27	00011011	1B	033
28	00011100	1C	034
29	00011101	1D	035
30	00011110	1E	036
31	00011111	1F	037
32	00100000	20	040
33	00100001	21	041
34	00100010	22	042
35	00100011	23	043
36	00100100	24	044
37	00100101	25	045
38	00100110	26	046
39	00100111	27	047
40	00101000	28	050

Decimal	Binary	Hexadecimal	Octal
41	00101001	29	051
42	00101010	2A	052
43	00101011	2B	053
44	00101100	2C	054
45	00101101	2D	055
46	00101110	2E	056
47	00101111	2F	057
48	00110000	30	060
49	00110001	31	061
50	00110010	32	062
51	00110011	33	063
52	00110100	34	064
53	00110101	35	065
54	00110110	36	066
55	00110111	37	067
56	00111000	38	070
57	00111001	39	071
58	00111010	3A	072
59	00111011	3B	073
60	00111100	3C	074
61	00111101	3D	075
62	00111110	3E	076
63	00111111	3F	077
64	01000000	40	100
65	01000001	41	101
66	01000010	42	102
67	01000011	43	103
68	01000100	44	104
69	01000101	45	105
70	01000110	46	106
71	01000111	47	107
72	01001000	48	110
73	01001001	49	111
74	01001010	4A	112
75	01001011	4B	113
76	01001100	4C	114
77	01001101	4D	115
78	01001110	4E	116
79	01001111	4F	117
80	01010000	50	120
81	01010001	51	121
82	01010010	52	122

Decimal	Binary	Hexadecimal	Octal
83	01010011	53	123
84	01010100	54	124
85	01010101	55	125
86	01010110	56	126
87	01010111	57	127
88	01011000	58	130
89	01011001	59	131
90	01011010	5A	132
91	01011011	5B	133
92	01011100	5C	134
93	01011101	5D	135
94	01011110	5E	136
95	01011111	5F	137
96	01100000	60	140
97	01100001	61	141
98	01100010	62	142
99	01100011	63	143
100	01100100	64	144
101	01100101	65	145
102	01100110	66	146
103	01100111	67	147
104	**01101000**	**68**	**150**
105	01101001	69	151
106	01101010	6A	152
107	01101011	6B	153
108	01101100	6C	154
109	01101101	6D	155
110	01101110	6E	156
111	01101111	6F	157
112	01110000	70	160
113	01110001	71	161
114	01110010	72	162
115	01110011	73	163
116	01110100	74	164
117	01110101	75	165
118	01110110	76	166
119	01110111	77	167
120	01111000	78	170
121	01111001	79	171
122	01111010	7A	172
123	01111011	7B	173
124	01111100	7C	174
125	01111101	7D	175

Decimal	Binary	Hexadecimal	Octal
126	01111110	7E	176
127	01111111	7F	177
128	10000000	80	200
129	10000001	81	201
130	10000010	82	202
131	10000011	83	203
132	10000100	84	204
133	10000101	85	205
134	10000110	86	206
135	10000111	87	207
136	10001000	88	210
137	10001001	89	211
138	10001010	8A	212
139	10001011	8B	213
140	10001100	8C	214
141	10001101	8D	215
142	10001110	8E	216
143	10001111	8F	217
144	10010000	90	220
145	10010001	91	221
146	10010010	92	222
147	10010011	93	223
148	10010100	94	224
149	10010101	95	225
150	10010110	96	226
151	10010111	97	227
152	10011000	98	230
153	10011001	99	231
154	10011010	9A	232
155	10011011	9B	233
156	10011100	9C	234
157	10011101	9D	235
158	10011110	9E	236
159	10011111	9F	237
160	10100000	A0	240
161	10100001	A1	241
162	10100010	A2	242
163	10100011	A3	243
164	10100100	A4	244
165	10100101	A5	245
166	10100110	A6	246
167	10100111	A7	247
168	10101000	A8	250

Decimal	Binary	Hexadecimal	Octal
169	10101001	A9	251
170	10101010	AA	252
171	10101011	AB	253
172	10101100	AC	254
173	10101101	AD	255
174	10101110	AE	256
175	10101111	AF	257
176	10110000	BO	260
177	10110001	B1	261
178	10110010	B2	262
179	10110011	B3	263
180	10110100	B4	264
181	10110101	B5	265
182	10110110	B6	266
183	10110111	B7	267
184	10111000	B8	270
185	10111001	B9	271
186	10111010	BA	272
187	10111011	BB	273
188	10111100	BC	274
189	10111101	BD	275
190	10111110	BE	276
191	10111111	BF	277
192	11000000	C0	300
193	11000001	C1	301
194	11000010	C2	302
195	11000011	C3	303
196	11000100	C4	304
197	11000101	C5	305
198	11000110	C6	306
199	11000111	C7	307
200	11001000	C8	310
201	11001001	C9	311
202	11001010	CA	312
203	11001011	CB	313
204	11001100	CC	314
205	11001101	CD	315
206	11001110	CE	316
207	11001111	CF	317
208	11010000	D0	320
209	11010001	D1	321
210	11010010	D2	322
211	11010011	D3	323

Decimal	Binary	Hexadecimal	Octal
212	11010100	D4	324
213	11010101	D5	325
214	11010110	D6	326
215	11010111	D7	327
216	11011000	D8	330
217	11011001	D9	331
218	11011010	DA	332
219	11011011	DB	333
220	11011100	DC	334
221	11011101	DD	335
222	11011110	DE	336
223	11011111	DF	337
224	11100000	EO	340
225	11100001	E1	341
226	11100010	E2	342
227	**11100011**	**E3**	**343**
228	11100100	E4	344
229	11100101	E5	345
230	11100110	E6	346
231	11100111	E7	347
232	11101000	E8	350
233	11101001	E9	351
234	11101010	EA	352
235	11101011	EB	353
236	11101100	EC	354
237	11101101	ED	355
238	11101110	EE	356
239	11101111	EF	357
240	11110000	F0	360
241	11110001	F1	361
242	11110010	F2	362
243	11110011	F3	363
244	11110100	F4	364
245	11110101	F5	365
246	11110110	F6	366
247	11110111	F7	367
248	11111000	F8	370
249	11111001	F9	371
250	11111010	FA	372
251	11111011	FB	373
252	11111100	FC	374
253	11111101	FD	375
254	11111110	FE	376
255	11111111	FF	377

IBM PERSONAL COMPUTER
STANDARD CONFIGURATIONS*

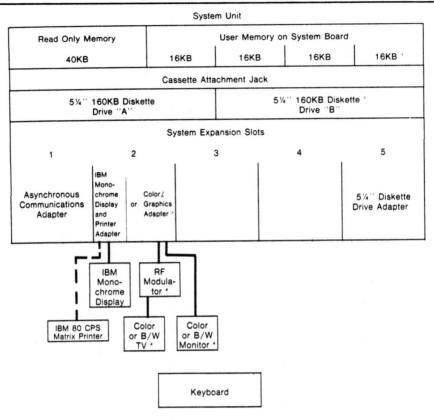

System Unit				
Read Only Memory	User Memory on System Board			
40KB	16KB	16KB	16KB	16KB '
Cassette Attachment Jack				
5¼'' 160KB Diskette Drive ''A''		5¼'' 160KB Diskette ' Drive ''B''		

System Expansion Slots

1 — Asynchronous Communications Adapter

IBM Monochrome Display and Printer Adapter

2 — Color/ Graphics Adapter ³ or

5 — 5¼'' Diskette Drive Adapter

IBM Monochrome Display

RF Modulator ⁴

IBM 80 CPS Matrix Printer

Color or B/W TV ⁴

Color or B/W Monitor ⁴

Keyboard

System Unit options not included in the above System Unit are shown below. Each requires one System Expansion Slot, except the 16KB Memory Expansion Kit which is installed on the System Board.

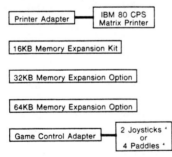

Printer Adapter — IBM 80 CPS Matrix Printer

16KB Memory Expansion Kit

32KB Memory Expansion Option

64KB Memory Expansion Option

Game Control Adapter — 2 Joysticks ⁴ or 4 Paddles ⁴

Notes:

¹ Included in Standard System Unit Configuration 2.

² Recommended for installation in the second from the left (as viewed from the front of the machine) System Expansion Slot since guides are provided to aid the installation.

³ Recommended for installation in the right hand (as viewed from the front of the machine) System Expansion Slot to minimize the distance from the adapter to the diskette drive.

⁴ Customer-supplied.

*(Courtesy IBM Corp.)

Glossary

access time—The interval between the application of an input pulse and the availability of data signals at the output is known as access time. In the IBM Personal Computer, access time is 250 nanoseconds.

Advanced Disk BASIC—Advanced Disk BASIC is the most extensive form of BASIC available on the IBM Personal Computer. Like Disk BASIC, it is a program on the DOS disk which must be loaded into memory for use. Advanced BASIC requires a disk-based machine with at least 48K of random access of memory.

algorithm—An algorithm is a precisely defined set of rules or a standard procedure which provides the solution to a problem in a finite number of steps.

alphanumeric—Alphanumeric describes characters that include the letters of the alphabet, numerals and symbols used for punctuation and mathematical operations.

alphanumeric mode—In the Personal Computer, the alphanumeric mode of operation is one which takes place in the Color/Graphics Monitor Adapter and the monochrome display adapter in which every display character position is defined by two bytes. Both adapters use the two-byte character/attribute format.

array—An array is a group or table of values referenced by the same name in BASIC. Each individual value in the array is called an element. Array elements are variables and can be used in expressions and in any BASIC statement or function which uses variables.

ASCII—ASCII is an abbreviation for American Standard Code for Information Interchange, an eight-level code (seven bits plus parity check). It is widely used for information interchange in data processing systems, communication systems, and associated equipment.

ASCII control codes—ASCII control codes are various types of computer inputs handled via the keyboard which are recognized by the printer and perform specified functions when they are received. For example, when the carriage return button is pressed on the keyboard, a CR code is transmitted to the print buffer. All data stored in the print buffer is then printed in hard copy form. The Personal Computer uses 16 different ASCII control codes, which include line feed (LF), vertical tab (VT), form feed (FF), etc.

assigned statement—An assigned statement is a line in a computer program that assigns a value of an expression to a variable. This can be done in one of two ways when programming in Personal Computer BASIC. The LET statement may be used, as in: 10 LET A=15. Alternately, the LET statement may be omitted and the equal sign (=) used, as in A=15. In both methods of programming, A is assigned the value of 15. This will hold true throughout the program.

asynchronous—Asynchronous is a mode of computer operation in which performance of the next command is started by a signal indicating that the previous command has been completed.

asynchronous communications adapter—In the IBM Personal Computer, the asynchronous communications adapter is a circuit board that plugs into the System Expansion Slot. It allows the computer to communicate with other terminals via phone lines, shortwave radio and other telecommunications modes, provided that the proper modem has been installed between the output of the computer and the input of the communications line. This adapter is programmable and supports asynchronous communications only. A programmable data rate generator allows operation over a range of 50 to 9600 baud.

backup disk—A backup disk contains information copied from another disk. It is used in case the original information is unintentionally altered or destroyed. When using the Personal Computer, a backup disk must first be formatted by using the FORMAT command. It is then ready to copy the information contained on the original disk by typing in the command DISKCOPY.

BASIC—BASIC is a programming language that is used to write programs or sets of instructions to tell the computer what to do. A BASIC program consists of one or more BASIC statements that are preceded by line numbers. These numbers are used by BASIC to control the sequence in which the statements are run.

batch processing—Batch processing is a method of processing in which a number of items are grouped for processing during the same machine run. Batch processing systems usually do not require immediate updating of files, as data is gathered up to a specific cutoff time and then processed.

baud—A baud is a unit of signalling speed. This term is quite often used when discussing communications transmit speed when microcomputers are involved. The IBM Personal Computer is capable of communicating at a rate of 50 baud on the low side to 9600 baud maximum. A baud is equal to the number of discrete conditions or signal events which occur during a one-second period.

bidirectional data bus—In the IBM Personal Computer, the bidirectional data bus accepts both input and output data signals on a single line.

bit—The term bit is an abbreviation for binary digit. This is an information unit which is equal to one binary decision or the designation of one or two possible values. These values may be referred to as high/low, 1/0, yes/no, off/on, etc. when dealing with digital processing.

Boolean algebra—Boolean algebra is a deductive system or process of reasoning named after George Boole, an English mathematician. It is a system of theorems which uses symbolic logic to denote classes of elements, true or false propositions, and on-off logic circuit elements. Symbols are used to represent operators such as AND, OR, NOT, EXCEPT, IF-THEN, etc. This system is now recognized as an effective method of handling single-valued functions with two possible output states. When Boolean algebra is applied to binary arithmetic, the two states become 0 and 1. When applied to switching theory, the two states become open and closed.

booting—Booting is a process of loading those segments of the IBM Disk Operating System (DOS) which will allow the system to operate.

bootstrap loader—A bootstrap loader is a routine that is input when there is no loader presently contained in system memory. It enables the entrance of data into the random access memory. The IBM Personal Computer contains its disk bootstrap loader on the system board. This will automatically locate the top of memory and then advance to that point. This allows program running from the top or 0 memory location.

buffer—A buffer is a device or unit that serves as an isolator or interface between two dissimilar elements. It is used to match impedances, speeds, or other characteristics while maintaining isolation between matched elements. As a register, the storage buffer would serve as an intermediary storage point between two registers or data handling systems with different access times or data formats.

bus—In its simplest form, a bus is a single conductor through which information is transmitted. In most digital computer applications, a bus will contain two or more conductors.

byte—Space on a disk and in a computer's memory is measured in bytes. One byte can hold one character; thus, the 5¼" disks used with the IBM Personal Computer can hold about 160,000 bytes, or 160,000 characters.

card—In IBM Personal Computer terminology, a card is a printed circuit board containing electronic components that form entire complex circuits. Each card is fitted with an edge connector to allow it to be simply plugged in place at a mating receptacle on the system board. The IBM Personal Computer uses printed circuit cards to expand machine capabilities. A 32K and 64K memory card is available, along with other cards which contain circuitry for an asynchronous communications adapter, Color/Graphics Monitor Adapter, disk drive adapter, monochrome monitor adapter, etc.

Cassette BASIC—Cassette BASIC is the nucleus of BASIC in the IBM Personal Computer. It is built into the machine in 32K of read-only storage. Information is saved in Cassette BASIC on a cassette tape recorder.

cassette storage—Cassette storage is a system for reading information from a previously programmed cassette tape and/or the ability to write information onto same.

cathode ray tube—A cathode-ray tube (CRT) is a device which contains electrodes surrounded by a glass sphere/cylinder and which will display information by creating a beam of electrons that strike the inside of the display surface. In the IBM Personal Computer, the monochrome adapter uses a cathode-ray tube with a P39 phosphor, which emits a yellow-green image.

central processor—The section of a computer that controls the interpretation and execution of instructions is the control processor. It is divided into three main sections:

1. Arithmetic and control, which performs the calculations, information routing, and control operations for the other sections.

2. Input and output, which handles information going into and out of the central processor while controlling all peripheral equipment.

3. Memory, which provides the temporary storage for data and instructions.

The memory cycle time usually determines the overall speed of the central processor.

character—A character corresponds to a key on a typewriter, usually including the decimal, digits 0 through 9, the letters A through Z, punctuation marks, operation symbols, and any other symbols that a computer may read, store, or write.

character set—A character set is an agreed set of representations, called characters, from which selections are made to denote and distinguish data. Each character differs from all others, and the total number of characters in a given set is fixed; e.g., a set may include the numerals 0 to 9, the letters A to Z, punctuation marks, and a blank or space.

chip—In its most basic form, a chip is a thin slab of silicon material. Solidstate devices use a single chip to produce highly complex circuits, all contained on the chip surface. More common terminology lets chip be used to describe integrated circuits.

code—A code is a system of symbols for representing data or instructions in a computer or tabulating machine. Code also means to translate the program for the solution of a problem on a given computer into a sequence of machine-language instructions or pseudo-instructions and addresses acceptable to that computer.

collate—An operation in which two or more ordered sets of data or cards are merged in order to produce one or more ordered sets which still reflect the original ordering relations. The collation process is the merging of two sequences of cards, each ordered on some mutual key, into a single sequence ordered on the mutual key.

color graphics monitor—A color graphics monitor is a television frequency monitor or television set capable of producing color images. IBM does not offer a color graphics monitor for their Personal Computer but has designed the Color/Graphics Monitor Adapter to interface with monitors made by other manufacturers and even color television receivers when a separate television modulator is used.

Color/Graphics Monitor Adapter—In the IBM Personal Computer, the monitor adapter is a plug-in circuit card which is designed to attach a variety of TV frequency monitors in standard television sets (with user-supplied rf modulator) for graphics and color output. This card operates in black and white or color modes and provides three video interfaces: a composite video port, a direct drive port, and connection interface for driving a user-supplied rf modulator. A light pen interface is also provided.

command—A command is an instruction that signals the machine to start, stop, or continue a specific operation. A command is not an instruction in the usual sense, but it is a portion of an instruction word which specifies the operation to be performed.

composite video—Composite video is television picture information and sync pulses combined. This is the equivalent of the output of a television camera. The IBM Personal Computer may be outfitted with a color/graphics adapter which will output computer information in composite video form. This output may be connected directly to a television monitor or to an rf modulator which will then feed a standard television receiver. The composite video output from this adapter board is rated at 1.5 V peak-to-peak.

concatenate—Concatenation is the process of linking together in a series. A concatenated data set is one formed by combining the contents of several data sets in a specific sequence.

cursor—The cursor is a small flashing hyphen which appears on the monitor screen to indicate to the user the point at which any characters or numerals input from the keyboard will be placed on the monitor.

cycle time—Cycle time is the period of time between the call for information and the delivery of data from storage. The IBM Personal Computer has a main storage cycle time of 410 nanoseconds with an access cycle time of 250 nanoseconds.

Cyclic Redundancy Check—In the IBM Personal Computer, a cyclic redundancy check (CRC) is an error detection method using redundant check bits. A cyclic redundancy generator is used to create a stream of check bits which are divided by the same polynomial as the data bits. A nonzero remainder indicates that an error has been detected.

DATA—DATA is a statement used in IBM Personal Computer BASIC. DATA statements are nonexecutable and may be placed anywhere in a program. A DATA statement may contain as many constants as will fit on a line, and any number of DATA statements may be used in a program.

data—In general, data is a graphic or textual representation of facts, concepts, numbers, letters, symbols, or instructions suitable for communication, interpretation, or processing. Data may be source data or raw data, which is then refined to suit the user by processing. Data is the basic element of information that is used to describe objects, ideas, conditions or situations.

data security—Any system which protects stored or hard copy data from being accidentally erased, damaged or falling into unauthorized hands is called data security. Since the IBM Personal Computer may be used to process sensitive or highly valuable information, simple security measures such as keeping backup copies of disks, removing disks when not in use or installing a locked disk and hard copy filing system should assure proper security.

debug—Debug is a term used to describe the detecting and removing of errors and malfunctions from a program, routine, or machine. Debugging usually involves the running and checkout of programs to detect the errors. Debugging aids are available to allow quick development of programs.

debug program—In IBM DOS, DEBUG is a program which is used to provide a controlled testing environment to monitor and control the execution of the program to be debugged. It will load, alter or display any file and execute object files. The latter are executable programs in machine language format.

default drive—In an IBM Personal Computer with more than one disk drive, the default drive is that drive where the Disk Operating System will look to find any filenames entered without a specified drive. Most often, it is indicated by the letter A followed by the symbol >. The default drive can be changed by entering the new designation letter (B) followed by a colon.

diagnostics—Diagnostics are programs used to check the operation of a computer system. The IBM Personal Computer uses a specially formulated Diagnostics Program which is contained on a prerecorded disk or cassette. When properly fed into the system, the Diagnostics Routine will allow the operator to check the entire system for any problems and to indicate in what area the problem lies. The latter is accomplished by an appropriate monitor display.

digital output register—The digital output register (DOR) is an output only register found on the disk drive adapter board. This circuit is used to control drive motors, drive selection and feature enable for up to four 5¼″ disk drives. All bits are cleared by the I/O interface reset line.

digital systems—Digital systems handle information in digital form whereby quantities and other data are assigned numerical values. Most digital systems operate on a binary number configuration using "2" as a base and the digits zero (0) and one (1) as values which are referred to as bits. Combinations of these bit values provide the code by which data can be processed through electronic circuitry.

DIP—DIP is an abbreviation for dual in-line package. This describes the case that contains a complex electronic circuit on a tiny silicon chip. This is known as an integrated circuit. The IBM Personal Computer contains hundreds of integrated circuits, most of which are mounted in DIP form. These include memory modules, the microprocessor itself and many other circuit elements. The 16K memory option consists of nine memory modules, each of which is mounted in a dual in-line package.

DIP switch—A DIP switch is a small rectangular device which contains many tiny switches in a single DIP package. DIP stands for dual in-line, which is a description of the physical makeup of switch construction. There are dual rows of pins on either side of the switch which are all in line with each other. The dual in-line package (DIP) switches used in the IBM Personal Computer are found on the system board and on the 32K and 64K memory cards. Each of these devices contains 8 discrete switches which may be placed in the on or off position. As new options are added to the computer system, the switch positions must be changed to allow the machine to have access to them. Switch changes are required for the addition (or deletion) of memory modules, memory cards, disk drives, etc.

Direct Memory Access—Abbreviated DMA, direct memory access is a technique for transferring data directly between memory and system peripherals. DMA permits transfers to take place without the central processing unit (CPU) intervening on a cycle-stealing basis. In the IBM Personal Computer, the microprocessor is supported by a set of high function support devices, providing four channels of 20-bit direct memory access. Three of the four DMA channels are available on the I/O bus and are provided to support high-speed data transfers between I/O devices and memory, again without processor intervention. The fourth DMA channel is programmed to refresh the system's dynamic memory. All DMA data transfers (with the exception of the refresh channel) take 5 processor clocks of 210 nanoseconds or 1.05 nanoseconds if the processor ready line is not deactivated. Refresh DMA cycles take 4 clocks or 840 nanoseconds.

direct mode—The direct mode is used when programming in BASIC when the user wants the computer to perform the request immediately after it is entered. This mode is operational when the program line is not preceded by a line number. It is important to note that the instructions themselves are not saved after they are executed. This mode can be used to display results of arithmetic and logical operations immediately. It is useful for debugging and quick computations that do not require a complete program.

directory—A directory is the system area on a disk in which the names of files are stored. Also included in a directory is pertinent information, such as the size of the file, its location on the disk, and the date it was created. The directory occupies four sectors at a specific location on each disk.

disk—A disk is a device which is used to store information. It is a flexible device which is coated with a magnetic substance. When in use, the disk spins inside its permanent pro-

tective jacket. The read/write head comes in contact with the recording surface through the long hole in the protective jacket, called the head slot. Information is written to or read from the magnetic surface of the disk.

Disk BASIC—Disk BASIC is a version of BASIC used with the IBM Personal Computer. It comes as a program on the IBM Disk Operating System (DOS) Disk and must be loaded into memory before it can be used. Disk BASIC requires a disk-based machine with at least 32K of random access memory.

disk drive adapter—In the IBM Personal Computer, the disk drive adapter is a long circuit card which allows the computer to control two internal disk drives and to read and write memory from and onto 5¼" disk. The adapter fits in one of the five system expansion slots on the system board and is attached to up to two internal drives by means of internal daisy-chained flat cable. The adapter has a second connector on its opposite end which extends through the rear panel of the system unit. This allows two additional and external disk drives to be used with the IBM Personal Computer.

disk operating system—The disk operating system (DOS) is a collection of programs for the IBM Personal Computer stored on the DOS disk. These programs process commands to allow the user to manage information and the hardware resources of the computing system. DOS must be loaded into the computer before starting either Disk BASIC or Advanced BASIC programs.

drive—In computer terminology, a drive is most often a mechanical device which manipulates data storage media. In the IBM Personal Computer, the drive is a disk type which is capable of spinning the disk so that

185

its electronic circuits may read the stored information.

edit—Editing is the process of rearranging data or information. Editing may involve the deletion of unwanted data, the selection of pertinent data, the application of format techniques, the insertion of symbols such as page numbers and typewriter characters, the application of standard processes, and the testing of data for reasonableness.

EDLIN—Using IBM DOS, EDLIN is an abbreviation for Line Editor. This is a portion of the program which is used to create, alter and display source or text files.

EPROM—EPROM is an abbreviation for erasable programmable read-only memory. It is a ROM in which the data pattern written in may be erased to allow a new pattern (and thus, new programming) to be used. In the IBM Personal Computer, the system board contains space for 48K by 8 of ROM or EPROM.

error message—An error message is a word or combination of words which appear on the monitor screen to indicate to the user that there is an error somewhere in the program. The IBM Personal Computer has a total of 73 different error messages that may occur. Most of these messages will inform the operator on which line the error has occured and may even print out the line on the screen to enable the user to study it and determine the cause of the error.

executable statement—In BASIC, all statements are either executable or non-executable. Executable statements are program instructions that tell BASIC what to do next while executing a program. For example, PRINT X is an executable statement.

file—A file is a collection of information which is kept somewhere other than in the random access memory of the IBM Personal Computer. For example, information can be stored in a file on disk or cassette. In order to use the information, it is necessary to open the file to tell BASIC where the information is. At this point, the file may be used for both input and output.

file attribute—File attribute is a term that is used to describe any of the characteristics of a file.

filename—A filename is the name given to a disk file. It must be one to eight characters long and may be immediately followed by a filename extension, which can be one to three characters long. When a directory is asked for, a list of filenames will appear on the monitor. A filename can be made up of any combination of letters and numerals, but it should be descriptive of what is contained in the file.

floppy disk controller—In the IBM Personal Computer, the floppy disk controller is a circuit card which contains a status register and a data register. The 8-bit main status register contains the status information of the floppy disk controller and may be accessed at any time. The data register stores data, commands, parameters and disk drive status information.

flowchart—A flowchart is a graphical representation of the definition or solution of a problem, in which symbols are used to represent functions, operations and flow. A flowchart might contain all of the logical steps in a routine or program in order to allow the designer to conceptualize and visualize each step. It defines the major phases of the processing, as well as the path to problem solution.

font—A font is a mechanical or electronic device which determines how printed characters will appear on computer printer forms. In the IBM Personal Computer, two character fonts are used on the character generator card and are selected by a card jumper, a small interconnecting wire.

formatting—Formatting is the process of initializing or preparing a disk to receive information. It checks the disk for bad spots, builds a directory to hold information about the files that will eventually be written on it. Formatting insures that bad areas are not used for files. Formatting erases a disk.

function keys—On the IBM Personal Computer keyboard, there are ten function keys (F1-F10) located on the far left-hand side. These keys serve many different purposes, depending upon the language being used. When programming in IBM BASIC, the function keys are used to save typing time. For example, to load a program from disk into disk BASIC, it is necessary to type load "(program name). However, typing time may be saved by depressing the third function key, F3, which will automatically input load". All that is necessary is to then type the name of the program. In this case, depressing F3 saves operator time by doing in one keystroke what would normally take five keystrokes using the standard character keys.

game control adapter—The game control adapter is a circuit board that allows the computer system to be controlled by game attachments such as paddles and joysticks. Up to four paddles or two joysticks may be attached and four inputs for switches are also provided.

graphics—Graphics is concerned with methods and techniques for converting data to or from a graphic display via a computer. In the IBM Personal Computer, this is made possible by means of their Color/Graphics Monitor Adapter, which allows the user to display text in 16 different colors.

handshaking—Handshaking is a term which implies an initial exchange between two units or items in a system connection. Handshaking usually requires a matching at an interface, as when signals are exchanged between data set devices when a connection is made. A typical handshaking procedure takes place when a connection between a modem and an ACIA (asynchronous communications interface adapter) channel is established.

hardware—Hardware refers to the physical components which make up a microcomputer, monitor, printer, etc. The hard components include microprocessors, semiconductors, integrated circuits, the mounting frame, etc.

high resolution—Using the IBM Color/Graphics Monitor Adapter, it is possible to use BASIC statements to draw in either medium or high resolution. In high resolution, there are 640 points horizontally and 200 points vertically. These points are numbered starting with 0 (zero) so that the lower right corner point is 639,199. High resolution consists of only two colors: 0 (zero) and 1 (one). Zero is always black, and one is always white. When text characters are displayed in high resolution, 80 characters per line can be obtained. 1 is the foreground color, and 0 is the background color. Thus, characters will always be white on black.

housecleaning—Housecleaning is when BASIC collects all of its useful data and frees up unused areas of memory that were once used for strings. The data is compressed so that the user can continue until there is no space left. BASIC will automatically do a housecleaning when it is running out of usable work area.

implication—Implication is a logical IF-THEN operation which states: If P and Q are statements, P inclusion Q is false if P is true and Q is false. P inclusion Q is true if P is false and Q is true, or P and Q are both true.

indirect mode—Indirect mode is the means of entering and running programs in BASIC. In this mode, each program line must begin with a line number. The line is then stored as part of the program in memory. The program can then be executed by entering the RUN command. This is the mode most commonly used when writing programs, as it stores each line for future use.

input—Input is data transferred from an external storage medium into the internal storage of the computer and vice versa.

instruction—An instruction is a set of characters which defines an operation that causes the computer to perform the operation.

integrated circuit—An integrated circuit or IC is an interconnected array of components fabricated from a single crystal of semiconductor material (usually silicon). The majority of components found in the Personal Computer are in integrated circuit form.

Intel 8088 microprocessor—The heart of the Personal Computer is the 8088 microprocessor, that features an 8-bit I/O bus but has 16-bit internal architecture, thus combining the features of a 16-bit microprocessor into a chip which has 8-bit communication capabilities. The processor supports 20 bits of addressing (1 megabyte of storage) and is implemented in maximum mode so a co-processor can be added as an optional feature. The processor is operated at 4.77 megahertz and is supported by a set of high-function support devices, providing four channels of 20-bit direct memory access, three 16-bit timer counter channels, and eight prioritized interrupt levels.

interface—An interface is a device which will allow one computer to operate into a communications line or another terminal. The interface, then, matches the output of the computer to the input of the desired line or terminal.

I/O channel—An input/output (I/O) channel is a circuit path which allows independent communication between the processor and external devices.

joystick—A joystick is a lever that provides coordinate data of a display surface. The data may be used to control operations such as the movement of one or more display elements.

keyboard—A keyboard contains keys for entering data or information into a system. Keyboards may be alphanumeric, as used for word processing, text processing, and data processing; or numeric, as used for touchtone telephones, accounting machines and calculators.

light pen—A photosensitive device that causes a computer to modify the display on a CRT screen. As the display information is selected by the operator, the light pen signals the computer using an electronically produced pulse. The light pen can be used to draw impressions on the computer monitor.

linker—The linker is a program that combines separately produced object modules, searches library files for definitions of unresolved external references, resolves external cross references, produces a printable listing that shows the resolution of external references and error messages, and produces a relocatable load module.

logical operator—Logical operators perform logical, or Boolean, operations on numeric values. Logical operators are usually used to connect two or more relations and return a true or false value to be used in a decision. A logical operator takes a combination of true-false values and returns a true or false result. An operand of a logical operator is considered to be true if it is not equal to zero, or false if it is equal to zero. The result of the logical operation is a number which is, again, true if it is not equal to zero, or false if it is equal to zero. The number is calculated by performing the operation bit by bit. The logical operators are NOT (logical complement), AND (conjunction), OR (disjunction), XOR (exclusive or), IMP (implication), and EQV (equivalence). Each operator returns results as indicated below. (T indicates a true, or non-zero value. F indicates a false, or zero value.)

logic expression—A logic expression consists of variable array elements, function references, logical constants and combinations of operands separated by logical operators and parentheses. Typically, logical expressions may contain arithmetic expressions separated by relational operators.

loop—A loop is the repeated execution of a series of instructions for a specific number of times.

LSB—LSB is an abbreviation for least significant bit, which is the rightmost bit in a word.

machine language—A machine language is a language that can be used directly by a microprocessor. All other languages must be translated or compiled into binary code before entering the processor. Users generally write the program in coded instructions that are more meaningful to them. Then assembly programs are used to translate the symbolic instructions into binary machine code.

matrix printer—A matrix printer is a device that uses an array of dots to form characters.

medium resolution—Medium resolution is a term used in describing computer graphics. There are 320 points horizontally and 200 points vertically in which BASIC statements can be drawn. These points are numbered from left to right and from top to bottom, starting with 0 (zero). That makes the upper left corner of the screen point (0,0), and the lower right corner point (319,199). Medium resolution is unusual because of its color features. When the user puts something on the screen in medium resolution, it is possible to specify a color number of 0,1,2, or 3. These colors are not fixed as are the 16 colors in text mode. It is possible to select the actual color number 0 and select one of two palettes for the other three colors using the COLOR statement.

memory—Memory is a basic component of a computer which stores information for future use.

microprocessor—A microprocessor is a solid-state central processing unit which is very much like a computer on a chip.

modem—A modem is an electronic device that performs the modulation and demodulation functions required for communications. A modem can be used to connect computers and terminals over telephone circuits.

module—A module is an assembly which contains a complete circuit or subcircuit. Technically, integrated circuits fall under the module category. Printed circuit boards which are designed to be plugged in to a computer or other electronic circuit may also be classified as modules.

modulo arithmetic—Modulo arithmetic is an arithmetic operator in IBM Personal Computer BASIC which performs an arithmetic function. It is denoted by the operator MOD and gives the integer value that is the remainder of an integer division.

monitor—A monitor is a unit in a computer which prepares machine instructions from a source code. It may use built-in compilers for one or more program languages. The machine instructions are sequenced into the processing unit once compiling is complete.

monochrome display—A monochrome display is most often a cathode-ray tube device which is capable of black and white output only.

MSB—MSB is an abbreviation for most significant bit, which is the leftmost bit in a word. The MSB contributes the most weight to the numerical value of the word in IBM coding.

multiple statement—A program line which is made up of two or more separate statements.

nanosecond—A nanosecond is an amount of time equal to 10^{-9} second. It is abbreviated ns and is equivalent to 1/1,000,000 of a second. A time interval of 1,000,000 nanoseconds is equal to 1 second.

negation—Negation is the monadic Boolean operation, the result of which has the Boolean value opposite to that of the operand. It is synonymous with NOT.

non-executable statement—Non-executable statements, such as DATA or REM, do not cause any program action when BASIC sees them.

numeric comparison—In numeric comparisons, when arithmetic and relational operators are combined in one expression, the arithmetic is always performed first. For example, the expression:
$$X+Y < (T-1)/Z$$
will be true (-1) if the value of X plus Y is less than the value of $T-1$ divided by Z.

numeric expression—A numeric expression may be simply a numeric constant or variable, or may be used to combine constants and variables using operators to produce a single numeric value. Numeric operators perform mathematical or logical operations mostly on numeric values, and sometimes on string values. They are referred to as numeric operators because they produce a value that is a number.

numeric function—A function is used like a variable in an expression to call a predetermined operation that is to be performed on one or more operands. BASIC has intrinsic functions that reside in the system, such as SQR (square root) or SIN (sine).

numeric keypad—The numeric keypad is located at the far right of the Personal Computer and is used for entering numeric data.

numeric constant—A numeric constant is an actual value used by BASIC during program execution. They are positive or negative numbers. Numeric constants in BASIC cannot contain commas. They may be indicated by an integer, fixed point, floating point, hexadecimal, or octal.

operator—The operator is that portion of the computer or program which tells the microprocessor what to do. An example of an operator in a program for the Personal Computer would be: 10 PRINT "THIS IS THE CORRECT ANSWER". This program line tells the computer to display, "THIS IS THE CORRECT ANSWER" on the monitor screen.

overscan—On the Personal Computer Color/Graphics Monitor Adapter, overscan is that area which is outside the area for characters. This overscan area is known as the border screen.

parallel printer adapter—The parallel printer adapter in the IBM Personal Computer is designed to attach printers with a parallel port interface, but it may also be used as a general input/output port for any device or application which matches its input/output capabilities.

program—A program is a set of instructions that direct a computer in performing a desired operation, such as the solution of a mathematical problem or the sorting of data.

program line—A program line is any line of text that is entered which begins with a number. A BASIC program line always begins with a line number and may contain a maximum of 255 characters.

protected file—A protected file is one which is stored within memory and cannot be listed or edited. This prevents persons from being able to gain access to the various program lines and copying the data.

power-on self test—When power is initially

applied, the computer will automatically scan and test many of its circuits and sound a beep from the internal speaker if this initial test indicates proper system performance. The power-on self test is really a check of the power supply to see if it is providing proper voltage to the unit.

power supply—A power supply is an electrical/electronic circuit which supplies all operating voltage and current to the computer system. Initial power is most often derived from the 115-volt household ac receptacle.

printer self test—The printer self test is activated by turning on the power switch of the IBM printer while simultaneously pressing the Line Feed switch. The printer then goes into an automatic test mode, providing a hard copy printout of all characters it is capable of producing. The complete test takes approximately ten minutes.

protocol—Protocol is the set of conventions between communications lines and links on the format and content of messages to be exchanged, especially those conventions which set the precedence among messages. Protocol can be used to define a complex hierarchy for the various levels of exchange encountered in information systems.

random access memory—Random access is the main internal memory of a computer. The computer can store values in distinct locations in random access memory (RAM) and recall them again, or alter and restore them. The values which are in RAM are lost when the power to the computer is turned off.

random file—A random file is a type of disk data file that may be created and accessed by a BASIC program. With random files, data too can be accessed randomly; i.e., anywhere on the disk. It is not necessary to read through all the information.

Read-Only Memory—This type of memory is usually used to hold important programs or data which must be available to the computer when the power is first turned on. Information in ROMs is unalterable and does not disappear when the power is turned off.

refresh cycle—Refreshing is the constant restoring of information that fades from RAM when left idle.

register—A register is a storage area in memory having a specified storage capacity, such as a bit, a byte, or a computer word, and usually intended for a special purpose.

REM—REM is a statement contained on a program line in IBM BASIC which stands for remark. When this statement is entered, the following text on the line provides an explanation of the use or function of the entire program. REM statements are not output to the monitor screen or printer during program execution. They serve as an explanation of the program when it is listed.

reserved word—Reserved words have special meaning. These include all BASIC commands, statements, function names and operator names. Reserved words may not be used as variable names. These reserved words should always be separated from data or other parts of a BASIC statement using spaces or other special characters.

rf modulator—An rf modulator is a device which will accept an audio or video input and then place this information on a carrier, usually at radio frequencies. They connect computers to TV sets.

ROM BIOS—The term ROM BIOS is an abbreviation for read-only memory basic input/output system. In the Personal Computer, this is a complex circuit that provides the device level control of the major I/O devices in the system unit. The BIOS routines allows the assembly language programmer to perform I/O operations without any concern for device address and operating characteristics.

routine—A routine is a set of instructions that are used frequently. A routine may be considered as a subdivision of a program with two or more instructions that are functionally related.

scratch disk—A scratch disk is one which contains no useful information and can thus be used as a backup disk.

scrolling—Scrolling is a process whereby information may be displayed on a screen even though the entire content of the information requires more screen space than is available at one time. When the screen is filled, the display will move upward one line at a time to allow additional lines to be input at the bottom. When this occurs, the top line disappears.

sequential file—A sequential file is a type of disk data file that may be created and accessed by a BASIC program. Sequential files are easier to create than random files but are limited in flexibility and speed when it comes to accessing the data. The data that is written to a sequential file is stored, one item after another (sequentially) in the order it is sent, and is read back in the same way.

single precision—Numeric constants may be stored internally as either integer, single precision, or double precision numbers. With single precision, seven digits are stored and up to seven digits are printed, although only six digits will be accurate.

software—Software includes computer languages, programs, storage, etc.

source disk—The source disk is the one which contains information that is to be copied onto another disk.

storage—Storage is used to describe a device or medium on or into which data can be entered, held and retrieved at a later time. Storage may use electrostatic, magnetic, acoustic, optical, electronic, or mechanical methods. This term is synonymous with memory.

string—A string is a linear sequence of items which are grouped in series according to certain rules. A string may be a set of records grouped in ascending or descending sequence according to a key contained in the records.

string constant—A string constant is a sequence of up to 255 characters enclosed in double quotation marks. It is a type of actual value which BASIC uses during execution.

subroutine—A subroutine is a segment of a program which can be executed by a single call. Subroutines are used to perform the same sequence of instructions at many different places in one program.

system board—In the Personal Computer, the system board is contained within the system unit and houses the microprocessor, ROM, read/write memory, and system expansion inputs.

system expansion slots—In computers, system expansion slots allow for the insertion of circuit cards which expand the capability of the computer. The IBM Personal Computer contains five slots.

system unit—The System Unit is the heart of the Personal Computer. It houses the microprocessor, read-only memory, read/write memory, power supply and system expansion slots for the attachment of up to five options. One or two 5¼" disk drives can be mounted on the System Unit.

task—A task is a basic unit of work to be accomplished by a computer.

telecommunication—Telecommunication is data transmission between a computer and remotely located devices via a unit that performs the necessary format conversion and controls the rate of transmission.

terminal unit—A terminal unit is a part of a computer system in a communications channel that may be used for inputting or outputting information to the channel.

timing generator—A timing generator is a circuit which outputs evenly spaced signals to be used for timing control throughout machine operations.

track—A track is a concentric circle on a disk. There are 40 tracks on a disk, and information is written onto the tracks. Each track is divided into eight sectors that are 512 bytes long.

truncation—Truncation is the deletion or omission of a leading or trailing portion of a string in accordance with specified criteria. It may also be the termination of a computation process before its final conclusion or natural termination, if any, in accordance with specified rules.

update—To update means to modify information already contained in a file or program with current information.

variables—Variables are names used to represent values that are used in a BASIC program. There are two types of variables: numeric and string. A numeric variable always has a value that is a number. A string variable may only have a character string value.

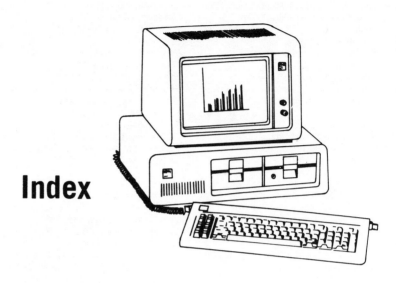

Index